DOUBLE EXPOSURE
Poverty & Race in America

DOUBLE EXPOSURE
Poverty & Race in America

Edited by Chester Hartman

Foreword by Bill Bradley

Preface by Julian Bond

M.E. Sharpe
Armonk, New York
London, England

Library of Congress Cataloging-in-Publication Data

Double exposure : poverty & race in America /
edited by Chester Hartman.
p. cm.
Includes index.
ISBN 1–56324–961–8 (hardcover : alk. paper). —
ISBN 1–56324–962–6 (paperback : alk. paper)
1. Racism—United States.
2. Poverty—United States.
3. United States—Race relations.
4. Afro-Americans—Economic conditions.
I. Hartman, Chester W.
E185.615.D657
1996
305.8′00973—dc20
96–31314
CIP

Printed in the United States of America

The paper used in this publication meets the minimum requirements of the
American National Standard for Information Sciences—
Permanence of Paper for Printed Library Materials,
ANSI Z 39.48-1984.

∞

BM (c)   10   9   8   7   6   5   4   3   2   1
BM (p)   10   9   8   7   6   5   4   3   2   1

Contents

Part 4. "The Underclass"

Part 5. Multiculturalism

Part 6. Affirmative Action

Foreword

Bill Bradley

Slavery was America's original sin, and race remains its unresolved dilemma. For the past year, three Black males have dominated the nation's focus on race. They are O.J. Simpson, Louis Farrakhan, and Colin Powell. Each in his own way fed America's appetite to live vicariously, and to shrink from confronting, our racial reality. Each said something different about the state of race relations in America. They allowed white Americans to ridicule, demonize, or idealize Black Americans. The O.J. case revealed an almost irrevocable division between Blacks and whites, with the same disparate percentages of Blacks and whites feeling he was guilty before and after the trial. Louis Farrakhan allowed whites to attack the messenger rather than confront the part of his message about the desperate conditions in much of Black America. Colin Powell permitted white America to fantasize that an answer to our racial divisions amounted to no more than "We like you; you do it for us."

The issue of race can never be a Black issue alone—not only because America is blessed by an abundance of Asian Americans, Latino Americans, and Native Americans, but also because a racial dialogue cannot take place without white Americans becoming full participants. White Americans have a race, too. Black separatists flourish where whites shut their doors to dialogue and assume no responsibility for their own stakes in racial healing.

The racial landscape of America seems full of land mines. Yet it is precisely at such moments of heightened awareness that we can make the greatest progress, because it is at those moments that the necessary pain of candor can be endured and then transcended.

Excerpt from "Race Relations in America: The Best and Worst of Times," a speech given at the Town Hall in Los Angeles, California, January 11, 1996.

So what is the state of Black–white relations in America? Both Black and white America are caught in a traumatic economic transformation in which millions of Americans feel insecure about their future, and for good reason. There are 130 million jobs in America, and 90 million of them involve repetitive tasks, which means that a computer can displace any of those jobholders. In a world where credit departments of three hundred people are routinely displaced by ten computer workstations, more and more Americans will lose good-paying jobs along with their health insurance and often their pensions, so that corporate profits can rise and productivity can increase. During the first six months of 1993, the Clinton administration announced that 1.3 million jobs had been created, to which a TWA machinist replied, "Yeah, my wife and I have four of them." And indeed, over half of the newly created jobs were part-time.

If you're an African American, you've seen it before. In the 1940s the cotton gin pushed Black field hands off the farms of the South, to the cities of the North. Labor-intensive manufacturing jobs seemed to be the Promised Land. Then automation arrived, and the last hired were the first fired; millions of unskilled Black workers lost their jobs. Still, many hung on in the manufacturing sector. Then, with the advent of information technology and foreign competition, labor unions, such as the multiracial steelworkers, saw their membership plummet from 750,000 in 1979 to 374,000 in 1990. Finally, in the 1960s and 1970s, government began to employ African Americans in sizable numbers, but in the 1980s and 1990s, with the fiscal crunch in full progress, government employees were let go. In the midst of the information revolution, just as in the midst of any recession, tough economic winds become a hurricane for African Americans.

Many white Americans who have been caught in the cold winds for the first time feel disoriented. Many become easy prey for politicians who want to explain deteriorating standards of living by stigmatizing Black Americans and immigrants. "You have lost your job," these mischief makers say, "because of affirmative action" or "because of the money government spends to help the poor." Instead of seeing the demographic reality—that only as all Americans advance will white Americans advance—they often fall into the scapegoating trap. It's an old story.

The fact is that, economically, Black America is in the best and the worst of times. Roughly a third of Black America can now be called middle class. Black Americans distinguish themselves in virtually every field of endeavor. Yet more than 30 percent of Black Americans live in grinding poverty. Many can't find a job, can't get credit to buy a house or start a business, and increasingly can't afford necessities, much less save for the future. Indeed, the unemployment rate for Blacks is routinely twice that for whites. Also, the earnings of Black college-educated men have only recently reached parity with those of white men with high school diplomas. Of greater significance is the fact that 46 percent of Black children live below the poverty line, compared with 17 percent of white youngsters.

Without question, disintegrating family structure contributes to Black poverty. The average income for a two-parent Black family is three times the income of a single-parent white family. But poverty is more than a Black problem. It is a broad national systemic issue flowing from inadequate economic growth unfairly shared. Indeed, there are 16 million more white Americans in poverty than there are Black Americans in poverty. But many whites feel it is primarily a Black problem. Because of lingering racial attitudes and stereotypes, marshaling resources to cope with poverty becomes more difficult. In that sense, racism contributes to Black poverty and to white poverty, too.

The conflict between generations in the Black community is real, and the primary responsibility for bridging it rests with the Black community. There is a breakdown in communication and a breakdown in values. When I left Missouri for college in 1961, the proportion of children in St. Louis born to a single mother was 13 percent; now it is 68 percent. Among Black children it is 86 percent. In some cities, such as Baltimore, 55 percent of African American males age 18–34 are in jail, on probation, or awaiting trial. The idealistic call of Martin Luther King, Jr., or the disciplined march of Muslims who have declared war on Black self-destruction, can't compete with the latest gangsta rapper who from the TV screen calls young people to a life of crime, violence, white hate, and female abuse. Increasingly, a generation with little to lose pulls the trigger without remorse, risks nothing for a neighbor, and invests little in the future. Some of them live for today because that's all they have ever done; others, because they believe that their tomorrow will only be worse.

Is the plight of this element of young Black America an isolated cancer, or a harbinger of all our futures? Is the message of these young

Black Americans pathological or prophetic? Will the rest of America respond or turn its back?

White Americans seem to have ignored the devastation in many American cities. Both government and the private sector have proved inadequate to the task of urban rejuvenation. It's almost as if the kids with AIDS, the gang members with guns, the teenagers lost to crack cocaine, the young rape victim whose only self-respect comes from having another child don't exist for most white Americans.

We have to recognize that the flip side of racial discrimination is racial privilege, which consists of all those things that come to white Americans in the normal course of living, all the things they take for granted that a Black person can never take for granted. Race privilege is a harder concept to grasp than racial discrimination, especially for whites, because it is more subtle. It is rooted in assumptions about every day, yet there is no denying it. For example, if I'm looking to buy a house and I'm white, I never fear someone will refuse me because of my race, but if I'm Black, I constantly make assessments about what is possible, problematic, or impossible. That freedom from fear is a white-skin privilege. If I'm white, I know that if I meet the economic criteria, I'll get the loan. If I'm Black, I know I might not. Skin privilege means that I don't have to worry that my behavior will reflect positively or negatively on my race; it will reflect only on me and on my family. Skin privilege means that I can relate to strangers without first having to put them at ease about my race. I know Black males who walk the street whistling classical music to let whites know they're not dangerous.

As long as white America remains blind to its own racial privilege, Black Americans will feel that the focus falls too heavily on them. As long as white America believes that the race problem is primarily a Black problem of meeting white standards to gain admittance to white society, things will never stabilize and endure. But the flip side of white-skin privilege is negative Black attitudes—reflected even in small things, such as coldness in daily interactions at work, slowdowns in providing services to whites, or gathering at separate tables in cafeterias—that cast any attempts by whites at racial dialogue as disingenuous and illegitimate. African Americans have to open up their worlds to whites just as whites have to open up their worlds to Blacks. Without that kind of candor, the dialogue will be phony. Without that kind of mutual interest, the ties will not bind. Without that kind of mutual commitment, racial hierarchy will persist.

The silence of good people in the face of continuing racism is often as harmful as the actions of bad people. Most people aren't racist, yet there are some white and Black people in America who do remain racists, spewing hostility toward other persons simply because of their race. There are white politicians who play the "race card," and there are Black politicians who play the "racist card." But the word "racist" is overused. Most people aren't brimming over with race hatred. To say that someone who opposes affirmative action is racist denies the possibility that the person may be ignorant or unknowledgeable. If one hurls the epithet "racist," a meaningful dialogue is unlikely to follow, and it is only out of candid conversations that whites will discover skin privilege, Blacks will accept constructive criticism from whites, and progress will come steadily.

Affirmative action occupies such a disproportionate place in our national politics because many whites cannot conceive of white-skin privilege and because discrimination, when it occurs, remains largely unaddressed. Why not deal with the underlying issue, which is discrimination, and facilitate remedies for discrimination? Affirmative action is a response to a discriminatory pattern over many years in institutions run by individuals who are confident that they don't have to change.

Today, many of the people who oppose affirmative action, state a preference for color blindness, and justify their position by reference to the American tradition of considering individuals equal before the law are often the same people who seldom have Black friends and who will choose the white teacher over the Black teacher for their children every time. When people shout "reverse discrimination," they ignore our history, the continuation of subtle white-skin privilege, and the fact that more white people lost their jobs in the 1982 recession than Blacks have gained jobs from court-ordered affirmative action since its inception. When people diminish real Black contributions to our society as if they were a threat to our historical canon, they diminish their own understanding of themselves and their country. What is at work here is another attempt to distort traditional American values in order to slow down progress on race.

Countering the human devastation in parts of urban America will take a heroic effort by thousands in the Black and white communities working together. It will take police departments that do their jobs conscientiously and with adequate resources. It will take schools that are teaching institutions, not simply warehouses for storing our children. It will take surrogate families who will express love for kids without parents. It might even take boarding schools for kids who can't make it in the neighborhood. Above all, it will take a new multiracial political vision that acts, because failure to act will stain our ideals, diminish our chances for long-term prosperity, and shortchange our children—all our children.

In the 1960s the civil rights movement thrived on the assumption that an America without racism would be a spiritually transformed America. That, after all, is what affirmative action affirms—that America can get over its racial nightmare; that few in America should be poor, ignorant, or violent because the rest of us have cared too little for them; that no persons in America should have a racial limit set on where their talents can take them; and that the process of seeing beyond skin color and eye shape allows us not to ignore race but to elevate the individual. A new political vision requires people to engage each other, endure the pain of candor, learn from each other's history, absorb each other's humanity, and move on to higher ground. Such is the task of those who care about racial healing. It won't happen overnight. It can never be just about numbers. Ultimately, it must always be about the human spirit. In other words, only together can we chart a brighter future.

Preface

Julian Bond

The scholar–activist W.E.B. Du Bois accurately predicted that "the problem of the 20th Century will be the problem of the color line." Not only was he correct, but his forecast is easily carried over to the century to come; race will continue to mark our society. The evidence of race's salience is everywhere.

The 1994 congressional election results were the product of an electorate divided even more than usual by race and gender. That Congress's new leadership was more hostile to equality than the Democrats they replaced. On a civil rights report card prepared by the NAACP, they fail: with 100 percent as a perfect grade, they averaged 21 percent in the House and 36 percent in the Senate. For racial minorities, the results have meant at least two years—maybe more—of revisiting and refighting battles many thought had already been fought and won.

That political shift will further segment Americans by race and wealth: tax cuts for the well-to-do; a noose around the neck of programs to aid low-income persons; slamming shut the courthouse door for poor Americans; a cutback in aid to cities, where most minorities live; and an assault on the laws and regulations that require fair hiring and equal opportunity.

Recent Supreme Court decisions have carried forward the assault on fairness, attacking affirmative action, limiting the scope of the historic 1954 school integration decision, and restricting application of the 1965 Voting Rights Act. Incidents of racial animus are everywhere, from church burnings to racially motivated denials of jobs, housing, education, and even service at fast-food restaurants.

The modern movement for civil rights and racial justice is rightly called the Second Reconstruction, named after the single period in modern American history, following the Civil War, when the national government insisted on and enforced civil rights for Black Americans. Today, Black Americans face prospects eerily similar to those they faced in the period following the first Reconstruction.

Then, white Americans grew tired of worrying about the welfare of the newly freed slaves, tired of fighting to secure their right to vote.

Then, as now, scientific racism and social Darwinism were in vogue.

Then, as now, a race-weary nation decided problems of race could best be solved if left to the individual states.

Then, as now, minorities and immigrants became scapegoats for real and imagined economic distress.

Then, a reign of state-sanctioned and private terror, including ritual human sacrifice, swept across the South to reinforce white supremacy. The heavy hand of legal racial segregation descended across the region, a cruel cotton curtain that separated Blacks from every opportunity. The modern civil rights movement vanquished legal racial exclusion by the mid-1960s. Blacks won access to public places and the voting booth, and the fabric of segregation began to come undone. The modern civil rights movement's origins lay in a bitter struggle for elemental civil rights. In the postsegregation era, it has largely become a movement for economic and political power. Today, Black women and men hold office and wield power in numbers barely dreamed of before.

But despite impressive increases in the number of Black people holding public office, despite the hard-won ability to eat, ride, vote, and go to school in places that used to bar Black faces, in some important ways nonwhite Americans face restrictions more difficult to attack now than in all preceding years.

Despite its victories, the modern civil rights movement foundered in several ways. The McCarthy period of the 1950s made anticommunism a secular religion; it permeated the popular discourse and isolated the civil rights movement from any economic critiques of the American order. The movement had wrongly classified segregation and racism as the same evil; banishing the first would shortly eliminate the second, advocates believed. By underestimating the endurance of racial supremacy, the movement celebrated too swiftly. It could not mount battles against extralegal white supremacy as effectively as it had against state-authorized apartheid.

While the movement floundered, race remained the organizing principle of American politics. As long ago as 1964, the Republican Party began to remake itself as the white people's party.

Today, the United Nations, Washington bureaucrats, homosexuals, and advocates for women's rights have replaced the Soviet Union as the Evil Empire. Neoracists found a winning electoral formula at the intersection of race and activist government.

The civil rights movement's very successes were its undoing. As more minorities and women pushed for, and gained, entry to the academy, media, business, and other traditionally white male institutions, a backlash was created in the discourse over race. The previously privileged majority exploded in angry resentment at having to cede space to the formerly excluded. Suddenly, white men became a victim class. Aggressive Blacks and pushy women were blamed for America's demise. Any indictment of white America was abandoned. Instead, a "Susan Smith defense" was adopted—Black people did it, did it to the country, did it to themselves. Black behavior, not white racism, became the reason why Blacks and whites lived in separate worlds. Racism retreated, and pathology advanced. The burden of racial problem-solving shifted from racism's creators to its victims. The failure of the lesser breeds to enjoy society's fruits became their fault alone.

In the 1890s, bruised and beaten, the movement for social justice and racial equality reached a nadir, seemingly devoid of hope. It rebounded, fought noble fights, and won great victories, but those victories need to be secured. Many of the battles must be fought and won again.

Yesterday's battlefield had many combatants who represented America's diversity. Today's battles cannot become fights of Blacks and other nonwhites against whites.

No one will win that fight.

Editor's Introduction

Chester Hartman

This volume is more than a collection of important, well-written contributions regarding what Senator Bradley, Gunnar Myrdal, and others
correctly identify as America's dilemma. Combating racism—and its
two-way, cause-and-effect relationship with poverty—is at the heart of
our mission at the Poverty & Race Research Action Council (PRRAC),
the organization I have headed virtually since its inception in 1990. It
was founded by committed advocates from the legal services and antipoverty communities who were seeking progressive solutions to what
we term "the intersectional trap": the ways our society creates and
maintains a large stratum of the population who are both poor and
subject to subordination by the dominant white majority.

As our name conveys, PRRAC deals not only with the intersection
of race and poverty but also with the intersection of research and
advocacy. We seek to enhance collaboration between those whose research is relevant to the fight against racism and poverty and those
activists who use the tools of litigation, community organizing, public
education, and legislation in that fight. We hope to encourage and
facilitate more, better, and more relevant social science research useful
to activists, and to persuade activists to shape their work in light of
what relevant research can impart regarding problems and solutions.

Our bimonthly newsletter, *Poverty & Race,* in which the writings
that comprise this volume earlier appeared, goes out to over eight
thousand activists, researchers, funders, and media people all over the
country, a list that grows steadily as word of PRRAC's existence,
mission, and products spreads. Through these writings, as well as reports on other aspects of our work and extensive listings of current
reports, studies, articles, and other resources, our periodical helps to
create an important interactive network among these various groups.

An extension of PRRAC's networking functions involves organizing local all-day meetings of race and poverty researchers and activists. Nine such gatherings have been held to date—in Philadelphia, Detroit, Atlanta, Los Angeles, Boston, San Francisco, Seattle/Portland, Chicago, and Washington, DC. These meetings serve to introduce people from each "world" to people from the others and lay the basis for subsequent contacts; identify community groups' urgent research needs, for adoption as projects by local academics; and, in several cities to date, lead to the creation of academic resource directories of ongoing and recent research efforts, available databases, expert witnesses and technical assistants, and internship possibilities that grassroots groups can draw upon, thus making universities accessible to low-income and minority communities and demystifying the world of academia.

Another of PRRAC's major activities is funding social science research designed directly to support a planned advocacy agenda. Some ninety such projects have been funded to date, for the most part small grants for unsolicited proposals. This is not classic disinterested research—there is enough support for that from government and foundation sources. As essentially an advocacy organization, PRRAC supports research designed to buttress advocacy goals. That is to say, it must be designed to be used to further a particular interest or cause. PRRAC's oversight task is to ensure that the methodology is sound and the results are credible, so that legislators, newspaper editors, courts, and the public will regard the research outcomes as convincing.

To cite two illustrative examples: First, the Legal Assistance Foundation of Chicago documented that city's failure to provide homeless children living in shelters with adequate schooling, as required under the federal McKinney Act; that research was then used to seek relief via state legislation and litigation. Second, Washington, DC's, Clínica Legal Latina interviewed immigrant women regarding domestic violence; the results were helpful in securing passage of federal legislation protecting the immigration status of women victimized by such abuse. A complete descriptive list of these PRRAC-funded projects, and of the successful advocacy work thereby fostered, is available from us. Our hope is to begin to replicate the more successful projects in several cities. Because PRRAC is closely allied with the advocacy community and has as a basic mission the building of relationships within the research and advocacy communities and across them, it is well situated to make and monitor these small grants and ensure the work is put to use. In this, PRRAC fills a clear need: most funders that support research shun advocacy; most funders that support advocacy fail to see the utility of targeted research.

In addition to these smaller research projects, PRRAC also commissions larger, Board-initiated research efforts (see page 247 for a list of PRRAC's current and former Board and Social Science Advisory Board members). One of these projects, currently nearing completion, is documenting the two-way, cause-and-effect relationship between housing segregation and school segregation. We have commissioned a comprehensive overview that assembles existing studies and litigation documents on the role of the federal government (via urban renewal, highways, public housing, and FHA and VA housing programs) in creating segregated residential patterns, and their impact on racial composition of schools. We also have commissioned a parallel set of studies on the impact of St. Louis's voluntary interdistrict school integration program (the nation's largest) that are being used in litigation to defend against state and local government attempts to terminate court supervision of this program—and, by extension, similar attempts by other localities to end school integration programs. The resultant research products will be used in further advocacy efforts, still to be determined, that may involve congressional hearings, media/public education work, and possibly litigation.

A second large, Board-initiated research project involves reconnaissance of federal and state government data collection efforts and sources on the impact of those governments' housing, education, health, and income-support programs on poor and minority beneficiaries. Undertaken in response to widespread complaints by advocates regarding the disappearance of impact data, the PRRAC project has commissioned surveys at the federal level and in five states (California, Alabama, Illinois, Texas, and North Carolina), to ascertain and identify the extent to which such data are collected and disseminated, how good and accessible the data are, what legal requirements exist with respect to data collection and how they are being met, and what advocates and researchers say they need with respect to data in these areas. The clear and serious shortcomings we are finding will be the basis for national and state-level advocacy efforts to improve data collection and dissemination, so that a sound basis will exist for evaluating programs, challenging poor performance, and working for program improvement.

We very much hope this volume can be a vehicle for stimulating creative thought *and* action to bring about swift and meaningful amelioration of America's historical and continuing twin shames of racism and poverty.

We welcome new contacts. The Poverty & Race Research Action Council can be reached at 1711 Connecticut Ave. NW, #207, Washington, DC 20009, 202/387-9887; fax: 202/387-0764; E-mail: prrac@aol.com.

Our small staff labored well and mightily to produce this book in time to meet the publisher's rapid production schedule. Thanks to Louisa Clark, Steven White, and especially Beth Ginsburg and Catherine Dorn—the latter leaving us after four years, having just received her law degree—for their stellar work.

DOUBLE EXPOSURE
Poverty & Race in America

Introduction

john a. powell

Race, racism, and racial equality have been, and continue to be, central to understanding what we are as a country, and who we are as a people and as individuals. Direct and indirect discussions of race are a great part of our public and private discourse. Yet we often have reservations about discussing race and even resent its intrusion into our conversations and considerations. Race can, and does, mean many things, and is almost always discussed with a degree of confusion that is both troubling and perplexing. Given how much time, energy, and thought we devote to issues related to race, one might think that we would at least have some clarity about our racial problems and some of the solutions.

Unfortunately, this has not been the case. We have failed to address our most pressing racial issues, and as a nation we not only lack a consensus about how race matters, we are deeply troubled by and fearful of race. And yet, because of the centrality of race to the way we are organized and how we are identified and identify ourselves, we cannot turn our attention too far away from it.

Indeed, part of the difficulty in addressing racial issues is the strong denial mechanism that we use to ignore, escape, or wish away race problems. We have tried unsuccessfully to assign racial issues to a distant past, fooling ourselves into thinking that racism can only faintly make claims on who we are today and should only peripherally inform our sense of justice. Although we are not all affected in the same way by race, we are all nonetheless affected in fundamental ways. Race is inescapable, regardless of whether we are white or people of color. Added to the confusion is that we see race in our lives differently, because our very understanding of what race means, the importance of it, our concern with it or lack thereof, is largely influenced by our race. Our very consciousness and perceptions are racialized.

This difficulty of addressing issues of race, racism, and racial equality is further confounded by how charged and raw these issues are. Most of us, whether or not we recognize it, feel deeply and profoundly about race and racial inequality/justice in our society. And these concerns, whether conscious or not, express or implied, shape how we vote, affect how we approach the law and make social policy, and impact how we articulate the moral claims we make on each other and ourselves. Our inability to have a rational conversation about race enflames these fears and undermines our hope for an inclusive democracy. The complexity and centrality of race to issues of justice, equality, and identity demand that we do more than simply assign blame. They demand that we pay serious attention to race and recognize that we have been unwilling or unable to discuss race in a constructive and sustained way.

Our failure has resulted in a chasm of misunderstanding. It is into this breach between recognition and dialogue that *Double Exposure: Poverty & Race in America* steps. In so doing, it makes an important and much-needed contribution. Without waiting for others to get it right, the contributors to this book have insightfully addressed a number of the most important racial questions that confront America, in an effort to try to make sense of race and its role in American society. In this vein, *Double Exposure* touches on racial debates that we recognize and reframes ostensibly nonracial debates within the historical context of American racial inequality and the legacy of slavery.

Double Exposure starts with a number of short essays that respond to the provocative claim put forth by Derrick Bell, Richard Delgado, and others that racism is a permanent, noneradicable feature of American life. Although a number of the contributors challenge the implications of this assertion, none of them claims that racism has been eradicated or will someday be eradicated in the United States. But conceding this point does not mean that racism as we know it is permanent. Howard Winant reminds us that racism, like race, is mutable. The racism that we are addressing today is very different from the racism of one hundred or even twenty years ago and, in all likelihood, different from the racism that will confront us in the next century. Indeed, one of the difficulties in addressing racism, according to Winant, is that we may not know what the term means, because racism is "not a static, obvious 'thing' anymore." Winant recasts the political and cultural dimensions of race to account for its changed manifestations and changing meaning, and challenges us to "reencounter the concept [racism] and disrupt its former meanings in order to understand it anew." As Winant points out, the changing meaning of race and racism not only has relabeled "Negroes" as "African Americans," but also has produced in whites the Du Boisian racial dualism that Blacks have long experienced. Whites must now consider how they are perceived by the racial Other. As one of the commentators puts it, whites are being "raced."

Paul Ong urges us to be pragmatic about racism. Without accepting its permanency or impermanency, he states that racism is mutable and progress can be made, but that the struggle against it is an intergenerational struggle. With this, José Padilla agrees. Furthermore, Ong says that it may not be so easy to know if we are making progress, but it is pessimistic and unwarranted to make "racial justice appear immutable and the goal of meaningful progressive social change appear unachievable." He challenges us to develop a more precise understanding of what we are fighting, recognizing that there is difficulty in establishing a baseline for identifying racism. S.M. Miller notes that racism is not permanent; rather, it is changing and durable. Miller sees a hope and a strategy: that if we employ both structural and personal change, we can move racism "into less pernicious forms—and even make some progress." In contrast to Miller's theory of racism's durability, Leslye Orloff puts racism on a continuum and points out that the real impediment to racial progress is in not recognizing racism's influence on us.

The question of the permanency of racism turns out to be complex. The contributors remind us that clearly there has been racial advancement since slavery. But they caution that the more recent changes have been good for some and devastating for others. Bernardine Dohrn notes that entry into the juvenile justice system is in large part racially defined; in Cook County, although white youth represent 64 percent of the juvenile population, over 80 percent of youth in detention are African American and 10 percent are Latino. And Daniel Levitas takes us to a small Southern town where Ku Klux Klan influence is open and powerful, and life for the African American community is wretched. He joins Derrick Bell in asserting that "the soul of a nation—and those of its citizens—is as much defined by the permanence of racism as by the struggle against it."

This issue of the permanence of racism in American society, despite the gains of the civil rights era, raises serious concerns for all of us, making us reconsider our civil rights successes and wonder whether our lives have been, as Kenneth Clark reluctantly concludes, a "series of glorious defeats" or the stuff of meaningful progress and victory. It beckons us, as John Brittain does, to recognize that because of the permanence of racism, civil rights work "will never end, only the battlefronts and tactics will change."

Whereas the meaning of race and racism informs much of the writing that explores the permanence of racism in Part 1, meaning becomes the central issue in exploring the significance of racial and ethnic categories in Part 2. All of the contributors to Part 2 apparently accept the insight that race is socially constructed. However, there is sharp divergence as to what racial categories should be or should mean, especially within the context of a discussion of racial and ethnic census categories.

The lack of biological mooring for the meaning of race might surprise some readers, in part because we experience race as a natural fact. Race seems obvious to us. The weakness of the scientific or biological bases for racial categories is quickly exposed as one realizes that not only does each country have different racial categories but that the categories in our country have continuously shifted since the Census Bureau first started collecting data on race and ethnicity over two hundred years ago.

The social construction of race may seem like an issue that would occupy late and postmodernist philosophical debates rather than the advocate and activist community that contributes to and reads PRRAC material. However, the division and the distinction are not so neat. Indeed, as pointed out by Lawrence Wright, it is the U.S. Census Bureau and the White House's Office of Management and Budget that have raised the question of whether race should be dropped completely from the census count or whether racial categories should be reconstructed to reflect our changing sense of race. This question, like many questions about race, is not a simple one because, as many of the contributors point out, racial categories touch both on issues of identity and self-identification and on the distribution of resources and protections under civil rights laws.

The contributors offer a number of critiques of the current census structure, as well as the possibility of changing the way we categorize race and ethnicity. One complaint about the current system that Libero Della Piana discusses is the way we categorize people of multiple races. There is currently no multiracial category in the census. Children who have parents of different races are forced to choose.

The issue becomes even more confounded when we look at Latinos. They are the fastest-growing minority in the United States, and accurate census data are important to designing and implementing programs to assist this community. Furthermore, they are a multiracial population and, as Raúl Yzaguirre and Sonia Pérez remind us, Latino "race and ethnicity are not easily recognized or distinguished by observable characteristics." Ethnicity then becomes the mode by which Latinos self-identify, which is problematic within the census count's Black–white paradigm. Latinos are caught between identifying in a manner that will be accurate and one that will be beneficial.

But if race is not a scientific fact, why not abandon it or let the subjects self-define? A number of the contributors address this question and point out the dangers and limitations of this approach. Part of the difficulty is that race is not a unitary concept. Its meaning and importance differ for how we identify ourselves, how we identify others, and how others identify us. Piana, whose parents are African American and Italian, states that he is never considered Italian outside of his family. The social construction of race, if it means anything, means that one is not given complete authority to self-define.

But if one shifts the focus from race to racism, the limits and dangers of dropping racial categories become even clearer. As a society, Samuel Myers says, we frequently misidentify the problem. Many of the contributors share the assumption that the problem is not race, it is racism. Not identifying race in the census count runs the serious risk of making it more difficult to attack the disease of racism as it continues to grow, spread, and change. It does not matter to the home mortgage loan officer, the police officer, or the taxi driver what we are called on the census. But if we do not collect the data, it will be more difficult to identify the racial disparity that exists in employment, education, and mortality. As Myers points out, when Donald Fraser, the former mayor of Minneapolis, instructed his police department not to supply state officials with data on the race of those arrested, did he think that racial disparity would go away? It won't. The racial disparity in arrests in Minneapolis remains the second worst in the country for large cities, not because of the categories that we use but because of "consistent and alarming discriminatory patterns of arrest." Moves such as that made by Mayor

Fraser only make it more difficult for the racial minorities to name and bring public attention to the issue.

The right and need to claim all of who we are for our identity may be a very different project from documenting racial discrimination and disparity in our society. Indeed, a number of the commentators suggest that some who would drop racial categories are all too aware of how the information has been used as an antiracism tool.

As pointed out in Part 3, immigration issues tie together national policies and international policies and events, and touch on our approach to the "racial other" and the changing world economy. Some would posit that the racial implications of our immigration policies only occasionally rise to the surface, but many commentators and contributors to this book agree with William Tamayo's assessment that "Racism has dominated and continues to dominate immigration polices in the United States." California's Proposition 187, which is currently under challenge in federal court, and the initiatives in Congress to deprive the children of undocumented immigrants of access to public education are aimed quite clearly at non-English-speaking, nonwhite Latinos and Asians, with little effort at trying to disguise their racial implications. Along with the federal requirements that employers certify the status of their workers as citizens or aliens, one can easily envision the negative impact of these changes on both new immigrants and American citizens who are "racial others." It is curious but not completely surprising that many of the anti-immigrant initiatives are born in California, which will be our first majority minority state.

As noted by the contributors to Part 3, the civil rights community has frayed in its response to immigration issues. Paul Ong and Abel Valenzuela find a "serious challenge to the simultaneous pursuit of civil rights for African Americans and upholding our heritage as a nation of immigrants." They tell us that this tension is likely to continue until and unless we develop a new civil rights agenda that deals with racial inequality and the scapegoating of immigrants. They insist that "Third World solidarity" is unfair and unlikely without considering the cost of immigration to African Americans and other minorities. And David Hayes-Bautista, Werner Schink, and Gregory Rodriguez make a strong argument that immigrants, especially Latinos, help instead of hurt the economy, whereas other contributors assert that this is less true in some areas than in others.

All of the commentators agree that racism has played, and continues to play, an important and even central role in our immigration policy. But some commentators assert that there are other nonracist issues that must be legitimately aired and addressed in order to make progress on this issue within the minority community. Failure to do this is likely to allow racism to continue to dominate while using the apparent concern of the domestic minority community as a cover.

One does not have to look any farther than California to see a vivid example of this danger. California has led the country in its attack on immigration policy, both in terms of keeping people of color out of the country and in terms of its treatment of people once they are here. Even though the competition for jobs between immigrants and African Americans in particular has been often cited by the anti-immigrant faction, the attack on programs that benefit African Americans and other minorities picked up steam and support from many of the supporters of Proposition 187. Although we are most sensitive to these immigration concerns that affect the United States, Howard Winant and other writers make it clear that the issue, with its racial center, is truly a worldwide phenomenon, along with a new plurality and a racism rising in opposition to it, which is based in part on domestic economic anxiety.

Although the dynamic of the interaction between race and class is uneven (for instance, the African American middle class may have interests that diverge from those of poor African Americans), race and class remain inextricably linked. In Part 4, Douglas Massey resituates the issue of race in the context of class and, importantly, space. Since the early debates of W.E.B. Du Bois and Booker T. Washington, there has been an effort to separate race from class and to reduce the issues confronting poor minorities to one or the other. Massey cuts against this grain by demonstrating that not only are they linked, but that the interaction of race and class has important implications for African Americans and, increasingly, Puerto Ricans. He contends that racial residential segregation is the key factor responsible for the social transformation of the Black community and the concentration of poverty in that community since the 1970s. Under conditions of racial segregation, economic downturns in Black neighborhoods produce devastating effects across a number of different indicators, to a degree unmatched in other minority or white communities. Race affects the social and economic well-being of Blacks, primarily through the housing market, and racial segregation concentrates social disadvantages, which become worse as a joint product of worsening economic conditions and increasing racial segregation. The communities left both racially segregated and under severe economic strain are the communities that for Massey compromise "the underclass." And it is not the outmigration of the Black middle class that is responsible for this. The racialization of poverty is the product of a dynamic relationship among racial segregation, Black socioeconomic status, and racial discrimination. Massey points out that the issue for public policy is not whether race and class are responsible for the current plight of Blacks in the United States, but how race and class interact to undermine the well-being of this group.

Whereas Massey seeks an accurate definition of who comprises the underclass and what dynamics have determined inclusion in this category, Herbert Gans takes a different tack, examining the use of such labels in the creation of policy. He describes the evolution of the term "underclass" from an economic concept to a behavioral concept and its use as such as a way to label the poor as undeserving of assistance and sympathy. Furthermore, Gans points out that the convenience of such labels is that they enable us to discuss issues such as race euphemistically. He notes that "underclass" has become a racial code word, because it is increasingly being applied to Blacks, and that although the public expression of racial prejudice is no longer respectable, "underclass" has become an acceptable euphemism and a way to disadvantage the racial poor without directly addressing the issue of race. In charting the use of underclass as a behavioral concept, Gans calls for social scientists to be sensitive to such terms and to the biases and assumptions that can be built into them a priori. He believes that the focus should be on the causes of poverty and not on a study of the behaviors of its victims.

The issue of racial and ethnic categories discussed in Part 2 raises interesting policy questions for our increasingly multicultural society. In Part 5, Manning Marable, Henry Hampton, and I tackle the normative questions raised by racism and the tensions that racism causes within a multicultural and democratic society. Marable makes it clear that racism within social structures and institutions is not accidental. And he correctly characterizes racism in America as both subordinating and systemic. But this is not a prescription for surrender. Rather, recognizing the changing demographics in our country and the dynamic quality of democracy, Marable challenges us to create a new and truly multicultural democracy. I agree with the need for and challenge of a multicultural democracy, and see its hope in creating a truly multicultural educational system. But I also point out some of the ways that multiculturalism can undermine an antiracism strategy, by allowing minority groups to focus exclusively on their own ethnic or racial history rather than on the history of all peoples. Hampton sees us at a critical juncture of meaningful possibilities, believing that with a "sustained assault on poverty and racism, we will free America and truly make it the powerful, humane, prosperous country we know it can be."

Issues such as the permanence of racism, the ramifications of racial and ethnic categories, and the role of racism in a multicultural democracy, although important to how we think about strategies and problems in fighting racial disparity, are only indirectly part of the national debate on race.

Other themes addressed in *Double Exposure,* however, have already exploded into our national debate, and are already restructuring, or may soon restructure, not only our collective conscience but also our laws. One such area is affirmative action. As with immigration, our affirmative action laws and policies are already undergoing massive changes that will affect the entire country for years to come. In Part 6, Congresswoman Maxine Waters points out that unemployment and economic anxiety are driving the anti–affirmative action initiative, and are also the source of much of the fear about immigration. Because affirmative action ideologically has been removed from issues of racial justice and discrimination, it has become more vulnerable to the claim of reverse discrimination, especially in economically unstable times. This implication that racism is over suffers from a number of serious defects. First, it fails to account for how racism constrains and defines the economic opportunity of all Americans, especially poor minorities. Second, it fails to appreciate the racialized aspect of white privilege. It fails to explain how whites have accumulated their wealth and opportunity. According to Salim Muwakkil, "By de-emphasizing affirmative action's racial aspects, liberals succeeded in making the programs more palatable but less effective." Indeed, a theme that resurfaces in many of the articles in this section is a questioning of the wisdom of avoiding direct discussion of racism even as the meaning of racism changes. This failure both adds to the confusion of discussions about racial categories and makes already hard issues unnecessarily complex by separating them from their core meaning and history.

A number of commentators try to correct this serious oversight. Roger Wilkins and William Taylor, in separate pieces, try to resituate the conversation about affirmative action in our racial/ethnic history and legacy of inequality. They, along with other contributors, consider the impact of affirmative action on white males, the group that has been most uniform in its attack on affirmative action. Representative Waters reminds us that white males comprise only one-third of the American population but make up 80 percent of the House of Representatives, 92 percent of the Senate, 92 percent of the senior executives at Fortune 500 companies, and 90 percent of newspaper editors. All this, despite the fact that only 15 percent of new job applicants are white males. The assumption that in a fair world white males would do this well or even better can be sustained only by both denying our history and accepting Brent Staples's "Presumption of Stupidity" or something equally derogatory.

Given even our weak attraction to equality, America's vast racial inequality requires an explanation. There is a need to engage in a dialogue about racial disparities and tie them to the affirmative-action issue. But even as we turn to history and the "fact" of race, there will continue to be areas of disagreement, in part because, as Wilkins points out, people of different races in America have very different views of America's past and present. We carry, as I stated earlier, racialized perceptions of our world and ourselves.

To understand the changing nature of race and racism in the United States, one must also look at the role of class and the relationship between race and class. Race and racism have had, and continue to have, a profound impact not only on who is poor in our society but also on the meaning of poverty and the policies that we adopt and fail to adopt. One has only to look at the current debate over welfare reform to appreciate the importance of race in understanding the dynamic of poverty in our society. Poverty in our society has always been racialized. But just as race has shaped the way we think about and deal with poverty, so poverty or class has shaped the way we think about race. As the civil rights movement has opened up opportunity to some racial minorities, there has been a renewed effort to separate our thinking on race and class issues. The gains of middle-class minorities are used as an excuse to abandon or ignore the needs of the racial poor.

Part 6 ends with a discussion of the complex subject of reparations for slavery, which might be regarded as an extreme form of affirmative action: what might constitute reparations, why they might be appropriate, how it might happen, and what role they might play in the civil rights movement. As the contributors point out, this proposal has a number of different implications and possibilities. Howard Winant wrestles with both the moral and the political issues raised by reparations, and suggests an alternative to address a number of the social problems as well as garner wider support because of benefits that would accrue to a broad coalition. Kalonji Olusegun sees reparations as necessary, as having to do with the relationship between America and Africans in America. David McReynolds believes that, although morally powerful, reparations would be divisive. Theodore Shaw shifts the reparations analysis from the practical to the symbolic and sees reparations as an opportunity for a necessary apology by America to African Americans. John Tateishi addresses reparations in the context of the Japanese American experience, noting that the symbolic value was far more significant than the actual money. Ronald Trosper does much the same regarding the Native American experience.

The racialized nature of wealth and opportunity, especially as it affects poor African Americans, is addressed in Part 7. Participation and opportunity are central to an effective democracy and necessary to equality. Without offering people an ability to participate effectively, democracy is a sham. Central to participation in our institutions are education, the ability to invest, and the opportunity to pass our success and gains to our children. The American story has long been one of individual achievement and gain, but the contributors to this section indicate how community assets and liabilities can act to stymie individual opportunity. There is a promise of equality, but at the same time, for Blacks, a systematic denial of it. Melvin Oliver and Thomas Shapiro write that median wealth data expose deep inequalities between whites and Blacks. The median white household controls almost seven thousand dollars in net financial assets (homes and vehicles excluded), whereas the median Black household retains no net financial assets whatsoever. The implications for democracy and equality are substantial. Parents with ample assets tend to use these assets to benefit their children, for such things as education. And the statistics indicate not only the plight of the Black poor but also the precariousness of the Black middle class, which has made gains in income but not in wealth. Oliver and Shapiro attempt to trace the causes of wealth disparities. White parents are in a much better position to pass along status to their children than are Black parents. This is especially true in the area of intergenerational occupational mobility. Thus, until wealth discrepancies are addressed and accounted for, the ability of the Black community to participate and get itself on equal footing is severely hampered.

Likewise, S.M. Miller and Karen Marie Ferroggiaro posit that collective respect is also unevenly distributed by race and, like wealth disparities, can have material ramifications for minorities. What is needed is a new thinking about respect and an understanding of the effect of disrespect on such things as individual and collective behavior. David Rusk shifts the discussion by looking at how the jurisdictional structure of our cities can operate to limit opportunity and access. He contends that only metropoliswide strategies will rescue cities and urban communities of color, and pushes for annexation, city–county consolidation strategies, and fair-share housing plans to open up the suburbs. In response, Eric Mann agrees with Rusk's analysis of the consequences of urban policy but points out that what is missing is an analysis of the political dynamics of why race and class inequality exists. Margaret Weir notes the contribution and importance of including regional considerations and solutions in policy work involving urban communities of color, but states that regional strategies are only part of the solution and must be combined with local strategies in order to be both effective and meaningful. John Calmore is more skeptical. He warns that Rusk's regional prescription and abandonment of local and community development initiatives risks subsuming minority concerns into the concerns of the larger community, and takes Rusk to task on the political viability of his proposal of city annexation.

The contributors to *Double Exposure* agree across the board that race and racism matter greatly in American society. There is virtual consensus that without confronting race in its structural and institutional manifestations, we will fail to create a racially just society. *Double Exposure* does not answer our questions about race. It sharpens them. It weighs in as a book for people who think about race and also for policy makers who deal with issues that touch on race. It clarifies how we think about race and helps us to find creative and constructive solutions to dealing with issues of racial and economic inequality in America.

Part 1

Is Racism Permanent?

A position put forth by Derrick Bell, Richard Delgado, Charles Washington, John Calmore, and others, and buttressed by Douglas Massey and Nancy Denton's recent research on "American apartheid," holds that racism is a permanent, ineradicable feature of American society. Several activists and thinkers were asked to express their agreement or disagreement with this view and its implications for their own work.

Howard Winant

Racism is not a static, obvious "thing" anymore, if it ever was. Its meaning and manifestations change as social conditions, state activity, and social movements confront it. There is a big tendency to assume we know what we mean by this term, and to address it as it was identified in the 1960s: as a matter of prejudice (beliefs and attitudes), discrimination (actions enforcing unequal treatment), and "institutional" phenomena (generally, the legacy of past racial inequality imposing inequalities automatically in the present). While these remain important aspects of the racism phenomenon, none of them is the same as it was a quarter-century and more ago. It is necessary to reencounter the concept and disrupt its former meanings in order to understand it anew.

Certainly racial injustice and inequality have not lessened in any overall way, yet they have been transformed and indeed rationalized in the quarter-century since the ambiguous triumph of the civil rights movement in the mid-1960s.

Any effective analysis of racism today has to address the following points:

- The existence of *real mobility* for more favored sectors (that is, certain class-based segments) of racially defined minority groups.
- The *substantial diversification* of the North American population (remember that immigration laws were reformed in 1965 to remove their overtly racist features).
- The significant *panethnic phenomena* among Asians, Latinos, and Native Americans, which have reconstituted the U.S. racial pan-

orama in a multipolar (as opposed to the old bipolar) direction. Arguments in defense of the white–Black bipolar analysis—for example, Andrew Hacker's claim that Latinos and Asians will attain such upward mobility that within one generation they will look more like white ethnics than like a racially defined minority—are quite unconvincing.

- The *problematization of white identity* (at least somewhat) for whites. What this means is that in the post–civil rights era whites have been forced to acquire a "pale" version of the Du Boisian racial dualism: they must consider how they are perceived by their racial "others." The idea that "whiteness" is in some sense the norm still persists, although it has been weakened. This is both dangerous (since it inspires tremendous anxieties among whites) and promising (since it involves the creation of common ground across racial lines and indeed transgresses racial barriers). Needless to say, white "racial dualism" remains a limited phenomenon at present.

- The *rise of social movements* to which the Black struggle gave initial impetus, notably feminism and gay liberation in their many forms, has developed to the point where a whole range of crosscutting subjectivities and tensions (as well as new alliances) has developed. This undercuts the insularity of racial identities in various ways, for example, by giving millions of whites a personal sense of what discrimination means, or by setting up limited but real zones of common interest across racial lines.

- Finally, and perhaps most important, a significant *racial reaction* has developed over the past twenty-five or so years. This reaction has reinterpreted the demands for equality and justice made by the Black movement and its allies in a conservative discourse of individualism, competition, and laissez-faire. It has therefore rationalized racism, depriving racially defined institutions of some of the legitimacy, some of the organic connectedness with the segregated community, which they formerly enjoyed, even though these institutions (Black political organizations, schools, etc.) also suffered under Jim Crow. We must recognize that the racial reaction—with its *individualistic* rhetoric of equality (opportunity, meritocracy, etc.)—is hegemonic today. The effect of this is that racism can be treated as largely an artifact of the past. My white students tell me, "My parents marched for civil rights. They took care of the problem back then."

To understand racism today, we must take these changed circumstances into account. Certainly we should never ignore economic or political inequality (what I would call the "social structural" dimensions of racism).

We should pay more attention to a whole series of other dimensions of racism, which I would awkwardly label the "signifying" dimensions of racism. These might include:

• The *changing meaning* of race and racial identity. Right now, stripped of euphemism, there are five color-based categories in the U.S. racial order: Black, white, brown, yellow, and red. Absurd as this is, it is real and critical in people's lives. Yet obviously it is not eternal, and also obviously, a lot of people don't fit (Arab Americans, "mixed race" folks, etc.). Both in terms of policy and in terms of experience, we have to look at the way these categories are constructed and inhabited (or not) by individuals and groups. At the policy level, such issues as census politics and hate speech regulation involve this stuff. At the experiential level, how much choice do variously identified individuals (and groups) have about how they are to be "named"?

• Our understanding of *power* as a racial phenomenon has to be tackled. Who has the power? may not be as straightforward a question as we used to think. My Black students tell me that Blacks cannot be racist, because racism equals prejudice plus power, and since Blacks don't have the power, at most they can be prejudiced. A lot of church groups and antiracist organizations think the same way. But power is not a "thing"; it's a complex field of relationships, including coercive ones, and the ability to produce ideas. Power involves the ability to resist as well as to rule; it involves challenging the meaning systems and "common sense" we use every minute to interpret the world. In this sense, racially defined minorities do have at least some power. In the long run it is very dangerous for a subordinated and oppressed group to think of itself as powerless.

• Ideas about race and racism are being raised at a high level by feminists, womanists, and gay activists. The intersection of these currents stems from their common bodily experience of being "the other" for the dominant (white, male, heterosexual, etc.) culture. This should lead us to think more about *the body*. Racism is, so to speak, written on the body; coercion always involves the body; and the race–gender–sexuality linkage, so central to racial meanings of all sorts, is about the body. In terms of race, *essentialism*—the belief in real and inherent human qualities impervious to historical or social context—always links such qualities to the racial body. It is a key to understanding racism.

In these observations, I have stressed the political and cultural dimensions of racism. I do not mean to de-emphasize the social structural aspects of the phenomenon—the material inequality, the widespread injustice—that continue to plague the United States. But I think we must recognize the profound disruption that racial "common sense" has undergone in the years since, say, 1960. The very need we experience to debate the question of racism's permanence testifies to the depth of the confusion and anxiety we experience today. Now that both the nightmare of legal separation and the limited reform of the civil rights movement have run their course, we confront a new and far more formidable racism, a "streamlined" model, as one of my students put it. We must understand it anew.

S.M. Miller

The *durability* of racism is inescapable. The charge of its permanence is too scary: I don't like acting—and living—with such little hope. "Bearing witness," which assumes that our endeavors are unlikely to prevail, at least at this time, is a much more difficult stance than activism that emerges from the belief that our efforts will produce significant change. Can emotional hope and hard-headed analysis be reconciled?

Racism's durability does not imply fixity. Racism waxes and (somewhat) wanes; it plays out and through many stages and forms. Today, awareness of the great advances that were made on many fronts in the 1960s and 1970s is overwhelmed by evidence of the terrible poverty of Black children, the internalized violence of many poor African American communities, and the political unwillingness to combat residential and job segregation, to invest in Black children, or to offer remedies other than prison for crime and violence.

Could racism's durability have been expected? (My focus is primarily on institutional racism, not racism as personal attitude.) In any process of social reform to improve the circumstances of those at the bottom, the inevitable tendency is to cream, to deal with the better-off of those who suffer poverty and discrimination. They are easier to deal with; the promises of "success" are greater and costs are limited; the route to their achievement requires at most only somewhat bending the rules rather than profoundly changing them; their success presumably encourages those left behind to move in the same way; and their advance is likely to dilute pressures for deeper changes. Individual mobility, frequently sponsored by some person or institution in the mainstream world, is the model: others should tread the path that has been established for what might be called, updating W.E.B. Du Bois, the talented quintile.

Ah, but what happens to those left behind? Are they in the same circumstances to advance as the talented quintile? Are openings still available to them, or are educational and employment opportunities scaled to deal with only limited numbers? The noncream cannot easily move ahead, for deeper changes are needed to make it possible for large numbers to improve their situations. That is expensive in terms of money and privilege. The result of the limited efforts is that African Americans have a much more varied economic situation than ever before. A quarter are doing quite well; another quarter are just getting by. But half are doing very badly. That and residential segregation are major sources of the feeling of the ineradicability of racism. (The undermining by colleagues of successful Blacks is another source.)

Are we at the end of possibilities of improving the situation of those left behind? I don't think so. Some stress the need for structural changes: the opening of employment, housing, and other opportunities; others are emphasizing that residents of unstable inner-city communities have to change their behavior. Personal change without structural change is likely to be overwhelmingly defeated, but structural change without behavioral change is likely to have limited appeal. Both are needed—in actuality, in concert.

Racism is durable, but we can move it into less pernicious forms— and even make some progress.

John C. Brittain

In his 1992 book *Faces at the Bottom of the Well,* Derrick Bell posited a provocative thesis:

> Black people will never gain full equality in this country. Even those Herculean efforts we hail as successful will produce no more than temporary "peaks of progress," short-lived victories that slide into irrelevance as racial patterns adapt in ways that maintain white dominance. This is a hard-to-accept fact that all history verifies. We must acknowledge it, not as a sign of submission, but as an act of ultimate defiance.

Other civil rights advocates have expressed similar views. Robert Carter, a veteran civil rights lawyer and later federal district court judge, once said that the pioneer civil rights leaders thought that racial segregation was the disease. Once the civil rights movement eliminated segregation, the society would achieve racial equality for the African American people. Instead, the leaders discovered that segregation was only the symptom, and white racism was the disease. Still further, Kenneth B. Clark, a brilliant psychologist who conducted the studies concerning the adverse impact of segregated education on the learning abilities of Black children, recently lamented (see his contribution in *Race in America: The Struggle for Equality,* Herbert Hill and James E. Jones, Jr., eds., 1993):

> Reluctantly, I am forced to face the likely possibility that the United States will never rid itself of racism and reach true integration. I look back and shudder at how naive we all were in our belief in the steady progress racial minorities would make through programs of litigation and education, and while I very much hope for the emergence of a revived civil rights movement with innovative programs and educated leaders, I am forced to recognize that my life has, in fact, been a series of glorious defeats.

I agree with the thoughts of these civil rights activists about the "permanence of racism" in America. The conditions of white racism remain the same, but some of the underlying assumptions may have changed.

The traditional civil rights ideology was founded on the unstated assumption that human beings are equal in the eyes of God—the same; and that human nature unites us all in a common *essence.* Together we will, in the words of Dr. Martin Luther King, reach the "promised land" of racial equality. The "permanence of racism" thesis attacks that "sameness" theory. Black feminists have stood up to say, "I am not the same as you and do not speak for me." This movement, dubbed anti-essentialism, suggests that no essence unites us as human beings. Rather, we are all individuals leading the attack with unique experiences that can be neither classified nor categorized. (For example, the Black lesbian faces a dilemma about which civil rights organizations to join. Should she join NOW, led by white women, or the NAACP, led by Black men, or ACT-UP, led by gay and lesbian white people?) Antiessentialists argue that unity must be built more by realistic connections, instead of relying on abstract and unreal notions of a common essence.

Similarly, the "permanence of racism" thesis criticizes the idea that most white people in America will grant Black people equal rights. In fact, according to Bell, African Americans advanced socially, politically, and economically when the particular principle appealed to white Americans' self-interest. This means that people of color cannot rely on the majority of white people for a shared commonality of all human beings for equal treatment.

The "permanence of racism" thesis exposes the idealist aspects that racial integration will lead to equality. Today, many commentators cite the failure of the civil rights movement in the past forty years to fully reach the promises and hopes of *Brown v. Board of Education* for racial integration and equality. While the goal that racial integration will lead to greater equality remains paramount, the reality of not achieving significant progress anytime soon more accurately reflects the nature of the struggle. To match racism's resolve of perpetuation, the antiracist forces must unite with equal strength of resistance. In *Possessing the Secret of Joy,* Alice Walker says that for African American people, "Resistance is the secret of joy." The battle against the permanence of racism will never end. Therefore society must continue to study racism and devise new strategies to combat it.

I recall a personal experience when I was a civil rights lawyer in Mississippi involving an old Black woman in Sunflower County with a fighting spirit like Fannie Lou Hamer. We came out of the federal courthouse one day after the judge praised the Black people for challenging some obvious vestige of racial segregation but denied their request for relief on some seemingly unpersuasive legal technicality. I sought to comfort her with condolences about the case that the people had lost. She taught me a lesson based on the knowledge that she acquired in life rather than by formal schooling. I never forgot. When she insisted that they had won, I tried to correct her on the legality of the decision, but she interrupted. She said they won because the Black people had the white people in town very scared about the potential impact of a favorable decision for them. True, everyone knew the white people were extremely concerned about a major change in the political relations with Black people. I thought to myself, how could this Black lady think that they won? Then she said, "Lawyer Brittain, I just lives to upset these white folks and today we upset them."

Hence, the "permanence of racism" theory means that this work will never end, only the battlefronts and tactics will change.

Leslye E. Orloff

As a Jewish woman who grew up in a diverse multiracial, multiethnic community and who has spent her professional career serving those communities, I have come to believe that racism is not an immutable characteristic of American life. Much of my career has been devoted to developing better understanding and bridging gaps between people of different racial and ethnic backgrounds. During years of working in organizations that have been striving to become multicultural in their approach and composition, I have come to develop a theory that racism in our society falls along a continuum that applies equally to persons of all backgrounds. The continuum runs from understanding to tolerance to intolerance, from persons who react instinctively to racism against others as if the racism were aimed at themselves to persons who are devoutly racist. Where we locate ourselves along the continuum is a function of our experiences with other racial and ethnic groups while we were growing up and our conscious efforts to think about, address, and deal with our own racism during our adult lives.

If the ultimate goal of our work as advocates is to improve and enrich the lives of all persons in our society, we must work together in a multicultural context to achieve this end. This is true whether the specific goal of our work is to fight racism, improve human rights at home or abroad, help battered women, reduce poverty, better our environment, or improve access to health care. However, our ability to work together effectively is greatly hindered if we fail to recognize that we are all raised with a certain level of racism. Our own racism affects our view of the world and each other. We cannot overcome racism unless we learn to recognize it in ourselves. It is for this reason that the most troubling group on the continuum is people who incorrectly believe they are not racist. For this group of people, what they view as objective and fair is in fact based on racist assumptions that they are unable to identify. If we are to move toward eradicating racism in our society, we must sensitize others to recognize their own racism so that they can move along the continuum toward racial tolerance.

Continuum of Racism

1	2	3	4	5
React instinctively to racism against others.	Work to successfully eradicate own racism.	Believe they have overcome racism but have not.	Do not think about racism.	Are devoutly racist.

In the first category of the continuum is a group of persons who have generally been raised or have spent a significant portion of their lives living among ethnic and/or racial groups that are different from their own. Many of these persons come from families who permitted and encouraged them to develop childhood friendships across racial and ethnic lines and attended schools that were ethnically diverse. This category generally includes people who were raised in racially and culturally mixed communities and people who moved during childhood from a community or culture where they were part of a racially dominant group to a community where they were members of a distinct minority. Persons who fall into this category on the continuum generally react viscerally when they experience racism against others, as if it were racism aimed at themselves. For this group of persons, racially biased thoughts against groups of persons with whom they were raised or have close ties seldom, if ever, enter their consciousness.

The second category is composed of many enlightened persons who have worked to overcome racism. This is the category that encompasses most progressives, activists, and civil rights advocates. These are people who have worked hard to recognize that we have all grown up with our own racism. They have looked inward to identify their own racial biases, and have taken what they have learned about themselves and used it to work toward eradicating racism in our society. They have developed friendships and close working relationships in their adult lives with persons of diverse backgrounds and have striven consciously to learn about other peoples and other cultures so that all of us may better understand each other. People in this category have taken concrete steps to remove racism and racially biased actions from their lives, their work, and the messages that they pass on to their children. It may be that persons in this category will occasionally think about making statements or undertaking actions that may be perceived by others to be racist, but because they have educated themselves about racism and worked to overcome it, they are able to recognize the racism in these thoughts and do not act on or articulate them. In time, as people become more attuned to racism, these thoughts cease to come to mind. If most people could strive to successfully address their own racial biases in the manner that people in this category have, we as a society would make great strides toward eradicating, if not all racism, practically all of the manifestations of racism that so dramatically affect and impede our lives.

The third category on the continuum is the most difficult to address and in some ways, for those of us committed to building positive relations among racial and ethnic groups in this country, the most destructive. This category is made up of people who understand that it is politically incorrect to be racist and who fervently believe they are not racist. Although they believe they are not racist, they have been unwilling or unable to identify and address their own racism, and therefore, despite their intellectual protestations, they repeatedly make statements and undertake actions that are based on racist assumptions. Persons in this group will think a racist thought and express it even in a multiethnic context, and will be completely unaware they have done so. They will fail to comprehend the racism in their statement or action and will become defensive when challenged. This defensiveness will in turn prevent them from identifying or addressing their own racism.

I have worked with multiethnic boards and staff in numerous organizations where the actions of this group of persons has significantly undermined the ability of others to further common goals as a multicultural whole and to approach our work in a manner that addresses the needs of all constituencies, and is infused with the rich flavor imbued by our diversity. Persons in this category need to become open to learning and not be ashamed to admit and identify their own racism. They must accept and not be threatened by the fact that if we are to end racism and work in a multicultural environment, each of us must recognize our own unique strengths. Those strengths are to some extent related to the racial and ethnic background we bring to our work. Those strengths are also related to the unique role each of us can play in a society that has not yet addressed its racism. Some persons, because of their own life experiences or because of our present society's attitude toward them, may be more effective than others in carrying out certain portions of our work. If we approach our work with an understanding of our own strengths and limitations, and a willingness to recognize and create room for the strengths others bring to our work, we can exponentially improve the quality of our work.

The fourth category contains persons who have made no effort to address or think about their racism. Many are well-meaning and do not necessarily intend to perpetrate racism. They were born and raised, and have continued to live their entire lives, in communities where racist assumptions are prevalent and go unchallenged. As adults they arrange their lives so that they have little or no contact with people of different racial or ethnic backgrounds. When their life experiences bring them into contact with persons from diverse backgrounds, they may begin to challenge the racist assumptions they have always accepted as true. Thus, it is incumbent upon all of us to encourage multiculturalism not only in our work but in our public schools, in PTAs, in our places of worship, and within groups working at a community level to solve problems facing our communities.

In the fifth category on the continuum are persons who are devoutly racist and make no effort to hide their racism. While changing attitudes of persons in this category may be impossible, their willingness to openly express their views may be constrained in a society where racist attitudes are not socially acceptable. We may, however, be able to interfere with their ability to pass unfettered racist attitudes on to their children by developing school-based programs aimed at fostering understanding and cooperation between children from diverse backgrounds.

It is important as well for us to keep in mind, as we strive to develop organizations that undertake work aimed at the betterment of the human experience for all in this country and around the world, that we cannot stop with creating organizations and boards that are multiracial and multicultural. Our ultimate goal must not be to achieve equality in numbers alone. Diversity in our workplaces, on our boards, and in our communities is only a significant step toward achieving a rich multicultural society in which the cultures, life experiences, and needs of all are addressed, respected, and valued equally. As we work together in organizations striving to achieve these goals, we must remain aware that the functioning of our workplaces and organizations will change. The organizational models and styles of operation for many of our institutions were developed in an era when white males dominated the board rooms of even our most progressive institutions. If we are to succeed in our struggle to eradicate racism and achieve multiculturalism, we must change the way we think about our lives and our work, and must be open to experimenting with, developing, and adopting approaches that incorporate the worldview and life experiences of persons from diverse backgrounds. This work will require each of us to address our own racism and identify the unique contributions we can make to our struggle. We must also be willing to relinquish control, share responsibility, and value the unique contributions that others will make in our struggle to achieve a multicultural society.

Paul Ong

I think the term "permanent racism" is unacceptable, not because I disagree with the assertion that racial inequality is a persistent feature of U.S. society but because the choice of words makes racial injustice appear immutable and the goal of meaningful progressive social change appear unachievable. My reading of U.S. history, and an understanding of my family's past, tell me that this implied pessimism is unwarranted.

We as a society have come a long way from the days when one of my great-granduncles and my grandfathers were prohibited from raising their children in this country because of their race, thus forcing them to commute over the Pacific Ocean to see their families once every few years. My maternal grandfather had the courage to attempt to bring his wife and children to Boston, but federal officials promptly deported him for his effort, thus ending a journey to the United States that had started in Mexico with an illegal crossing of the Rio Grande with the help of an African American, whose name unfortunately has been lost to our family. My parents immigrated using false documents, and we the children told outsiders that a family friend who had provided the papers was our father. I still recall the nights my mother cried during the early 1960s when the U.S. government went after the "illegals" in Chinatown(s). Their problems were not limited to the fear of being expelled. My father was deeply disappointed when he could not buy a simple home in a moderate-income neighborhood because he was not white. Urban decay and later urban renewal were destroying our Chinatown and the surrounding minority neighborhood in Sacramento. One of the few areas where my parents could relocate was "tipping" from white to Black—that neighborhood became our home for most of my childhood.

This family history, which is also U.S. history, tells me that progress is possible, thus enabling me to find purpose in my antiracism work. Despite the persistence of racial discrimination, each successive generation encountered a less formidable form of racism, and this progress was made possible by reforms won by earlier activists. I see my work not in terms of changing the world today or tomorrow, but as part of a multigenerational struggle. My expectations are tempered by this sense of history and by the understanding that one must fight mightily for small gains. I am not, however, so naive as to believe that change is simply linear and that racism can be eliminated. There are tremendous institutional forces and economic interests that maintain and reproduce racial inequality. I accept that we will suffer minor and major setbacks.

One final note. As I implied above, I believe that the nature of racial injustice changes from one historical period to another. Our generation faces a racism that is incredibly complex in a racially pluralistic urban setting such as Los Angeles. The confounding effects of ethnicity and disparate class standing have made it exceedingly difficult to formulate effective strategies. One major challenge is to develop a more precise understanding of what we are fighting.

Daniel Levitas

If anyone needs convincing about the permanent nature of racism, I recommend a visit to Blakely, Georgia. Located a three-and-a-half-hour drive south of Atlanta, this small, rural community distinguished itself by allowing its fire department to be run by the Ku Klux Klan. The fire chief told coworkers that fires in the Black community "beautify the neighborhood."

Until recently, Blakely's African American community—which comprises fully half the town's population—had been completely disenfranchised by decades of segregation and at-large voting. It took a federal voting rights lawsuit to force the city council to create single-member districts. Further courageous organizing by a handful of Black activists helped ensure an end to more than one hundred years of all-white government.

Blakely's school board is still chosen in secret by an anonymous grand jury, a practice that continues in nineteen Georgia counties. The result is that although the school system is majority Black, only one person on the five-member board is African American.

Cross burnings were frequent in the town and surrounding county. The targets were usually white families who socialized with Blacks. The local police chief refused to investigate.

In 1990 and 1991, I made that three-and-a-half-hour trip more times than I care to remember. On one of those visits, I interviewed Charles Weatherford, the regional Klan organizer. Dissatisfied with the administration of the local Klavern, he was eager to spill the beans on the fire chief. Weatherford's disclosures—and those of other Klansmen who were similarly coaxed and cajoled into talking—laid the groundwork for yet another federal civil rights lawsuit.

After the town spent nearly fifty thousand dollars in legal fees to defend itself and its racist fire chief, the suit was settled and all three Klan firefighters were dismissed. The lawsuit sparked an FBI investigation, indictments followed, and Weatherford and several of his compatriots earned felony convictions.

I had the luxury of leaving Blakely before sundown, but for millions of people of color who must endure racism's debilitating and oftentimes deadly effects, there is no escape. And, unlike Blakely, their struggles usually do not reach the federal courts, the pages of the *New York Times,* or network television.

While white social scientists, conservatives, politicians, and media pundits debate to what extent—and sometimes even whether—racism exists, more than half their fellow citizens remain convinced that Blacks breed crime, prefer welfare to hard work, and are less patriotic than whites, according to the National Opinion Research Center. Numerous other objective indicators of racism exist, measuring everything from discrimination in housing and employment to car purchases and bank loans.

Racism must be fought because it—like anti-Semitism, homophobia, and sexism—is inherently unjust and destroys both human potential and lives. These evils must also be challenged to preserve what humanity remains in all of us. The soul of a nation—and those of its citizens—is as much defined by the permanence of racism as by the struggle against it.

José Padilla

Early in my life, I believed that were we to rid the world of railroad tracks, racism would walk away down the same path. The daily crossing from the Mexican east side to the other side of town to attend Catholic school was an education on the way there and on the crossing back. Upon graduating from Catholic middle school, I failed to understand the warning about local racism when my mother offered her prophetic wisdom, explaining that my white Catholic school friends would abandon me for other social circles at the mixed public high school. I also failed to see when I learned that perfect grades and bilingual skills were "too Mexican," the reason given when I was denied the honor of representing this country through the foreign exchange program that was sending a student from our high school to Costa Rica.

Then a civil rights problem walked onto the high school campus in 1969 when the Chicano high school students decided to wear buttons that called for "Chicano Liberation." At that moment, the near riot was mediated by an invisible line separating brown teenagers from their Anglo peers, both enraged because the unspoken differences between them were now in the open, expressed through words on yellow-brown buttons. The following June, I let go of the naive railroad track theory just before college when the mother of a white friend reminded me that it was not stellar grades that got me (and not her daughter) into the prestigious university, but rather "race."

I repeat this purely personal exposé of a racial journey from rural youth to midlife because it persists as a personal learning and as the formative experience that introduced me to racism. Twenty-some years later this race education continues evolving with increasing complexity. New notions mix class and race, race and nationalism, and nationalism and indigenous background. The latter describes the phenomenon in California where Mexican mestizo farmworkers will discriminate against Mexican Indian farmworkers because of language and other cultural differences. Among the indigenous groups represented in California are Mixtec and Zapotec Indians from southern Mexico and Kanjobal and Mam Indians from Guatemala.

In my youth, poverty confused the issue because the railroad tracks didn't keep just Mexicans, but poor Mexican and Black families, on their side. And although it was true that the social circles at the high school were largely richer kids going around and around with each other, other circles mixed on the athletic field, in the college-prep classes, in student body governance, even in limited interracial dating. These social separations masked deeper racial divisions. The exceptions to the rule that race molded the character of interracial relations made many of us less aware of the existence of the rule and its extent.

I have concluded that so long as racial, ethnic, and national origin differences exist in American society, racism will fester because it is an effective means through which the economic class system is maintained. Through these differences, the supposed superiority of one group will act to subordinate another. Where there is economic advantage to be had, potential beneficiaries will use these differences to advantage. Concurrently, other "isms" (e.g., sexism, militarism) will play enhancing roles that accomplish the same thing. In other words, groups seeking to remedy their particular "ism" issues fail to collaborate effectively with other change advocates to mutual benefit. At the same time, because each "ism" agenda cuts across class categories, it is much more difficult to collaborate on multi-issue or class-defined agendas. Class and social division is enhanced in that way.

In an economically stratified society, the urge to get ahead and its possibility will feed racism at all class levels. Through the eyes of an outsider, the American wealthy and powerful do not appear to fully accept those of certain religious or ethnic backgrounds, despite their riches. At the midlevel of society, racial difference will be used to both include and exclude ethnic individuals in that competition for a limited economic pie. In the last half century, the difference was used to expand the beneficiaries of the class status, and more recently race is being used in reverse. Among the poor, racial difference feeds human esteem by assisting those of different color to perceive themselves as better off than others in the same depraved economic state. Beyond that, in our welfare state, the distribution of resources to help alleviate the effects of poverty was done racially and again enhanced racial division to the extent that the benefits were distributed with racial disparity. Yet were we to eliminate class difference, racism would not exist to separate economically but might exist to separate socially.

As to solution, laws will get some of color up the ladder nearer the ceiling. Legal force will also get us into tolerance but not love of neighbor. Marriage might get some nearer to power or into more prestigious social circles, as will becoming middle-class or being prestigiously schooled. Interethnic marriages will mask the persistence of racism, as will mixed friendships. These all help the perception that race relations are improving. But on the edges, raw hatred will continue to characterize American racism. An "edge," for example, is where white-on-Black violence sets a Black man on fire. It also is where Black-on-white violence bashes a truck driver senseless on the pavement, as happened during the Los Angeles rebellion. In our Anglo-dominated society, the second expression of hatred is not racism. It is pure brutishness that some perpetrators justify as a by-product of a race-driven society. It is "reverse hatred." Five generations hence, can the same hate event justifiably be called racism when the Anglo victim pleads for remedy to humans of color running the country with similar domination? Or will the shift in power control effectively eliminate the applicability of racism as a term for describing those racial relations?

There are other edges today where racial competition leaves little room for sharing of the bone (e.g., on the edges where racial candidates compete for political, corporate, or governmental presence and advantage). Is it racism when one subordinated group uses racial difference to its advantage at the expense of another racial or national origin group, or is it a simple question of racial politics?

Another edge exists where the immigration debate meets racial difference. At a recent academic debate on immigrant-bashing, an enraged Latina advocate called the root cause of immigrant hatred racism. In that context, some Latino advocates try to understand the difference between a white politician using anti-immigrant sentiments to bring suffering to Latino or Asian communities and an African American politician doing the same thing. It is perceived as racism on both counts. It is still racism, despite the effort to intellectualize the debate as a question of "citizenship" and "illegality" when the impact falls disproportionately on those immigrant communities of color. But what if a Latino politician joined the debate on the anti-immigrant side? Would the perpetrator be called racist or simply a facilitator of another's racism?

The immigrant history of the nation indicates that hatred expressed as anti-immigrant sentiment varies in the cycle only with the nationality, the color, or the religion of the victim. Immigrant history argues for persistence of racism, although the oppressive treatment of immigrants may not always be labeled racism. It goes without saying that the two centuries of persistent African American oppression following the forced emigration into slavery is a historical fact different from the Mejicano/Chicano or Native American experience as victims of conquest through war.

Yet the quality of the racial oppression experienced by different ethnic groups is not dissimilar. Latinos share with African Americans the mistreatment due to color and culture. With our Native American brethren we share mistreatment due to cultural and linguistic differences that clash with mainstream American cultural expectation. With our Asian brethren we share all of these, adding immigrant status. In this view, the necessity for the nation to feed its economic needs or to feed its democratic tradition with immigrants would argue for persistence, as most immigrants will enter at the economic bottom and their accentuated difference will somewhere breed contempt. If the difference is one of color, the victim may well use the term "racism" to describe the maltreatment. In our times, the Latino community prefers to use that term.

Racial justice prevails in that nation where the tolerant govern, dominate the debate, and outyell the intolerant citizens voicing hatred. Yet the intolerant always carry racism in the heart. There is a solution. It is an intergenerational struggle evolving to end the injustices of all intolerant "isms." It is the affirmative promotion of cultural humanism and pluralism. The yearning to be respected and treated "the same" will always come from a minority of color or religion or nationality and a higher human value; a human right must exist to provide for it. And only where there exists a cultural leadership that learns to communicate across ethnic lines, that learns to mediate across the language obstacles and across the multicolored masses of people, will racism be defeated and left to the economics of our time. There we shall all be rich. We shall all be poor. But there we may yet embrace Maya Angelou's prophetic words, looking into each other's face, saying, "Very simply / With hope— Good morning."*

Bernardine Dohrn

Watching children chained to each other in Chicago's juvenile court causes me to think of Derrick Bell.

The racialized image of bondage, slavery, and chain gangs evoked by the passage of these youths is unavoidable. Yet hundreds of committed employees carry on each day, undismayed by this silent assault on the dignity of children. I hear Professor Bell whisper to me when I rage at this treatment of young men, whisper that I've focused on symbol rather than substance. Surely, Bell would point out, even unchained these young people would be arrested, detained, and adjudicated in heartbreaking disproportion: 80 percent of the youth in

---

*From the inaugural poem "On the Pulse of Morning," read January 20, 1993, by Maya Angelou.

detention are African American and 10 percent are Hispanic, in a county where 64 percent of the juveniles are white. Entry into the juvenile justice system is in large part racially defined, and foretells an impoverished future. This year, nearly half of all African American children are born into poverty, and Blacks are three times as likely as whites to be poor.

The causes of this overrepresentation of children of color in juvenile court are multiple and intertwined, but the machinery and message of racism permeate the apparatus. These youths are disposable, dangerous, and doomed. Another, private system operates for white youth. The public pretends that the solutions are mysterious or expensive, but our own middle-class children have access to the schools, health care, security, and dreams that all youth deserve. These children are denied.

By placing the permanence of racism squarely in the frame, Bell calls not for acceptance but for resistance as an existential act, consciously determined, based neither on sentiment nor on victory, but taken nonetheless as ethical "makers-of-meaning." This notion involves creating a public space by acting, by imagining racial equality, by forging an engaged citizenry based on "committed living." Poet/author bell hooks tells her students, "If you can't imagine something, it can't come into being." Derrick Bell insists that we acknowledge the impossibility yet act through conviction—what the South African revolutionaries called "tunnelling from both ends."

Cornel West notes that "the notion that we are all part of one garment of destiny is discredited. . . . There is no escape from our interracial interdependence, yet enforced racial hierarchy dooms us as a nation to collective paranoia and hysteria—the unmaking of any democratic order." For white people, resistance includes disrupting the "taken-for-granted" and the "care-less-ness" of privilege. It requires humility, acceptance of inadequacy, and doses of good humor.

At the end of the 1900s, described best by W.E.B. Du Bois as a century defined by "the issue of the color line," my worldview based on certain understandings of racism, sexism, and imperialism seems inadequate. How to understand the mass cultures of religious fundamentalism, endemic violence, or the collapse of highly unsatisfactory socialism? Increasingly, I choose based on a stubborn sense of allying with the oppressed, identifying with the "other": what Toni Morrison calls "entering what one is estranged from." I fight for strategy and vision, but no longer insist that there is a rational fit.

I work with and for children because they require "futuring"—thinking beyond the bottom line and next year's election. They mirror back to us our failures and limitations, and our small, ragged mortality. The honest observations of my three sons spur me to chart the unsettling course of who I am. They spotlight the multiple hypocrisies. They tease me for obsessing about the paradigm of race in sports, music, and film and for choosing sides correspondingly. They watch.

James Baldwin wrote (in *The Fire Next Time*): "To be sensual . . . is to respect and rejoice in the force of life, or life itself, and to be present in all that one does, from the effort of loving to the breaking of bread." Yes.

john a. powell

There is a growing sense within the minority community that the condition of African Americans has not improved and, worse still, that it will not get any better. An increasing number of minority thinkers voice this sentiment. Indeed, one scholar, whom I greatly respect, has stated not only that racism is a permanent fixture on the American landscape, but also that equality rhetoric itself does not produce real change, and instead causes despair. While these sentiments are understandable, especially given the declining living conditions of African Americans, they are wrong and dangerous.

Regardless of the difficulty in defining that racial baseline and comparing the African American circumstance during two different periods of time, one would have to ignore history to assert that the conditions and status of Blacks in America have not improved since slavery. This should not be our central focus, though. The more important point we must consider is to what extent we can reasonably expect to affect the future living conditions of Blacks and what role equality will play in realizing that change.

Racial subordination and racial hostility still pervade American society. Yet many people, including powerful members of the courts and the political structure, suggest that racial equality has already been achieved. How is it that society can look at the condition of Blacks, some seeing racial equality, others seeing racial inequality? One reason is that many people are *not* aware of the racial disparity. If they see disparity at all, they see economic disparity that just happens to disproportionately affect Blacks.

Another reason hinges on the way we think about equality. Many people believe that inequality is determined by formal laws and intentional individual practices. The removal of explicit racial barriers during the civil rights era, such as laws prohibiting Blacks from living in certain neighborhoods or going to certain schools, engendered a belief that the vast majority of racial inequality had been corrected because of the advance in the level of *formal equality*. However, while some Blacks clearly benefited from this change, a substantial number did not. Indeed, most Blacks continued to go to segregated schools and live in segregated neighborhoods. This was not by choice.

This phenomenon calls into question the role of equality and equality rhetoric in changing or maintaining the racial status quo. Conditions in many of the de facto apartheid schools and segregated neighborhoods are as bad as, if not worse than, the conditions before the civil rights movement. But it is not equality per se we need to move beyond; rather, it is the pursuit of formal equality we should put aside. We must still focus on real equality by concentrating on the underlying conditions and causes of racial disparity. The goal of the civil rights movement was not simply to repeal racist laws but to end actual racial subordination. Clearly, removing racist laws was only part of the effort. It is the struggle for actual equality, substantive equality, that remains.

Certainly, the African American condition has improved since slavery. This is little cause to celebrate, though. The struggle for the majority of African Americans remains to be fought. The problem is not simply equality, and certainly not substantive equality, but the more subtle structural barriers that continue to maintain racial disparity. It is the condition of African Americans and racism that cause despair. It is that removal that must be our goal. Equality is not just an empty ideal; it is a social and human imperative. It must be part of us and part of our future. Will this struggle be won? Who knows? This future is not something to be discovered; it is to be made.

Put on a Happy Face
Masking the Differences Between Blacks and Whites

Benjamin DeMott

At the movies these days, questions about racial injustice have been amicably resolved. Watch any recent film in which both Blacks and whites are primary characters and you can, if you want, forget about race. Whites and Blacks greet one another on the screen with loving candor, revealing their common humanity. In *Pulp Fiction,* an armed Black mobster (played by Samuel L. Jackson) looks deep into the eyes of an armed white thief (played by Tim Roth) in the middle of the holdup and shares his version of God's word in Ezekiel, whereupon the two men lay aside their weapons, both more or less redeemed. The moment inverts an earlier scene in which a white boxer (played by Bruce Willis) risks his life to save another Black mobster (played by Ving Rhames), who is being sexually tortured as a prelude to his execution.

Pulp Fiction is one of a series of films suggesting that the beast of American racism is tamed and harmless. Close to the start of *Die Hard with a Vengeance* the camera finds a white man wearing a sandwich board on the corner of Amsterdam Avenue and 138th Street in Harlem. The board carries a horrific legend: I HATE NIGGERS. A group of young Blacks approach the man with murderous intent, bearing guns and knives. They are figures straight out of a national nightmare— ugly, enraged, terrifying. No problem. A Black man, again played by Jackson, appears and rescues the white man, played by Willis. The Black man and white man come to know each other well. In time the white man declares flatly to the Black, "I need you more than you need me." A moment later he charges the Black with being a racist—with not liking whites as much as the white man likes Blacks—and the two talk frankly about their racial prejudices. Near the end of the film, the men have grown so close that each volunteers to die for the other.

Benjamin DeMott's "Put on a Happy Face: Masking the Differences Between Blacks and Whites" (excerpts) appeared in the September 1995 *Harper's.*

Pulp Fiction and *Die Hard with a Vengeance* follow the pattern of *Lethal Weapon 1, 2,* and *3,* the Danny Glover/Mel Gibson buddy vehicles that collectively grossed $357 million, and *White Men Can't Jump,* which, in the year of the L.A. riots, grossed $76 million. In *White Men Can't Jump,* a white dropout, played by Woody Harrelson, ekes out a living on Black-dominated basketball courts in Los Angeles. He's arrogant and aggressive but never in danger because he has a Black protector and friend, played by Wesley Snipes. At the movie's end, the white, flying above the hoop like a stereotypical Black player, scores the winning basket in a two-on-two pickup game on an alley-oop pass from his Black chum, whereupon the two men fall into each other's arms in joy. Later, the Black friend agrees to find work for the white at the store he manages.

> WHITE (helpless): I gotta get a job. Can you get me a job?
> BLACK (affectionately teasing): Got any references?
> WHITE (shy grin): You.

Such dialogue is the stuff of romance. What's dreamed of and gained is a place where whites are unafraid of Blacks, where Blacks ask for and need nothing from whites, and where the sameness of the races creates a common fund of sweet content. The details of the dream matter less than the force that makes it come true for both races, eliminating the constraints of objective reality and redistributing resources, status, and capabilities. That cleansing social force supersedes political and economic fact or policy; that force, improbably enough, is friendship.

The good news at the movies obscures the bad news in the streets and confirms the Supreme Court's recent decisions on busing, affirmative action, and redistricting. Like the plot of *White Men Can't Jump,* the Court postulates the existence of a society no longer troubled by racism. Because Black–white friendship is now understood to be the rule, there is no need for integrated schools or a Congressional Black Caucus or affirmative action. The Congress and state governors can guiltlessly cut welfare, food assistance, fuel assistance, Head Start, housing money, fellowship money, vaccine money. Justice Anthony Kennedy can declare, speaking for the Supreme Court majority, that creating a world of genuine equality and sameness requires only that "our political system and our society cleanse themselves . . . of discrimination."

The movies reflect the larger dynamic of wish and dream. Day after day the nation's corporate ministries of culture churn out images of racial harmony. Millions awaken each morning to the friendly sight of Katie Couric nudging a perky elbow into good buddy Bryant Gumbel's side. My mailbox and millions of demographically similar others are choked with flyers from companies (Wal-Mart, Victoria's Secret) bent on publicizing both their wares and their social bona fides by displaying Black and white models at cordial ease with each other. BellSouth TV commercials present children singing "I am the keeper of the world"—first a white child, then a Black child, then a white child, then a Black child. Because Dow Chemical likes Black America, it recruits young Black college grads for its research division and dramatizes, in TV commercials, their tearful–joyful partings from home. ("Son, show 'em what you got," says a Black lad's father.) American Express shows an elegant Black couple and an elegant white couple sitting together in a theater, happy in each other's company. During the evening news I watch a Black mom offer Robitussin to a miserably coughing white mom. On *The 700 Club,* Pat Robertson joshes Ben Kinchlow, his Black sidekick, about Ben's far-out ties.

What counts here is not the saccharine clumsiness of the interchanges but the bulk of them—the ceaseless, self-validating gestures of friendship, the humming, buzzing background theme: All decent Americans extend the hand of friendship to African Americans; nothing, but nothing, is more auspicious for the African American future than this extended hand. Faith in the miracle cure of racism by change of heart turns out to be so familiar as to have become unnoticeable. And yes, the faith has its benign aspect. Even as they nudge me and others toward belief in magic (instant pals and no-money-down equality), the images and messages of devoted relationships between Blacks and whites do exert a humanizing influence.

Nonetheless, through these same images and messages the comfortable majority tells itself a fatuous untruth. Promoting the fantasy of painless answers, inspiring groundless self-approval among whites, joining the Supreme Court in treating "cleansing" as inevitable, the new orthodoxy of friendship incites culturewide evasion, justifies one political step backward after another, and greases the skids along which, tomorrow, welfare block grants will slide into state highway-resurfacing budgets. Whites are part of the solution, says this orthodoxy, if we break out of the prison of our skin color; say hello, as equals, one on one, to a Black stranger and make a Black friend. We're part of the problem if we have an aversion to Black people; or are frightened of them; or if we feel that the more distance we put between them and us, the better; or if we're in the habit of asserting our superiority rather than acknowledging our common humanity. Thus we shift the problem away from politics—from Black experience and the history of slavery—and perceive it as a matter of the suspicion and fear found within the white heart; solving the problem asks no more of us than that we work on ourselves, scrubbing off the dirt of ill will.

The approach miniaturizes, personalizes, and moralizes; it removes the large and complex dilemmas of race from the public sphere. It tempts audiences to see history as irrelevant and to regard feelings as decisive—to believe that the fate of Black Americans is shaped mainly by events occurring in the hearts and minds of the privileged. And let's be frank: the orthodoxy of friendship feels *nice*. It practically *consecrates* self-flattery. People forget the theoretically unforgettable—the caste history of American Blacks, the connection between no schools for longer than a century and bad school performance now, between hateful social attitudes and zero employment opportunities, between minority anguish and majority fear.

In the civil rights era, the experience for many millions of Americans was one of discovery. A hitherto unimagined continent of human reality and history came into view, inducing genuine concern and at least a temporary setting aside of self-importance. I remember with utter clarity what I felt at Mary Holmes College in West Point, Mississippi, when a Black student of mine was killed by tailgating rednecks; my fellow tutors and I were overwhelmed with how shamefully wrong a wrong could be. For a time, we were released from the prisons of moral weakness and ambiguity. In the year or two that followed—the mid-1960s—the notion that some humans are more human than others, whites more human than Blacks, appeared to have been overturned. The next step seemed obvious: society would have to admit that when one race deprives another of its humanity for centuries, those who have done the depriving are obligated to do what they can to restore the humanity of the deprived. The obligation clearly entailed the mounting of comprehensive, long-term programs of developmental assistance—not guilt money handouts—for nearly the entire Black population. The path forward was unavoidable.

It was avoided. Shortly after the award of civil rights and the institution, in 1966, of limited preferential treatment to remedy employment and educational discrimination against African Americans, a measure of economic progress for Blacks did appear in census reports. Not much, but enough to stimulate glowing tales of universal Black advance and to launch the good-news barrage that continues to this day (headline in the *New York Times,* June 18, 1995: "Moving On Up: The Greening of America's Black Middle Class").

After Ronald Reagan was elected to his first term, the new dogma of Black–white sameness found ideological support in the form of criticism of so-called coddling. Liberal activists of both races were berated by critics of both races for fostering an allegedly enfeebling psychology of dependency that discouraged African Americans from committing themselves to individual self-development. Most Blacks, it was claimed, could make it on their own—as voluntary immigrants have done—were they not held back by devitalizing programs that presented them, to themselves and others, as somehow dissimilar to and weaker than other Americans. This argument was all-in-the-same-boatism in a different key; the claim remained that progress depends upon recognition of Black–white sameness. Let us see through superficial differences to the underlying, equally distributed gift for success. Let us teach ourselves—in the words of the Garth Brooks tune—to ignore "the color of skin" and "look for . . . the beauty within."

Yet more powerful has been the ceaseless assault, over the past generation, on our knowledge of the historical situation of Black Americans. On the face of things it seems improbable that the cumulative weight of documented historical injury to African Americans could ever be lightly assessed. Gifted Black writers continue to show, in scene after scene—in their studies of middle-class Blacks interacting with whites—how historical realities shape the lives of their Black characters. In *Killer of Sheep,* the brilliant Black filmmaker Charles Bumett dramatizes the daily encounters that suck poor Blacks into will-lessness and contempt for white fairy tales of interracial harmony; he quickens his historical themes with images of faceless Black meat processors gutting undifferentiated, unchoosing animal life. Here, say these images, as though talking back to Clarence Thomas, here is a basic level of Black life unchanged over generations. Where there's work, it's miserably paid and ugly. Space allotments at home and at work cramp body and mind. Positive expectation withers in infancy. People fall into the habit of jeering at aspiration as though at the bidding of a physical law. Obstacles at every hand prevent people from loving and being loved in decent ways, prevent children from believing their parents, prevent parents from believing they themselves know anything worth knowing. The only true self, now as in the long past, is the one mocked by one's own race. "Shit on you, nigger," says a voice in *Killer of Sheep.* "Nothing you say matters a good goddamn."

For whites, these works produce guilt, and for Blacks, I can only assume, pain and despair. During the last two decades, the entertainment industry has conducted a siege on the pertinent past, systematically excising knowledge of the consequences of the historical exploitation of African Americans. Factitious renderings of the American past blur the outlines of Black–white conflict, redefine the ground of Black grievances for the purpose of diminishing the grievances, restage Black life in accordance with the illusory conventions of American success mythology, and present the operative influences on race history as the same as those implied to be pivotal in *White Men Can't Jump* or a BellSouth advertisement.

Mass-media treatments of the civil rights protest years carried forward the process, contributing to the "positive" erasure of difference. Big-budget films like *Mississippi Burning,* together with an array of TV biographical specials on Dr. Martin Luther King and others, presented the long-running struggle between disenfranchised Blacks and the majority white culture as a heartwarming episode of interracial unity; the speed and caringness of white response to the oppression of Blacks demonstrated that broad-scale race conflict or race difference was inconceivable.

A consciousness that ingests either a part or the whole of this revisionism loses touch with the two fundamental truths of race in America: namely, that because of what happened in the past, Blacks and whites cannot yet be the same; and that because what happened in the past was no mere matter of ill will or insult, but the outcome of an established caste structure that has only very recently begun to be dismantled, it is not reparable by one-on-one goodwill. The word "slavery" comes to induce stock responses with no vital sense of a grinding devastation of mind visited upon generation after generation. Hoodwinked by the orthodoxy of friendship, the nation either ignores the past, summons for it a detached, correct "compassion," or gazes at it as though it were a set of aesthetic conventions, like twisted trees and fragmented rocks in nineteenth-century picturesque painting—lifeless phenomena without bearing on the present.

The chance of striking through the mask of corporate-underwritten, feel-good, ahistorical racism grows daily more remote. The trade-off—whites promise friendship, Blacks accept the status quo—begins to seem like a good deal.

Cosseted by Hollywood's magic lantern and soothed by press releases from Washington and the American Enterprise Institute, we should never forget what we see and hear for ourselves. Broken out by race, the results of every social tabulation from unemployment to life expectancy add up to a chronicle of atrocity. The history of Black America fully explains—to anyone who approaches it honestly—how the disaster happened and why neither guilt money nor lectures on personal responsibility can, in and of themselves, repair the damage. The vision of friendship and sympathy placing Blacks and whites "all in the same boat," rendering them equally able to do each other favors, "to give rides to one another," is a smiling but monstrous lie.

The New International Dynamics of Race

Howard Winant

The new world order, such as it is, is increasingly and complexly a racial order, and we ought to work on understanding its dynamics better.

Let me begin by summarizing my argument:

- In the last quarter-century, migration to the Northern societies has reached the point where de facto plural societies are in place just about everywhere.
- Racial heterogeneity is linked with other forms of economic and social crisis; furthermore, it calls into question previous concepts of national identity and the role of the state.
- The centrist elites in power in the North do not possess the strategic resources or vision required to deal with this expanded (and in many cases, quite racialized and already politicized) social heterogeneity.

- The traditional Left oppositions also are not equipped to address the new racial dynamics; their failure is due in part to their susceptibility to economic crisis, and in part to their own complicity with racism.
- In this situation, the Right is ascendant, because it can express the anxieties and reiterate the familiar national-popular themes, which the center and Left cannot so easily assert.
- The ascendance of the Right also involves some modifications or rearticulations of its traditional racial ideology; new forms of racism have emerged to incorporate elements of past "egalitarian" positions, and fascism is again a real threat.
- Recognizing these dynamics can help us mobilize against the resurgent Right, against the rising tide of a renovated and newly diversified racism, and against the specter of fascism.

The Empire Strikes Back

From a global point of view, the last two or three decades have established that indeed "the empire strikes back." The postcolonial era has witnessed unprecedented population movements, creating societies that are considerably more diverse than they were only a few years before. This pluralized and heterogeneous situation, this multiplication of group identities, furthermore, is racialized throughout the developed world. In the Americas, of course, racialized heterogeneity is a millennial phenomenon, dating back to the conquest and the inception of African slavery. But in Europe, with the notable and significant exception of anti-Semitism, this phenomenon of a pluralized and racialized population is actually quite new. Though a few colonial subjects were always present in the European metropolis, the influx of substantial numbers in the postwar, postcolonial period has deeply altered a dynamic in which the racial order and the imperial order had been one, in which the "other" was by and large kept outside the gates of the "mother country." Those days are now gone forever.

The challenges posed by this new and often racialized heterogeneity reach around the globe. They extend, for example, to Japan, where Yamato hegemony is coming in for renewed questioning. They apply to Australia, where Asian populations are expanding and native peoples are more organized than ever. They resonate in countries that have long histories of Eurocentric orientation and white supremacy, such as South Africa, Zimbabwe, Mexico, and Brazil.

Of course, there are enormous variations in the local situations I am describing: the degree to which minorities are racialized varies; in fact, the meaning of race varies among, and indeed within, the various societies I've mentioned. As always, the meaning of race has to be understood as a prime theme of political contestation. But the main point stands: that throughout the world, and especially in the North, a new and politicized racial heterogeneity is the norm, and that this is going to remain the case for the foreseeable future.

Racial Heterogeneity Is Linked
with Other Forms of Crisis

At present, world population is growing at about 100 million/year. While population growth is quite modest in the North, it is very rapid in the South, where the "demographic transition" is still an outcome devoutly to be wished. Since there is no appreciable improvement in Southern "life chances"—with a few well-known exceptions—the "push" pressures for migration to the North can hardly be expected to abate.

Meanwhile, the earlier, postwar "pull" factors that existed in the North have largely evaporated. These arose in the earlier postwar period from relative labor shortages and from the high growth rates that permitted various pacts (or tacit agreements for cooperation) between capital and labor. European "guest worker" programs, the repeal of restrictive (and racist) U.S. immigration laws in 1965 (leading to extensive inflows of Latin American, Caribbean, and Asian immigrants), the active British recruitment of labor in the West Indies from the late 1940s into the 1960s, the French absorption of widespread numbers of Maghrebines in the wake of the Algerian defeat, the creation of a large Korean community in Japan—all these took shape at a time when "pull" strategies were organized and administered by Northern governments.

Today all this is in the past.

Proposition 187 in California, restrictions on so-called *extracommunitarios* in Italy, Margaret Thatcher's famous speech about the "swamping" of the English by aliens (persons who only a few years before had been entitled, as Commonwealth citizens, to full rights under British law)—all these developments highlight the disappearance of official support for immigration toward the North. More yet:

they reveal the confusion and conflict which ex-imperialist states face when confronted by the mobility of their former subjects, and by the claims of those whose political rights were only recently restricted by racial caste systems that have now lost their grip.

The Center Cannot Hold

The political center cannot hold against this tide of racialized plurality. To the extent that all the Northern countries are under the rule of technocratic state elites whose chief objective is to keep the bow of the ship of state pointed smartly into the economic wind, the presence of ex-colonials, as citizens, as permanent residents, or as increasingly expensive and demanding erstwhile peasants and subproletarians, is not a happy prospect. It threatens or even obliterates a whole range of formerly stability-oriented policies, transforming them into openly conflicting and contradictory policy imperatives.

Therefore, faced not only with a rising tide of immigration but also with a far more developed and politicized heterogeneity among their populations (something true even in the United States), governments have sought to reframe social policies in a host of related areas: to organize labor supplies; to control immigration flows, in order to distinguish among desirable and undesirable migrant workers; to handle social problems such as housing, education, and public health; to orient and restrict welfare outlays to impoverished minority groups; to integrate them into social and political institutions (or to set up parallel institutions, or to handle the disruption costs of failing to achieve this integration); and, finally, to reconceptualize themes of national identity and the logic of the nation-state.

In the real world of today, where the tides that lift all boats have been out for twenty years, these tasks are beyond the capabilities of the centrist and technocratic elites that hold power throughout the developed North. After all, to maintain a labor force divided by race into high- and low-wage sectors may depress wages, but will certainly also fuel social conflict. To handle social problems like housing and education shortfalls means taxing established residents to pay for newcomers. Yet to restrict social welfare programs means fostering crime and social antagonism. To integrate minorities is either to problematize their identities or to problematize the identities of established residents, as we can see in the English-only movement in the United States, the general fear of Muslims throughout the North, and so on. Managing these problems is simply too difficult for most of the present Northern governments.

The Traditional Left Is Not Up to the Task

Just as the center cannot hold, so the traditional Lefts are not up to the task of mobilizing these heterogeneous populations for change, either reformist or radical, precisely because of the narrowness of their social base.

The Northern Lefts have always been suspicious of transformations in the composition of the labor force. Often in the past they have resisted the incursions of freedmen, immigrants, women, ex-colonials, and various combinations thereof. Always fearful of low-wage competition, the Left is threatened everywhere by the emergence of a "lean and mean" capitalism that is less dependent on the "mass worker" than ever before. It is less inclined, therefore, not only to hire and train workers but also to support the welfare state, which working-class reformist movements had secured in the past as a price for their submission to capitalist discipline.

Native (more accurately, white) workers everywhere in the North are thus more subject than ever to the blandishments of nativism and exclusionary politics. This is the home turf of the Right, which presents the welfare state and the low-income (racialized) strata as the enemies of the "salt of the earth" types who "play by the rules," "go to work each day," "pay their taxes," and end up "getting screwed" by the "freeloaders" who "don't even belong in this country."

Many examples attest to the bankruptcy of the Left in the face of racism and nativism: the British Labour Party's resistance to the Black sections (a type of caucus); the anti-immigrant compromises of the German and French Socialists (not to mention the French Communists); and the complicity of the Clinton Democrats in welfare "reform," to name but a few. In most of the developed countries, there is a significant current of hostility and racism built into the Left.

The Right Is Ascendant

In the Northern countries, the Right has been the chief beneficiary of the conflicts framed by the increasing racialization of politics. The

Right today is the repository of nationalism, whose core concepts of "autonomy, unity, identity" marked the rise and consolidation of nation-states throughout the early modern period. These concepts are put in question by the racialized heterogeneity I am discussing here.

The racialized challenge to national identity takes various forms. It reflects the shrinking and knitting together of the contemporary world. It mirrors the ever greater internationalization of the movement of capital and labor and the transnational phenomenon of diaspora, with its globalization of various identities: Jewish, Chinese, South Asian, Filipino, Greek, Palestinian, as well as African.

We can see these challenges to the established Northern nationalism framed by immigration, to be sure, but also by egalitarianism, by affirmative action (however called), by feminism and gay liberation (sexuality and race are deeply linked in nationalism), and by all forms of transnational identification that compete for loyalty with the national–patriotic.

Today, in all the advanced countries, the established working classes are fearful and resentful. In the United States, this is the "angry white male" phenomenon; elsewhere, it focuses more particularly on immigration or on Islam, but these are largely superficial differences. The "angry white males," the nativists, believed for a long time that their race, their gender, their religion more or less guaranteed them a middle-class standard of living, a well-paying job, a secure home in a safe neighborhood, access to quality education and health care, paid vacations, a comfortable retirement.

These prospects are slipping away. Children are worse off than their parents were. The policies of the welfare state no longer appear able to fend off the unease in the heartland. Thus, they look for someone to blame. In the tradition of American nativism and European colonialism, racialized minorities and immigrants furnish the ready scapegoat.

It hardly seems necessary to repeat that the real culprit in this situation is not the racialized "other"; rather, it is large-scale capital, which since the 1970s has openly declared its intention to redistribute income regressively, to maintain higher levels of unemployment, to break unions, to dismantle the welfare states, and to increase levels of repression, both political and "criminal." The turn to the political Right, then, and to the nationalism this turn entails is in many respects a clear political consequence of the capitalist-class program in many of the developed countries.

But in other respects what has been characterized in the U.S. context as "white racial nationalism" is a much broader phenomenon. It is a vision or an ideology of community, of an "imagined community" that emerges from revulsion at late modernity and seeks to turn back the clock toward the white supremacy of the past.

The Right still sees the nation as a "white man's country." Its patriotism is identified with "blood": with whiteness, with imperialism, with masculinity, and with heterosexuality.

The Right thus attempts to hold pluralistic and heterogeneous concepts of national identity, or of internationalism, at bay, but this is a difficult task to carry out in a democratic polity. Therefore, there's an uneasy tension on the Right between the "people" and the citizenry. This is one of the central conflicts, perhaps *the* central conflict, that race poses for the Right. At its core it is a conflict between democracy and fascism. The identification of the nation as the primary collective entity involves an emphasis on homogeneity, on national frontiers actually dividing putatively "different" peoples. It therefore assumes that there is a basic distinctiveness among groups, which is always potentially available for racialization.

In short, both in the United States and elsewhere, right-wing currents are being pushed further to the right by the racialization of national politics.

Racism Takes on New Forms: Fascism Is a Real Threat

New forms of racism are developing as these racialized political dynamics work themselves out. In the United States, we have a lot of experience by now with "egalitarian racism"; the "color-blind" politics that have characterized neoconservative appeals are by now so familiar that they have become "grassroots" ideologies, "common sense." A comfortable if shallow veneer of egalitarianism can thus be maintained over the deep structures of racial privilege; one can convince oneself, with the help of endless assertions of the point in the media and the halls of power, that one has overcome racism. Indeed, from such a perspective, the true racists are those—often racialized minorities themselves—who "bring up race all the time" and who "inject it into everything."

Another form of racism is "differentialist," not egalitarian. More common in Europe than in the United States, it asserts that while certainly all peoples are equal, it is "natural" for every group to prefer its own kind, to be averse to those who are different, and to prefer to stay separate from them. In contrast with traditional forms of racism, which claimed that there were fundamental inequalities among human groups, "differentialist racism" adopts and rearticulates egalitarian notions of difference. In this perspective, it is not racial equality but "race mixing" that is the supreme mistake.

In short, throughout the North, in a complex response to the heterogeneity I have discussed, there is a new variety of racism(s). The older, discriminatory, hierarchized racism still flourishes, retaining its commitment to biologism and notions of racial superiority and inferiority. Alongside this, coexisting more or less harmoniously for decades in the United States, there has been neoconservatism, which operates as a "soft" racism, advocating a "color-blind," individualistic, conservative approach to race. Its egalitarian claims consist at best in its preferred combination of racial policies: sanctions for active discrimination and laissez-faire with respect to the results. It often adopts a "blame the victim" strategy, which also has the advantage of justifying ongoing white privilege.

Counterarguments need to be posed to both these "streamlined" and "rationalized" forms of racism, but neither in the United States nor in Europe can they be decisive. What will determine the long-term success of these "new racisms" (or "neoracism") is the extent to which they can be implanted as the "common sense" or hegemonic discourses of race in the various countries with which we are concerned. And this in turn depends on the degree of political momentum that can be mobilized in favor of or against this or that articulation of the meaning of race in each national setting.

Some Political Conclusions

At present, lamentably, very little popular mobilization is under way against the racial nationalism of the Right. Given the analysis I have made, it is quite understandable why this is so: the center and the Left do not have the tools to carry out the job, and racially defined minorities must confront the high degree of racial chauvinism that the Northern "democratic" national cultures still contain.

Racial minorities often find it difficult to reinterpret national identity and national culture in a progressive, "multicultural" way (although that term has been somewhat debased). From the standpoint of racialized minorities, it is not so easy to embrace what is still in many ways a "white man's country." This remains true in the United States, even for those who have been here for centuries. It is especially true for more recent arrivals: the immigrant Pakistani or second-generation Trinidadian in England, the French Muslim, the Korean or Salvadoran newly settled in Los Angeles.

For this reason among many others, antiracist opposition, for a long time to come, will probably take on a "nationalist" and diasporic character. Consciousness of the world-historical nature of white supremacy is not a relic of the postwar anticolonial struggles or of an earlier pan-Africanism, but a well established and likely permanent feature of the new international racial dynamics.

On the other side of the equation, at a certain point racism also involves the Right in internal conflicts and divisions. These are the divisions between a "softer," conservative, democratic Right, one that perhaps believes in civic duty and firm patriarchal authority, but that doesn't necessarily capitulate to the irrational politics of fascism. That's on the one hand.

On the other hand, developing throughout the North, there's a "hard" Right, which has serious protofascist tendencies. This "hard" Right includes people who are armed and dangerous. It includes militant and millennarian religious sects (more so in the United States). And it includes groups that survived the debacle of European fascism and regrouped (more so in Europe).

There are potentially some major conflicts on the Right, but for the present they have been far more successfully papered over than have conflicts on the Left. We (racially defined minorities, progressive workers, intellectuals and artists, feminists, gays, students, etc.—that's crudely who "we" are) must learn how to exploit the divisions and antagonisms that persist on the Right, particularly where race is concerned.

For example, in the United States the Right confronts a significant secular–religious conflict in its own ranks. Capital in general is secular, is not so anti-immigrant, and in fact requires a low-wage workforce, which it expects to be multiracial and to include women. Capital is often explicitly multicultural. On the other hand, authoritarian, populist, and religious rightism, "grassroots" rightism, is often more explicitly racist, prone to violence, and "workerist." It represents threatened sectors of labor, small farmers, and vulnerable middle-class sectors, the traditional fascist base.

Any mobilization against the Right will necessarily take on different forms in different countries.

In the United States, where the welfare state is far less advanced, struggles over racism will focus on drawing the line between productive and unproductive members of society. There will be comparatively less focus on "differentialist racism," and more on individualism, meritocracy, equality of opportunity vs. equality of result (i.e., neoconservatism). The "soft" Right will deny its racism by stressing absolute individualism, color-blindness, secularism, and the primacy of market forces. It will be at pains to deny not only racism but also anti-Semitism. In contrast, the "hard" Right will increasingly avow a biologistic form of racism that harks back to eugenics; that stresses old-fashioned beliefs about superiority and inferiority; that embraces the authority of a "righteous" nation rather than that of a "soulless" marketplace; that emphasizes sexual racism; that accommodates, if it does not actively promote, anti-Semitism; and that explicitly links itself to religious fanaticism and fascism.

In Europe, where the welfare state is far more entrenched and European unity is a powerful (if embattled) trend, struggles over racism will focus on citizenship and immigration, on "Europe and its others." The "soft" Right will stress the impossibility of assimilation and the need for secure borders. It will deny its racism by emphasizing the necessity of unified national–cultural identities. The "hard" Right will increasingly work to recuperate fascist tendencies, anti-Semitism, and hard-core nationalism.

Race splits "us"; class splits "them." We do not need to be class reductionists to see that a progressive racial politics must address the dynamics of class. We must understand the struggle for racial justice as central to the struggle for social justice, as central to any resistance to capital's drive to dominate, to discipline, to control not only labor but society as a whole. We must understand that logic in order to resist it.

Part 2

Racial/Ethnic Categories

One Drop of Blood

Lawrence Wright

The United States in the millennial years is a nation of warring racial and ethnic groups fighting for recognition, protection, and entitlements. This war has been fought throughout the second half of the twentieth century largely by Black Americans. How much this contest has widened, how bitter it has turned, how complex and baffling it is, and how far-reaching its consequences are became evident in a series of 1993 congressional hearings held by the House Subcommittee on Census, Statistics, and Postal Personnel, chaired by Representative Thomas C. Sawyer, Democrat of Ohio.

Although the Sawyer hearings were scarcely reported in the news and sparsely attended even by other members of the subcommittee, they opened what may become the most searching examination of racial questions in this country since the 1960s. Related federal agency hearings, and meetings that will be held in Washington and other cities around the country to prepare for the 2000 census, are considering not only modifications to existing racial categories but also the larger question of whether it is proper for the government to classify people according to arbitrary distinctions of skin color and ancestry. This discussion arises at a time when profound debates are occurring in minority communities about the rightfulness of group entitlements, some government officials are questioning the usefulness of race data, and scientists are debating whether race exists at all.

"We are unique in this country in the way we describe and define race and ascribe to it characteristics that other cultures view very differently," Sawyer says. He points out that the country is in the midst of its most profound demographic shift since the 1890s—a time that opened "a period of the greatest immigration we have ever seen, whose numbers have not been matched until right now." A deluge of new Americans from every part of the world is overwhelming our traditional racial distinctions, Sawyer believes. "The categories themselves inevitably reflect the temporal bias of every age. That becomes

Lawrence Wright's "One Drop of Blood" (excerpts) appeared in the July 25, 1994, *New Yorker*.

a problem when the nation itself is undergoing deep and historic diversification."

Looming over the shoulder of Sawyer's subcommittee is the Office of Management and Budget (OMB), the federal agency that happens to be responsible for determining standard classifications for racial and ethnic data. Since 1977, those categories have been set by OMB Statistical Directive 15, which controls the racial and ethnic standards on all federal forms and statistics. Directive 15 acknowledges four general racial groups in the United States: American Indian or Alaskan Native; Asian or Pacific Islander; Black; and White. It also breaks down ethnicity into Hispanic Origin and Not of Hispanic Origin. These categories, or versions of them, are present on enrollment forms for schoolchildren; on application forms for jobs, scholarships, loans, and mortgages; and, of course, on United States census forms. The categories ask that every American fit himself or herself into one racial and one ethnic box. From this comes the information that is used to monitor and enforce civil rights legislation, most notably the Voting Rights Act of 1965, but also a smorgasbord of set-asides and entitlements and affirmative-action programs. "The numbers drive the dollars," Sawyer observes, repeating a well-worn Washington adage.

The truth of that statement was abundantly evident in the hearings, in which a variety of racial and ethnic groups were bidding to increase their portion of the federal pot. The National Coalition for an Accurate Count of Asian Pacific Americans lobbied to add Cambodians and Lao to the nine nationalities already listed on the census forms under the heading of Asian or Pacific Islander. The National Council of La Raza proposed that Hispanics be considered a race, not just an ethnic group. The Arab American Institute asked that persons from the Middle East, now counted as white, be given a separate, protected category of their own. Senator Daniel K. Akaka, a Native Hawaiian, urged that his people be moved from the Asian or Pacific Islander box to the American Indian or Alaskan Native box. "There is the misperception that Native Hawaiians, who number well over two hundred thousand, somehow 'immigrated' to the United States like other Asian or Pacific Island groups," the senator testified. "This leads to the erroneous impression that Native Hawaiians, the original inhabitants of the Hawaiian Islands, no longer exist." In the senator's opinion, being placed in the same category as other Native Americans would help rectify that situation. (He did not mention that certain American Indian tribes enjoy privileges concerning gambling concessions that Native Hawaiians currently don't enjoy.) The National Congress of American Indians would like the Hawaiians to stay where they are. In every case, issues of money, but also of identity, are at stake.

In this battle over racial turf, a disturbing new contender has appeared. "When I received my 1990 census form, I realized that there was no race category for my children," Susan Graham, who is a white woman married to a Black man in Roswell, Georgia, testified. "I called the Census Bureau. After checking with supervisors, the bureau finally gave me their answer: the children should take the race of their mother. When I objected and asked why my children should be classified as their mother's race only, the Census Bureau representative said to me, in a very hushed voice, 'Because, in cases like these, we always know who the mother is and not always the father.' "

Graham went on to say, "I could not make a race choice from the basic categories when I enrolled my son in kindergarten in Georgia. The only choice I had, like most other parents of multiracial children, was to leave race blank. I later found that my child's teacher was instructed to choose for him based on her knowledge and observation of my child. Ironically, my child has been white on the United States census, Black at school, and multiracial at home—all at the same time."

Graham and others were asking that a *multiracial* box be added to the racial categories specified by Directive 15—a proposal that alarmed representatives of the other racial groups for a number of reasons, not least of which was that multiracialism threatened to undermine the concept of racial classification altogether.

According to various estimates, at least 75 percent to more than 90 percent of the people who now check the *Black* box could check *multiracial,* because of their mixed genetic heritage. If a certain proportion of those people—say, 10 percent—should elect to identify themselves as multiracial, legislative districts in many parts of the country might need to be redrawn. The entire civil rights regulatory program concerning housing, employment, and education would have to be reassessed. School desegregation plans would be thrown into the air. Of course, it is possible that only a small number of Americans will elect to choose the *multiracial* option, if it is offered, with little social effect. Merely placing such an option on the census form invites people to consider choosing it, however. When the census listed *Cajun* as one of several examples under the ancestry question, the number of Cajuns jumped nearly 2,000 percent. To remind people of the possibility is to encourage enormous change.

Those who are charged with enforcing civil rights laws see the *multiracial* box as a wrecking ball aimed at affirmative action, and they hold those in the mixed-race movement responsible. "There's no concern on any of these people's part about the effect on policy—it's just a subjective feeling that their identity needs to be stroked," one government analyst said. "What they don't understand is that it's going to cost their own groups"—by losing the advantages that accrue to minorities by way of affirmative-action programs, for instance. Graham contends that the object of her movement is not to create another protected category. In any case, she said, multiracial people know "to check the right box to get the goodies."

Of course, races have been mixing in America since Columbus arrived. Visitors to colonial America found plantation slaves who were as light-skinned as their masters. Patrick Henry actually proposed, in 1784, that the state of Virginia encourage intermarriage between whites and Indians, through the use of tax incentives and cash stipends. The legacy of this intermingling is that Americans who are descendants of early settlers, of slaves, or of Indians often have ancestors of different races in their family tree.

Thomas Jefferson supervised the original census, in 1790. The population then was broken down into free white males, free white females, other persons (these included free Blacks and "taxable Indians," which meant those living in or around white settlements), and slaves. How unsettled this country has always been about its racial categories is evident in the fact that nearly every census since has measured race differently. For most of the nineteenth century, the census reflected an American obsession with miscegenation. The color of slaves was to be specified as "B," for Black, or "M," for mulatto. In the 1890 census, gradations of mulattoes were further broken down into quadroons and octoroons. After 1920, however, the Census Bureau gave up on such distinctions, estimating that three-quarters of all Blacks in the United States were racially mixed already, and that pure Blacks would soon disappear. Henceforth, anyone with any Black ancestry at all would be counted as Black.

Actual interracial marriages, however, were historically rare. Multiracial children were often marginalized as illegitimate half-breeds who didn't fit comfortably into any racial community. This was particularly true of the offspring of Black–white unions. "In my family, like many families with African American ancestry, there is a history of multiracial offspring associated with rape and concubinage," G. Reginald Daniel, who teaches a course in multiracial identity at the University of California at Los Angeles, says. "I was reared in the segregationist South. Both sides of my family have been mixed for at least three generations. I struggled as a child over the question of why I had to exclude my East Indian and Irish and Native American and French ancestry, and could include only African."

Until recently, people like Daniel were identified as Black because of a peculiarly American institution known informally as the "one-drop rule," which defines as Black a person with as little as a single drop of "Black blood." This notion derives from a long-discredited belief that each race has its own blood type, which is correlated with physical appearance and social behavior. The antebellum South promoted the rule as a way of enlarging the slave population with the children of slaveholders. By the 1920s, in Jim Crow America the one-drop rule was well established as the law of the land. It still is, according to a United States Supreme Court decision as late as 1986, which refused to review a lower court's ruling that a Louisiana woman whose great-great-great-great-grandmother had been the mistress of a French planter was Black—even though that proportion of her ancestry amounted to no more than 3/32 of her genetic heritage. "We are the only country in the world that applies the one-drop rule, and the only group that the one-drop rule applies to is people of African descent," Daniel observes.

People of mixed Black and white ancestry were rejected by whites and found acceptance by Blacks. Many of the most notable "Black" leaders over the last century and a half were "white" to some extent, from Booker T. Washington to Frederick Douglass (both of whom had white fathers) to W.E.B. Du Bois, Malcolm X, and Martin Luther King (who had an Irish grandmother and some American Indian ancestry as well). The fact that Lani Guinier, Louis Farrakhan, and Virginia's former governor Douglas Wilder are defined as Black, and define themselves that way, though they have light skin or "European" features, demonstrates how enduring the one-drop rule has proved to be in America, not only among whites but among Blacks as well. Daniel sees this as "a double-edged sword." While the one-drop rule encouraged racism, it also galvanized the Black community.

"But the one-drop rule is racist," Daniel says. "There's no way you can get away from the fact that it was historically implemented to create as many slaves as possible. No one leaped over to the white community—that was simply the mentality of the nation, and people of African descent internalized it. What this current discourse is about is lifting the lid of racial oppression in our institutions and letting people identify with the totality of their heritage. We have created a nightmare for human dignity. Multiracialism has the potential for undermining the very basis of racism, which is its categories."

But multiracialism introduces nightmares of its own. If people are to be counted as something other than completely Black, for instance, how will affirmative-action programs be implemented? Suppose a court orders a city to hire additional Black police officers to make up for past discrimination. Will mixed-race officers count? Will they count wholly or partly? Far from solving the problem of fragmenting identities, multiracialism could open the door to fractional races, such as we already have in the case of the American Indians. In order to be eligible for certain federal benefits, such as housing improvement programs, a person must prove that he or she either is a member of a federally recognized Indian tribe or has 50 percent "Indian blood." One can envision a situation in which nonwhiteness itself becomes the only valued quality, to be compensated in various ways depending on a person's pedigree.

Kwame Anthony Appiah, of Harvard's philosophy and Afro-American studies departments, says, "What the *multiracial* category aims for is not people of mixed ancestry, because a majority of Americans are actually products of mixed ancestry. This category goes after people who have parents who are socially recognized as belonging to different races. That's O.K.—that's an interesting social category. But then you have to ask what happens to their children. Do we want to have more boxes, depending upon whether they marry back into one group or the other? What are the children of these people supposed to say? I think about these things because—look, my mother is English, my father is Ghanaian. My sisters are married to a Nigerian and a Norwegian. I have nephews who range from blond-haired kids to very Black kids. They are all first cousins. Now, according to the American scheme of things, they're all Black, even the guy with blond hair who skis in Oslo. That's what the one-drop rule says. The *multiracial* scheme, which is meant to solve anomalies, simply creates more anomalies of its own, and that's because the fundamental concept—that you should be able to assign every American to one of three or four races reliably—is crazy."

These are sentiments that Representative Sawyer agrees with profoundly. "It [the one-drop rule] is so embedded in our perception and policy, but it doesn't allow for the blurring that is the reality of our population. Just look at—What are the numbers?" he said in his congressional office as he leafed through a briefing book. "Thirty-eight percent of American Japanese females and 18 percent of American Japanese males marry outside their traditional ethnic and nationality group. Seventy percent of American Indians marry outside. I grant you that the enormous growth potential of multiracial marriages starts from a relatively small base, but the truth is it starts from a fiction to begin with; that is, what we think of as Black-and-white marriages are not marriages between people who come from anything like a clearly defined ethnic, racial, or genetic base."

The United States Supreme Court struck down the last vestige of antimiscegenation laws in 1967, in *Loving v. Virginia*. At that time, interracial marriages were rare; only sixty-five thousand marriages between Blacks and whites were recorded in the 1970 census. Marriages between Asians and non-Asian Americans tended to be between soldiers and war brides. Since then, mixed marriages between many racial and ethnic groups have risen to the point where they have eroded the distinctions between such peoples. Among American Indians, people are more likely to marry outside their race than within it, as Representative Sawyer noted. The number of children living in families where one parent is white and the other is Black, Asian, or American Indian, to use one measure, has tripled—from fewer than four hundred thousand in 1970 to 1.5 million in 1990—this doesn't count the children of single parents or children whose parents are divorced.

Blacks are conspicuously less likely to marry outside their group, yet marriages between Blacks and whites have tripled in the last thirty years. Matthijs Kalmijn, a Dutch sociologist, analyzed marriage certificates filed in this country's non-Southern states since the *Loving* decision and found that in the 1980s the rate at which Black men were marrying white women had reached approximately 10 percent. (The rate for Black women marrying white men was about half that figure.) In the 1990 census, 6 percent of Black householders nationwide had non-Black spouses—still a small percentage, but a significant one.

Multiracial people, because they are now both unable and unwilling
to be ignored, and because many of them refuse to be confined to
traditional racial categories, inevitably undermine the entire concept of
race as an irreducible difference between peoples. The continual mod-
ulation of racial differences in America is increasing the jumble created by centuries of ethnic intermarriage. The resulting dilemma is a
profound one. If we choose to measure the mixing by counting people
as multiracial, we pull the teeth of the civil rights laws. Are we ready
for that? Is it even possible to make changes in the way we count
Americans, given the legislative mandates already built into law? "I
don't know," Sawyer concedes. "At this point, my purpose is not so
much to alter the laws that underlie these kinds of questions as to raise
the question of whether or not the way in which we currently define who
we are reflects the reality of the nation we are and who we are becoming.
If it does not, then the policies underlying the terms of measurement are
doomed to be flawed. What you measure is what you get."

Science has put forward many different racial models, the most
enduring being the division of humanity into three broad groupings:
the Mongoloid, the Negroid, and the Caucasoid. An influential paper
by Masatoshi Nei and Arun K. Roychoudhury, "Gene Differences between Caucasian, Negro, and Japanese Populations," which appeared
in *Science* in 1972, found that the genetic variation among individuals
from these racial groups was only slightly greater than the variation
within the groups.

In 1965, the anthropologist Stanley Garn proposed hundreds, even
thousands, of racial groups, which he saw as gene clusters separated by
geography or culture, some with only minor variations between them.
The paleontologist Stephen Jay Gould, for one, has proposed doing
away with all racial classifications and identifying people by clines—
regional divisions that are used to account for the diversity of snails
and of songbirds, among many other species. In this, Gould follows the
anthropologist Ashley Montagu, who waged a lifelong campaign to rid
science of the term "race" altogether and never used it except in quota-
tion marks. Montagu would have substituted the term "ethnic group,"
which he believed carried less odious baggage.

Race, in the common understanding, draws upon differences not
only of skin color and physical attributes but also of language, nationality, and religion. At times, we have counted as "races" different
national groups, such as Mexicans and Filipinos. Some Asian Indians

were counted as members of a *Hindu* race in the censuses from 1920 to 1940; then they became *white* for three decades. Racial categories are often used as ethnic intensifiers, with the aim of justifying the exploitation of one group by another. One can trace the ominous example of Jews in prewar Germany; they were counted as *Israelites,* a religious group, until the Nazis came to power and turned them into a race. Mixtures of first- and second-degree Jewishness were distinguished, much as quadroons and octoroons had been in the United States. In fact, the Nazi experience ultimately caused a widespread reexamination of the idea of race. Canada dropped the race question from its census in 1951 and has so far resisted all attempts to reinstitute it. People who were working in the United States Bureau of the Census in the 1950s and early 1960s remember that there was speculation that the race question would soon be phased out in America as well. The American Civil Liberties Union tried to get the race question dropped from the census in 1960, and the state of New Jersey stopped entering race information on birth and death certificates in 1962 and 1963. In 1964, however, the architecture of civil rights laws began to be erected, and many of the new laws—particularly the Voting Rights Act of 1965—required highly detailed information about minority participation that could be gathered only by the decennial census, the nation's supreme instrument for gathering demographic statistics. The expectation that the race question would wither away surrendered to the realization that race data were fundamental to monitoring and enforcing desegregation. The census soon acquired a political importance that it had never had in the past.

Unfortunately, the sloppiness and multiplicity of racial and ethnic categories rendered them practically meaningless for statistical purposes. In 1973, Secretary of Health, Education and Welfare Caspar Weinberger asked the Federal Interagency Committee on Education (FICE) to develop some standards for classifying race and ethnicity. An ad hoc committee sprang into being and proposed creation of an intellectual grid that would sort all Americans into five racial and ethnic categories. The first category was *American Indian or Alaskan Native.* Some members of the committee wanted the category to be called *original peoples of the Western Hemisphere,* in order to include Indians of South American origin, but the distinction that this category was seeking was "Federal Indians," who were eligible for government benefits; to include Indians of any other origin, even though they might be genetically quite similar, would confuse the collecting of data. To accommodate the various, highly diverse peoples who originated in the Far East, Southeast Asia, and the Pacific Islands, the committee proposed a category called *Asian or Pacific Islander,* thus sweeping into one massive basket Chinese, Samoans, Cambodians, Filipinos, and others—peoples who had little or nothing in common and many of whom were, indeed, traditional enemies. The fact that American Indians and Alaskan Natives originated from the same Mongoloid stock as many of these peoples did not stop the committee from putting them in a separate racial category. *Black* was defined as "a person having origins in any of the Black racial groups of Africa," and *white,* initially, as "a person having origins in any of the original peoples of Europe, North Africa, the Middle East, or the Indian subcontinent"— everybody else, in other words. Because the *Black* category contained anyone with any African heritage at all, the range of actual skin colors covered the entire spectrum, as did the *white* category, which included Arabs, Asian Indians, and various other darker-skinned peoples.

The final classification, *Hispanic,* was the most problematic of all. In the 1960 census, people whose ancestry was Latin American were counted as white. Then people of Spanish origin became a protected group, requiring the census to gather data in order to monitor their civil rights. But how to define them? People who spoke Spanish? Defining the population that way would have included millions of Americans who spoke the language but had no actual roots in Hispanic culture, and it excluded Brazilians and children of immigrants who were not taught Spanish in their homes. One approach was to count persons with Spanish surnames, but that created a number of difficulties: marriage made some non-Hispanic women into instant minorities and stripped other women of their Hispanic status. The 1970 census inquired about people from "Central or South America," and more than a million people checked the box who were not Hispanic—they were from Kansas, Alabama, Mississippi—the central and southern United States, in other words.

The greatest dilemma was that there was no conceivable justification for calling Hispanics a race. There were Black Hispanics from the Dominican Republic, Argentines who were almost entirely European whites, Mexicans who would have been counted as American Indians if they had been born north of the Rio Grande. The great preponderance of Hispanics are mestizos—a continuum of many different genetic backgrounds. Moreover, the fluid Latin American concept of race differs from the rigid United States idea of biologically determined and highly distinct human divisions. In most Latin cultures, skin color is an individual variable—not a group marker—so that within the same family one sibling might be considered white and another Black. By 1960, the United States census, which counts the population of Puerto Rico, gave up asking the race question on the island, because race did not carry the same distinction there that it did on the mainland. The ad hoc committee decided to dodge riddles like these by calling Hispanics an ethnic group, not a race.

In 1977, OMB Statistical Directive 15 adopted the FICE suggestions practically verbatim, with one principal exception: Asian Indians were moved to the *Asian or Pacific Islander* category. Thus, with little political discussion, the identities of Americans were fixed in five broad groupings. Those racial and ethnic categories that were dreamed up almost twenty years ago were not neutral in their effect. By attempting to provide a way for Americans to describe themselves, the categories actually began to shape those identities. The categories became political entities, with their own constituencies, lobbies, and vested interests. What was even more significant, they caused people to think of themselves in new ways—as being members of "races" that were little more than statistical devices. In 1974, the year the ad hoc committee set to work, few people referred to themselves as Hispanic; rather, people who fell into that grouping tended to identify themselves by nationality—Mexican or Dominican, for instance. Such small categories, however, are inconvenient for statistics and politics, and the creation of the meta-concept "Hispanic" has resulted in the formation of a peculiarly American group. "It is a mixture of ethnicity, culture, history, birth, and a presumption of language," Sawyer contends.

Largely because of immigration, the *Asian or Pacific Islander* group is considered the fastest-growing racial group in the United States, but it is a "racial" category that in all likelihood exists nowhere else in the world. The third-fastest-growing category is *other*—made up of the nearly 10 million people, most of them Hispanics, who refused to check any of the prescribed racial boxes. American Indian groups are also growing at a rate that far exceeds the growth of the population as a whole: from about half a million people in 1960 to nearly 2 million in 1990—a 255 percent increase, which was demographically impossible. It seemed to be accounted for by improvements in the census-taking procedure and also by the fact that Native Americans had become fashionable, so that people now wished to identify with them. To make matters even more confounding, only 74 percent of those who identified themselves as American Indian by race reported having Indian ancestry.

Whatever the word "race" might mean elsewhere in the world, or to the world of science, it is clear that in America the categories are arbitrary, confused, and hopelessly intermingled. In many cases, Americans don't know who they are, racially speaking. A National Center for Health Statistics study found that 5.8 percent of people who called themselves Black were seen as white by a census interviewer. Nearly a third of the people identifying themselves as Asian were classified as white or Black by independent observers. That was true of 70 percent of people who identified themselves as American Indians. Robert A. Hahn, an epidemiologist at the Centers for Disease Control and Prevention, analyzed deaths of infants born from 1983 through 1985. In an astounding number of cases, the infant had a different race on its death certificate than on its birth certificate, and this finding led to staggering increases in the infant-mortality rate for minority populations—46.9 percent greater for American Indians, 48.8 percent greater for Japanese Americans, 78.7 percent greater for Filipinos—over what had been previously recorded.

Such disparities cast doubt on the dependability of race as a criterion for any statistical survey. "It seems to me that we have to go back and evaluate the whole system," says Hahn. "We have to ask, 'What do these categories mean?' We are not talking about race in the way that geneticists might use the term, because we're not making any kind of biological assessment. It's closer to self-perceived membership in a population—which is essentially what ethnicity is." There are genetic variations in disease patterns, Hahn points out, and he goes on to say, "But these variations don't always correspond to so-called races. What's really important is, essentially, two things. One, people from different ancestral backgrounds have different behaviors—diets, ideas about what to do when you're sick—that lead them to different health statuses. Two, people are discriminated against because of other people's perception of who they are and how they should be treated. There's still a lot of discrimination in the health care system."

Racial statistics do serve an important purpose in the monitoring and enforcement of civil rights laws; indeed, that has become the main justification for such data. A routine example is the Home Mortgage

Disclosure Act. Because of race questions on loan applications, the federal government has been able to document the continued practice of redlining by financial institutions. The Federal Reserve found that, for conventional mortgages, in 1992 the denial rate for Blacks and Hispanics was roughly double the rate for whites. Hiring practices, jury selections, discriminatory housing patterns, apportionment of political power—in all these areas, and more, the government patrols society, armed with little more than statistical information to ensure equal and fair treatment. "We need these categories essentially to get rid of them," says Hahn.

The unwanted corollary of slotting people by race is that such officially sanctioned classifications may actually worsen racial strife. By creating social welfare programs based on race rather than need, the government sets citizens against each other precisely because of perceived racial differences. "It is not 'race,' but a *practice* of racial classification that bedevils the society," writes Yehudi Webster, a sociologist at California State University, Los Angeles, and the author of *The Racialization of America.* The use of racial statistics, he and others have argued, creates a reality of racial divisions, which then require solutions, such as busing, affirmative action, and multicultural education, all of which are bound to fail because they heighten the racial awareness that leads to contention. Webster believes that adding a *multiracial* box would be "another leap into absurdity," because it reinforces the concept of race in the first place. "In a way, it's a continuation of the one-drop principle. Anybody can say, 'I've got one drop of *something*—I must be multiracial.' " It may be a good thing. It may finally convince Americans of the absurdity of racial classification.

In 1990, Itabari Njeri, who writes about interethnic relations for the *Los Angeles Times,* organized a symposium for the National Association of Black Journalists. She recounts a presentation given by Charles Stewart, a Democratic Party activist: "If you consider yourself Black for political reasons, raise your hand." The vast majority raised their hands. When Stewart then asked how many people present believed they were of pure African descent, without any mixture, no hands were raised. Stewart commented later, "If you advocate a category that includes people who are multiracial to the detriment of their Black identification, you will replicate what you saw—an empty room. We cannot afford to have an empty room."

Njeri maintains that the social and economic gap between light-skinned Blacks and dark-skinned Blacks is as great as the gap between all Blacks and all whites in America. If people of more obviously mixed backgrounds were to migrate to a *multiracial* box, she says, they would be politically abandoning their former allies and the people who needed their help the most. Instead of draining the established categories of their influence, Njeri and others believe, it would be better to eliminate racial categories altogether.

That possibility is actually being discussed in the corridors of government. "It's quite strange—the original idea of OMB Directive 15 has nothing to do with current efforts to 'define' race," says Sally Katzen, the director of the Office of Information and Regulatory Affairs at OMB, who has the onerous responsibility of making the final recommendation on revising the racial categories. "When OMB got into the business of establishing categories, it was purely statistical, not programmatic—purely for the purpose of data gathering, not for defining or protecting different categories. It was certainly never meant to *define* a race." And yet for more than twenty years Directive 15 did exactly that, with relatively little outcry. "Recently, a question has been raised about the increasing number of multiracial children. I personally have received pictures of beautiful children who are part Asian and part Black, or part American Indian and part Asian, with these letters saying, 'I don't want to check just one box. I don't want to deny part of my heritage.' It's very compelling."

In 1994, Katzen convened a new interagency committee to consider how races should be categorized, and even whether racial information should be sought at all. "To me it's *offensive*—because I think of the Holocaust—for someone to say what a Jew is," says Katzen. "I don't think a government agency should be defining racial and ethnic categories—that certainly was not what was ever intended by these standards."

Is it any accident that racial and ethnic categories should come under attack now—when being a member of a minority group brings certain advantages? The white colonizers of North America conquered the indigenous people, imported African slaves, brought in Asians as laborers and then excluded them with prejudicial immigration laws, and appropriated Mexican land and the people who were living on it. In short, the nonwhite population of America has historically been subjugated and treated as second-class citizens by the white majority. It is to redress the social and economic inequalities of our history that we have civil rights laws and affirmative-action plans in the first place.

Advocates of various racial and ethnic groups point out that many of the people now calling for a race-blind society are political conservatives, who may have an interest in undermining the advancement of nonwhites in our society. Suddenly, the conservatives have adopted the language of integration, it seems, and the left-leaning racial-identity advocates have adopted the language of separatism. It amounts to a polar reversal of political rhetoric.

Jon Michael Spencer, a professor in the African and Afro-American studies curriculum at the University of North Carolina at Chapel Hill, wrote an article in *The Black Scholar* lamenting what he calls "the postmodern conspiracy to explode racial identity." The article ignited a passionate debate in the magazine over the nature and the future of race. Spencer believes that race is a useful metaphor for cultural and historic difference, because it permits a level of social cohesion among oppressed classes. "To relinquish the notion of race—even though it's a cruel hoax—at this particular time is to relinquish our fortress against the powers and principalities that still try to undermine us," he says. He sees the *multiracial* box as politically damaging "to those who need to galvanize peoples around the racial idea of Black."

There are some Black cultural nationalists who might welcome the *multiracial* category. "In terms of the African American population, it could be very, very useful, because there is a need to clarify who is in and who is not," Molefi Kete Asante, who is the chairperson of the Department of African-American Studies at Temple University, says. "In fact, I would think they should go further than that—identify those people who are in interracial marriages."

Spencer, however, thinks that it might be better to eliminate racial categories altogether than to create an additional category that empties the others of meaning. "If you had who knows how many thousands or tens of thousands or millions of people claiming to be multiracial, you would lessen the number who are Black," Spencer says. "There's no end in sight. There's no limit to which one can go in claiming to be multiracial. For instance, I happen to be very brown in complexion, but when I go to the continent of Africa, Blacks and whites there claim that I would be 'colored' rather than Black, which means that somewhere in my distant past—probably during the era of slavery—I could have one or more white ancestors. So does that mean that I, too, could check *multiracial?* Certainly light-skin Black people might perhaps see this as a way out of being included among a despised racial group. The result could be the creation of another class of people, who are betwixt and between Black and white."

Whatever comes out of this discussion, the nation is likely to engage in the most profound debate of racial questions in decades. "We recognize the importance of racial categories in correcting clear injustices under the law," Representative Sawyer says. "The dilemma we face is trying to assure the fundamental guarantees of equality of opportunity while at the same time recognizing that the populations themselves are changing as we seek to categorize them. It reaches the point where it becomes an absurd counting game. Part of the difficulty is that we are dealing with the illusion of precision. We wind up with precise counts of everybody in the country, and they are precisely wrong. They don't reflect who we are as a people. To be effective, the concepts of individual and group identity need to reflect not only who we have been but who we are becoming. The more these categories distort our perception of reality, the less useful they are. We act as if we knew what we're talking about when we talk about race, and we don't."

The Limitations of Directive 15

Juanita Tamayo Lott

The development of OMB Statistical Policy Directive 15, "Race and Ethnic Standards for Federal Agencies and Administrative Reporting," is grounded in the United States' historical and continuing differential treatment of selected populations. The directive represents the most current attempt to better classify racial and ethnic minority groups vis-à-vis a white majority group. It is not an absolute or final standard, and thus is subject to change.

Racial and ethnic categories have been used in the United States to distinguish groups in relation to a white majority. This differential treatment has been used for both exclusion and inclusion. Historically, these categories were used to denote a different civil status for persons who were not among the initial settlers of this nation. Broad groups of people, including native tribes, slaves from Africa, residents of Spanish America, Southern Europeans, and Asians were excluded from becoming full citizens. For example, a three-way racial classification was embedded in the first census of 1790, which identified whites, American Indians, and slaves. For apportionment purposes, a slave was counted as three-fifths of a white person. American Indians who were not taxed were not included in the count.

Since World War II, with the broad enactment of civil rights statutes, racial and ethnic data have been used to monitor discrimination against minorities and to support their inclusion and full citizenship participation. In general, civil rights laws do not specify individual racial and ethnic groups but rather forbid discrimination on the basis of race, color, or national origin. In the enforcement of such laws, however, racial and ethnic groups are classified and minority groups are designated.

Minority group status has been most associated with the Black population. For over two hundred years, the United States has been described as a Black and white society, with a white majority and a Black minority. Minority group status is also identified with American Indians, particularly with tribes that maintain legal relationships with the federal government. With statehood, the minority group status of Aleuts and Eskimos in Alaska and Hawaiians in Hawaii has become prominent. These groups represent resident populations who predated American settlers. The minority group status of Asians is more recent due to their historically fewer numbers, their concentration in the West, and a perception that they are new settlers. The latter view is reinforced with continuing immigration from Asian countries. Hispanics as a minority group are both distinct from and similar to the above racial groups. Hispanics are a multiracial group, with European, African, and Indian origins. In the Southwest, a Hispanic presence dates back to Spanish America, giving Hispanics a residential status similar to American Indians. Like Asians, they also include new settlers, with steady immigration from Mexico and Latin America. Finally, despite European origins, their historical treatment of being less than equal to whites is similar to the treatment of Blacks.

Given this history, it was appropriate that in formulating Directive 15 in the 1970s federal agencies directed special attention to the

Black, Latino, American Indian/Alaskan Native, and Asian/Pacific populations. Disparities between these groups and the white population were documented in the 1960 and 1970 censuses and the 1976 Survey of Income and Education. These disparities were in large part due to earlier policies of limited or total exclusion in various areas—such as citizenship, property rights, and immigration. The civil rights compliance purposes of these categories have been paramount.

Both civil rights laws and Directive 15 have potentially wide and flexible coverage in their present forms. Protected groups are not necessarily limited to historically disadvantaged racial and ethnic minorities. Rather, they can include other groups that assume a national policy importance: for example, new refugees. Similarly, although Directive 15 does specify groups, the four racial categories and the Hispanic category are defined as minimum categories. Data on subgroups can be collected and reported as long as they can be aggregated to the minimum categories for federal reporting purposes. Additionally, exceptions to these categories can be obtained from OMB. The Census Bureau has requested and been granted use of an *other* category for the 1980 and 1990 censuses. Finally, the directive does not preclude the use of other categories for nonfederal reporting.

From a historical perspective, the current categories are relatively new and have been in use for less than two decades. Implementation of these categories has surfaced both the significance and the limitations of this classification system. For the most part, these categories have been adhered to for a variety of data collection activities at the federal, state, and local levels, and in the public and private sectors. They have been useful in documenting the growth of minority populations. When Directive 15 was promulgated, racial and ethnic minorities were a stable but small proportion of the American population. Between 1970 and 1990, however, they increased from about one-eighth to one-fourth of the total population. They will continue to grow and diversify for the foreseeable future.

During this period, the limitations of Directive 15, on several levels, have become more visible. One entails changing the terminology of existing groups to reflect contemporary usage, such as "African American" for "Black." While these terms are not conceptually synonymous and point out the ambiguity and fluidity of labels, such changes do not threaten the existing standards. A second limitation is the inclusion of particular groups in a category. The most prominent example is the reclassification of Pacific Islanders from an *Asian or Pacific Islander* category to one with American Indians and Alaskan Natives. On the one hand, Pacific Islanders, particularly Hawaiians, share an indigenous status with American Indians and Alaskan Natives, and specific relationships with the federal government. On the other hand, an *Asian or Pacific Islander* category reflects a popular geographic usage referring to an Asia Pacific region. These types of limitations are not insurmountable.

A more challenging limitation of this policy is whether the current categories are exhaustive. Any new category undermines the extant classification, for it entails the addition of new groups that not only may not self-identify with the current categories but also may not self-identify as a minority group. Critics contend that a new category would also diminish the numbers of existing groups. Nonetheless, the experience of the decennial census with the *other* race category does not encourage new groups. While the numbers of the American population reporting in this category increased between 1970 and 1990 (from less than one million to almost ten million), over 95 percent of persons reporting in the *other* race category in 1990 were Hispanic. In addition, despite the general perception of a sizable multiracial population, about 253,000, or only 0.10 percent in the 1990 census, provided multiple race responses. In the past, federal statistical systems (notably those of the Census Bureau and the National Center for Health Statistics) have generally classified persons of mixed backgrounds as nonwhite and, more recently, in terms of a mother's race, rather than as a separate category. (When both parents were nonwhite, however, children were assigned the father's race, except if either parent was Hawaiian; then the children were designated Hawaiian.)

Another limitation is whether the *Hispanic origin* category can continue to hold a preferential status. In distinguishing *Hispanic origin* as a separate ethnic category, Directive 15 set a precedent that selected ethnicity as primary over racial identity. Specifically, when a combination of race and ethnicity is used, Hispanics who are Black or white are excluded from the *Black* and *white* categories and counted under

Hispanic. While Hispanics can be of any race, the white population in the last two decades has evolved to be defined as non-Hispanic.

Perhaps the most challenging limitation of this directive is whether such a policy has outlived its utility. In the current debate on revising Directive 15, the focus has shifted from measuring the disparities between majority and minority groups to highlighting benefits and entitlement of minority status. Such a shift may lead to the conclusion that disparities are minimal or no longer exist between the majority group and minority groups, despite evidence that both continuation and reduction of disparities exist. With emphasis on the latter, the monitoring of disparity and subsequent action to remedy disparities would no longer be primary policy objectives.

An equally popular reason for the outdatedness of this directive is that it does not reflect the groups with which individuals identify. New immigrants, for example, identify primarily with their nationality rather than race or ethnicity. For other individuals, race or ethnicity is not primary to their identification and thus assumes an optional status. Furthermore, in a heterogeneous society, persons can have a multiplicity of identities shaped not only by official categories but also by the individual's self-identification and definitions of a particular racial or ethnic community, the media, and other groups.

In summary, race continues to be a major organizing principle in the United States. It is used as a basic demographic variable in defining the American population. Its origin, however, is as a legal status defining a majority and a minority. The intersection of demography and policy forces us to raise the question "Do racial and ethnic categories matter?" An initial answer is "It depends." For the racial and ethnic minority groups identified in OMB Statistical Directive 15, it is clear that racial and ethnic categories continue to matter in tracking their political inclusion and access to resources. For other groups, however, it is less clear that racial and ethnic categories per se matter or that the official federal categories defined in Statistical Directive 15 are the only ones that matter.

It is clear that, for the whole nation, racial and ethnic categories will continue to matter as long as Directive 15's purpose is to provide racial and ethnic data to support policies of inclusion, among them policies related to disadvantage and discrimination as stated in legislative and program requirements. To continue to be effective, Directive 15 must reconcile the historic need for differential attention to selected groups with the reality of greater interaction among existing categories and the probability of new racial/ethnic categories.

The Error of the Third Type

Samuel L. Myers, Jr.

Policy analysts talk of what William Dunn calls "The Error of the Third Type." Unlike Type I and Type II errors, well known to students of statistics, errors of the third type refer not to rejecting or accepting null hypotheses when they are true or false. These errors refer to finding the right answer to the wrong question.

The debate illuminated in Lawrence Wright's essay "One Drop of Blood" is an excellent example of the error of the third type. The entire discussion of the utility of racial classification is a misguided and often dangerous exercise in trying to find the right answer to the wrong question.

Take, for example, former Minneapolis mayor Don Fraser's attempt to solve the crime problem by refusing to submit to the state racial data on arrests. Minneapolis has the distinction of having the second highest racial disparity in arrest rates among the nation's cities with populations over 250,000. (Sister city St. Paul has the highest.) The Black arrest rate is twenty-four times the white arrest rate. And why? Because, presumably, "racial identities may be arbitrarily assigned by those who are required to collect such information or reported inconsistently by affected individuals," as Mayor Fraser wrote to Attorney General Janet Reno, urging her to change the way racial statistics are collected.

When Mayor Fraser instructed his chief of police to refuse to supply to state officials figures concerning the race of arrested persons, what could he possibly have had in mind? That many of the persons labeled "Black" were really not Black at all? That by reclassification to some other category—perhaps mixed race—the racial disparity would disappear?

Unfortunately, the consistent and alarming discriminatory patterns of arrest will not go away if we simply stop collecting statistics by race. Worse, analysts who wish to document these patterns will be forced to abandon these efforts, and antidiscrimination litigation will be dealt a fatal blow.

Why, one wonders, has so little been done in the nearly twenty years since passage of the Equal Credit Opportunity Act to force lenders to cease discriminating against Blacks and other nonwhites in mortgage loan approvals? Why only in the past few years have the *Atlanta Constitution, Wall Street Journal,* and *New York Times* reported definitively on racially disparate loan rejection rates? Quite simply, the answer is that until 1990 lenders were not required to report race on individual loan applications, so that no one knew for sure whether there existed racial disparities in loan approval rates.

In several recent papers, my graduate students at the University of Minnesota and I have been examining racial disparities in loan approval rates in the upper Midwest. We are fortunate to know not just the race of the applicant but also the race of the co-applicant. Does being in a mixed-race household afford the applicant an advantage in the marketplace for loans? The answer is a resounding *no!* We have documented a pervasive pattern of racial discrimination in mortgage lending in the upper Midwest. And we find a definite disadvantage faced by mixed-race or biracial households.

If people think that separating mixed-race peoples from the rest of the universe of nonwhites will somehow make these persons better off, they are fooling themselves.

Perhaps there lingers in the minds of some the false belief that either by chance or by design biracial or multiracial persons are better off financially or economically than the rest of us colored folk. Lawrence Wright quotes Itabari Njeri as saying as much. I don't know where Njeri gets her numbers, but they do not confirm the Minnesota experience. We examined the 1990 Public Use Micro Sample (PUMS) census data for Minnesota. Minnesota happens to have one of the highest rates of interracial marriages in the nation. It also happens to have a very small population of African Americans, Asian Americans, and American Indians, who collectively account for less than 3 percent of all married-couple households. Unlike what Lawrence Wright will have you believe, it is really very easy to glean from existing census information mixed-race and biracial classifications. We looked at persons who listed themselves as Black but who then listed as their ancestry one of many Northern and Western European nations. Not surprisingly, given what we know of the historically large percentages of mixed-race marriages in Minnesota, there were more Black married heads of households who identified their ethnic ancestries as European than those who were simply Black with either no identified ethnic ancestry or with African or other ancestries.

We even calculated the mean household incomes of the "European Blacks" and the "Non-European Blacks." And we found that the "European Blacks," or essentially the mixed-race or biracial Blacks who nevertheless accept the label "Black," consistently have lower household incomes than the "non-European Blacks." Of course, this is a tricky exercise because the numbers are all very small in this sample—the PUMS sample is a 5 percent sample of the state's population, which has only 940,000 married-couple households, of which only 0.9 percent are Black. Still, it is not obviously the case that mixed-race persons are any better off than the rest of us colored folks. If there is a need or desire to prove or disprove this, existing classification schemes already exist for these purposes.

While the issue of racial classification has interest as a theoretical *curiosum,* as a practical matter the debate is focusing on the wrong question. It matters not whether I have $\frac{1}{32}$ Cherokee "blood," $\frac{19}{32}$ Black "blood," and who knows how much Irish, French, Spanish, Cuban, and perhaps German (note the name Myers) blood. What matters is that I am Black. My mother and father are Black. My sisters and my daughter are Black. And regardless of whom my daughter eventually marries, her children will also be Black. And as Black people in America, we are deemed less able, less deserving, and less equal than whites. What matters is race. What matters is not being endowed indisputably with white privilege in America. When biracials, mixed-race persons, or Asians and Latinos come to this conclusion, as American Indians long ago came to this conclusion, they will see the benefits of joining forces with other minorities and whites of goodwill to fight racism and racial discrimination. Not by clever-handed racial redesignations or schemes, but by litigation and legislation on the battlefields of employment, housing, lending, and education.

Categories Count

Libero Della Piana

In the summer of 1993, several groups, spearheaded by the American Multi-Ethnic Association and Project RACE (Reclassify All Children Equally), urged the House Subcommittee on Census, Statistics, and Postal Personnel to add *multiracial* as a category to the U.S. census. These groups and others have won multiracial identification in school districts in Georgia and Illinois. In Ohio, there is now statewide legislation making *multiracial* an official racial category on all school forms.

Advocates for a *multiracial* category cite a number of statistics to back their case. In 1992, there were an estimated 1.2 million interracial marriages, which constitutes a 365 percent increase over 310,000 in 1970. In 1989 alone, 110,500 children were born into interracial families. Given the dramatic increase in interracial marriage, estimates of the number of people with multiracial backgrounds range between 600,000 and 5 million. However, this does not mean that all of these people self-identify as multiracial. Maria P.P. Root writes in *Racially Mixed People in America* that 30–70 percent of all African Americans, virtually all Latinos and Filipinos, and the majority of Native Americans are multiracial. The point is clear: while multiracial individuals have existed as long as the concept of race, there is today a new awareness of large numbers of multiracial people. Multiracial advocates want to have this reality reflected in the U.S. census.

A box for the racial designation of mixed-race people threatens federal funds earmarked for specific racial groups, according to some monoracial organizations. Henry Der, executive director of Chinese for Affirmative Action (CAA), argued before the House subcommittee mentioned above that it is difficult to ascertain which benefits people of multiracial backgrounds are entitled to, given the fact that federal civil rights legislation and programs are premised on exclusive membership in one racial group. Although Movimiento Estudiantil de Chicanos en Aztlán (a Chicano student organization), the National Urban League, and CAA, to name a few, oppose the

Libero Della Piana's "Categories Count" appeared in the March/April 1994 *RaceFile*.

new *multiracial* census category in the interests of protecting political apportionment for their constituents, there are dimensions of the demand for a *multiracial* category that have implications beyond the political sphere.

Issues raised in the racial categorization debate are not new. For at least two centuries, "one drop of Black blood" made one Black in the United States. A 1930s court case in California found a Filipino exempt from a state miscegenation law because he was defined as a *Malay* (not covered under the law at the time) and not a *Mongolian.* Three weeks after the decision, the California state legislature modified the law to include the racial category *Malay.* Twelve other states soon followed suit. From overtly racist notions of mongrelization by "mud people," to liberal concerns about "how difficult life is for children of mixed heritage," to increased ethnocentricity in communities of color, whose advocates argue that "out-marriage" weakens the race, racial categorization is about power.

The question is, Do multiracial people have the power to force recognition? New magazines like *Interrace, New People,* and *Interracial Classified* have all been founded to increase the positive images of multiracial people in society. As the editor of *Interrace* noted in the November 1993 issue: "We created *Interrace* not to challenge a racist society . . . but to bring balance to the negative depictions of our families and children in the mass media." *New People* addresses the politics of multiracial identity. Its October 1993 issue ran articles addressing the effects of Afrocentric ideology on multiracial people.

Two main trends flow through these publications: the naively uncritical celebration of all dimensions of multiracial identity, and challenges to the existing notions of race. These trends also flourish in organizations of multiracial people at more than a dozen liberal arts colleges. These include MISC (the Multiethnic/Interracial Students' Coalition) at U.C.–Berkeley, the Union of Multiracial Students at U.C.–Santa Cruz, and Brown University's Brown Organization of Multiracial & Biracial Students (BOMBS). These groups have influenced the universities to recognize multiracial identity on application forms, in transition programs, and in other ways. These identity-based organizations function to aid young multiracial people's personal development and to educate other people about multiracial identity. In addition, multiracial campus groups often pressure monoracial (Black, Latino, etc.) student groups to hold forums with them on multiracial issues, get multiracial people into counseling positions, or organize their own awareness week. Multiracial advocacy is primarily identity-based organizing. The groups are not necessarily working for social justice, but for recognition.

Multiracial people confront the difference between racial categorization and self-identification every day. I know this experience personally. My mother is African American and my father is Italian American. I identify as both Black and Italian, not "half-and-half" and not one or the other. However, on a regular basis I am faced with forms, applications, and check-boxes that do not allow me to identify as both. They don't allow me to identify as multiracial either. If you're lucky, they provide an *other* and maybe a space to fill in. The most wrenching choices that have to be made, however, are not on paper. I, like most biracial and multiracial people, must choose to identify with my mother or my father.

Even though I know that identity has more to do with history and consciousness than with appearance, I also know that in order for me to survive in a racially polarized society, I have to react to how others perceive me, as well as how I perceive myself. For instance, I have never been treated as an Italian by someone who wasn't family. I know that as long as I look Black, I am Black to the world. Therefore, I experience racist verbal attacks and discriminatory treatment.

For many multiracial people, there is tension between how one identifies oneself and how one is labeled by both the dominant and the subordinate cultures. Because of this, we are often called confused. The classical representation of our existence is the "tragic mulatto," condemned to be torn between two worlds, psychologically and morally perverse. The fact is, multiracial people are literally forced by this society to choose one reality over the other. Although for the majority of society, racial categories are static and racial identity is a "done deal," the questions raised by multiracial people challenge these assumptions.

Unquestionably, there are problems with the tendency in the multiracial movement to confuse issues related to multiracial identity with the desire to pursue relations with members of a different race and to glamorize the "multicultural melting pot" and multiracial existence. On the other hand, it is clear that conflict over racial categorization in the census articulated by this new multicultural movement is one way to expand the boundaries of how we think about race.

At the Races
The Multiracial Proposal

Ibrahim K. Sundiata

For more than two years, the federal government has been considering revising race in America. Among the most controversial proposals is one calling for creation of a mixed-race *multiracial* category. The debate on this subject promises to establish the context for race relations for the next century and beyond.

The Office of Management and Budget, which oversees establishment of official race categories, has several options. It could urge abolition of all racial data gathering. Conversely, it could multiply the number of new ethnolinguistic categories. Neither approach would solve any long-range problems. Abolition of race is not feasible. The collection of racial data is essential for antidiscrimination measures— for instance, the 1965 Voting Rights Act. At the same time, creation of ever greater numbers of categories meets political demands, but it also creates confusion as categories overlap. This would be the chief problem if the proposed *multiracial* category were to become law.

It must be directly faced that any multiracial proposal would "deconstruct" the historic Black category, due to undercounting and reclassification. Legally enumerated Black populations have all but disappeared in several countries, most notably Brazil, Argentina, and Costa Rica. Significantly, the U.S. census has been acclaimed because it did not, for a large part of the twentieth century, have a *mixed-race* category. In 1972, Carl Degler, in his Pulitzer Prize–winning book *Neither Black nor White,* argued that U.S. race relations were better than those in Latin America because the U.S. census made no distinction between Blacks and people of mixed Black descent. According to Degler's thesis, racial segregation, antimiscegenation laws, and legalized Jim Crow led to intense group solidarity. The civil rights movement was one outcome of this unity, a unity that contrasted with the fragmented nature of racial identity in Brazil, for instance. There, he argued, the "Mulatto Escape Hatch" siphoned off much of the potential "Black" leadership. Civil rights legislation and affirmative action could emerge in the United States because of the very fixity of racial boundaries.

Creation of a *mixed-race* category for the year 2000 census would answer the demands of many individuals—especially the offspring of whites and Blacks—who are not included in any of the present "racial" categories. It would also serve to limit the number of Blacks. Degler observed: "All offspring of Whites and Negroes are Negroes. Therefore, if intermarriage did become widespread, the result would be a Negro majority—or a change in the definition of a Negro." We have reached the latter point with the proposal now before the government.

Conceptually, the multiracial proposal presents several problems. For one, who would be counted? The African American population already has varying amounts of European ancestry. In addition, many persons are of partially Native American ancestry. Frederick Douglass, Booker T. Washington, W.E.B. Du Bois, Walter White, Adam Clayton Powell, Martin Luther King, Malcolm X, Thurgood Marshall, and Lani Guinier were, or are, all "multiracial." If the new category lacked widespread public support, it would tell us very little. Because membership would be on the basis of self-declaration, census numbers would still not reflect the actual number of "mixed-race" persons within the general population. Also, would the category be retroactive or would it apply to offspring conceived after the prescribed date? Very important, how would the new category affect implementation of existing civil rights legislation?

Advocates of the "multiracial" proposal insist that it recognizes biology. What they fail to realize is that the term itself posits the existence of two or more "pure" races, a situation that is chimerical. The proposal accepts antiquated notions of ideal racial essences and then proposes to rectify racism by multiplying categories. What has been labeled "race" in the United States represents ongoing "ethnic" communities that have a shared history and often a common experience of legalized discrimination. The supposed problem of what to do with the offspring of mixed marriages presents, at bottom, a problem no greater or smaller than that presented by other types of interethnic marriages—for instance, Hispanic/non-Hispanic. The individual, under the policy of self-selection that has been operative since 1960, is free to choose the category of primary identification—or none at all.

If "multiracial" were to be anything more than a euphemism for the old *mulatto* category, abolished after 1910, it would have to be defined in such a way as to include large numbers of people from the present Hispanic and Asian groups. What would be the effect of change on Asians, Hispanics, and Native Americans? Asian/Pacific Islanders and American Indians have comparatively high rates of out-marriage. There is little evidence that these groups wish to place interracial offspring in a new *multiracial* designation. Indeed, the proposed category is opposed by La Raza and the Asian American Legal Defense Fund.

One of the most deleterious effects of a *multiracial* category would be that it would disaggregate one group while others were in the process of government-managed aggregation. The *Asian/Pacific Islander* category includes individuals from Pakistan to Fiji who have no common racial, religious, or linguistic link. The *Hispanic* category, created in 1980, has been defined very broadly for political reasons. It now stretches to include Mayas in Guatemala and the children of German immigrants in Argentina. This administrative creation is not the ethnic label chosen by most people within the group (e.g., Chicanos and Puerto Ricans) and has served chiefly as a means of transethnic political mobilization in an era of civil rights legislation.

The disaggregation of Blacks would drive a wedge into the community that would only increase the isolation of its most disadvantaged members. The flight of the Black middle class from inner-city neighborhoods has already been noted by numerous scholars. Some have also found a relationship between skin color and socioeconomic status within the African American community. Creating a North American version of the "Mulatto Escape Hatch" would have the effect of legally hastening the proliferation of caste boundaries in a society that is already a "pigmentocracy." In a review of Richard Herrnstein and Charles Murray's *The Bell Curve* in the conservative *National Review,* historian Eugene Genovese predicted a "caste war between mulattoes and Blacks." Without a doubt, any split in the community will be acted on by those inimical to its interests. The manipulation of the *coloured (mixed-race)* category by South Africa's former apartheid regime should stand as a caveat to those who would advocate its introduction here.

Accurate Racial/Ethnic Data Should Drive Category Review

Raúl Yzaguirre and Sonia M. Pérez

The review of the racial and ethnic categories listed on most official government forms comes at a time when the demographics of the nation are changing rapidly. In the span between 1980 and 1990, for example, the Hispanic population in the United States increased by 53 percent, and the Census Bureau predicts that by 2007, Hispanics will become the nation's largest "minority" group.

But why is it important to know such data? Why should research and advocacy organizations, or those that represent community-based agencies, care about how the census and other government agencies collect these data? How do proposed changes to racial and ethnic categories improve or reduce the quality and accuracy of data about significant segments of the population, like Latinos? And how can government forms best capture not only demographic characteristics of a population, but also cultural or ethnic identity?

As the only official source of detailed data on the U.S. population, census data serve many important purposes. From the perspective of the U.S. Latino community—the only ethnic group for whom data are independently compiled—such data confirm the role we are playing in the workforce, in schools, and in society as a whole. These data also allow researchers, schools, states and municipalities, and others to assess and analyze the social, health, and economic status of specific population groups. For instance, we know through the collection of census data that the poverty rates for Latinos have steadily increased since 1980, even when Black and white poverty rates experienced declines. From a research and public policy perspective, we count on these data to determine how policy makers and other officials can more effectively address the issues that affect their constituencies. Schools, industries, and employers require these data for planning purposes in order to match their needs to changing population characteristics.

And, of course, these data are crucial to the racial and ethnic populations themselves. As frequent users of these data, we at the National Council of La Raza (NCLR), as well as our community-based affiliates, rely on timely and accurate information about U.S. Latinos to enhance our research, advocacy, and ability to adequately provide needed services. Without such data, NCLR affiliates would be poorly positioned either to design and implement needed programs or to offer services to their Latino communities. In a political climate which suggests that individuals will have to rely more on private "charities" and less on public policy interventions, such data are critical. For NCLR, knowledge of Latino socioeconomic status through these specific data allows us to focus our advocacy efforts on what is most needed to improve the status of Hispanics.

Accurate racial and ethnic data are also necessary for protection of our civil rights. Decades ago, the nation understood that in order to remedy social and economic inequality, and ensure the rights of groups that had been historically discriminated against, we needed civil rights protections—which can be implemented and monitored only with the collection of such data. Many civil rights laws rely on race and ethnic data to ensure equitable compliance and effective enforcement in key areas, including education, voting, employment, and housing.

But we and other researchers and advocates recognize that the existing racial and ethnic categories are narrow and limited. With respect to Hispanics, results from the 1990 census show that the census questions on race and Hispanic origin are problematic for several reasons. First, Hispanics are a multiracial population, and race and ethnicity are not easily recognized or distinguished by observable characteristics. Observers who identify Hispanics based on physical characteristics find that such identification may differ from the way the person identifies him/herself.

Second, many Hispanics, especially those who are not U.S.-mainland born, have difficulty classifying themselves by race. For many Hispanic subgroups, particularly those from Central and South America and the Caribbean, choosing one race category is problematic, since they self-identify principally by subgroup (i.e., ethnicity) and descend from multiracial origins. Moreover, in the case of Central and South Americans who may also represent a number of indigenous Indian groups, the classification *Indian* may be selected. A related issue concerns Puerto Ricans, who, when they live in Puerto Rico, are not asked about their race, yet, if they move to the U.S. mainland, are required to answer a race question on the census form.

Third, the category *other race* is primarily checked by Hispanics, who must then be reclassified by the Census Bureau. According to the General Accounting Office, fully 98 percent of respondents who classified themselves as *other race* in the 1990 census were Hispanic. In addition, research suggests that Hispanics and other population groups who may not identify with any of the options offered may have simply skipped or ignored the question. If follow-up was not done for that household or if the allocation procedure was used—the practice of assigning a characteristic to a respondent who did not answer the question or whose answer was incomplete or illegible—this may have contributed to the misclassification of Hispanics and others, and, therefore, to the undercount or inaccurate count of these populations.

Moreover, national and other data collection efforts inconsistently use race and ethnic terms. Such inconsistency is problematic for Hispanics, who are considered, in most daily and practical applications, a "race" but who, on census forms, are designated an "ethnic group." The reliance on the concept of race, as defined in the United States by using a "Black–white" paradigm, ignores the growing importance of large American ethnic groups—like Hispanics.

Any decisions made regarding the race and Hispanic origin questions must be carefully weighed and evaluated, especially if such changes are being considered for the 2000 census.

NCLR:

• *Advocates the selection of identifiers that research and testing determine would ensure the most accurate response rate.* It is critical that the racial and/or ethnic identifiers proposed for the 2000 census and beyond be based on well-researched analysis and findings. While it is important to update the census and revise it to reflect changing demographics, it is also important not to adopt terms simply because they may be preferable to some according to the political and social climate of the time.

• *Favors additional research to test different versions of the race and Hispanic origin questions.* With respect to the Hispanic population, we believe focus group research conducted regionally and by Hispanic subgroup would assist in disentangling the nuances related to these questions. In addition, we encourage further investigation of the growing Central and South American populations, who may have a different perspective regarding the identification of race.

• *Does* not *support including Hispanic as a racial designation, rather than as a separate ethnic category.* Hispanics are a multiracial population and do not constitute a single race. NCLR recognizes that the terms "race" and "ethnicity" are frequently used interchangeably and would support a question that included both terms. However, many Hispanics might not respond to a question that listed *Hispanic* solely as a race. On census and other federal forms, we recommend maintaining use of the term "Hispanic" to denote an ethnic group.

• *Would be inclined to support combination of the race and Hispanic origin questions into a question relabeled "Race/Ethnicity," if testing indicates that such a question elicits a greater and more accurate response rate to the census survey compared with the 1990 census.* As a way to reduce the large proportion of Hispanics who marked *other race* in the 1990 census or who did not answer the race question, NCLR suggests testing a combination of the questions. Before large-scale changes are made, however, it is critical that the Census Bureau and the Office of Management and Budget determine which version of the questions accommodates the largest number of respondents and provides the most accurate data.

• *Strongly urges the census to continue to collect Hispanic sub-group data.* Hispanics are not a monolithic ethnic group. In fact, there is much diversity among the four principal Hispanic subgroups—Mexican American, Puerto Rican, Cuban, and Central and South American. Data for each group are critical to addressing and improving their status and should continue to be gathered. As certain groups increase in number, additional data collection may be warranted.

• *Does not support an open-ended question regarding race and ethnicity.* An open-ended question would negatively affect the quality of the data collected for purposes of understanding the status of Americans relative to each other. Moreover, data that could not be aggregated would hinder the efforts of existing civil rights laws meant to protect specific "minority" groups from employment, housing, and other forms of discrimination.

• *Does not support the addition of a* multiracial *category.* As a multiracial population, Hispanics understand and appreciate the complexity of issues of identity, and know that race and ethnicity are not necessarily distinguishable by physical characteristics. However, the original intent in collecting racial and ethnic data resulted, in part, from the lack of information on particular groups and the concern over the discrimination these groups face. Careful consideration must be given to the implications such categories would have on civil rights issues involving equitable representation and affirmative action, for which census data are often used to determine coverage according to affected group. Double-counting of an individual (for twice-protected groups) may present a problem; additionally, such a category might encourage misclassification of people who may mark it without truly identifying as such. Furthermore, such a category would limit the usefulness of data collected about "multiracial" residents, since it would be difficult to address the needs of a profoundly heterogeneous group. For example, how would public policy address the theoretical 15 percent unemployment rate of "multiracials"?

• *Suggests a review of the purpose of the* other race *category.* The purpose of the *other race* category is unclear. Although this category is presented for individuals who do not identify with the options presented, we understand that the Census Bureau currently reclassifies these data into one of the other categories. We wonder about the effectiveness of such a category.

Finally, in the challenge to document race/ethnicity, a major problem exists in trying to address the concerns related to identity expressed by the growing number of multiracial/multiethnic individuals. As the federal government seeks to be responsive to these concerns, we should all remember the need for and uses of accurate, reliable data about our country's makeup. As a first step in understanding and addressing how identity fits into the redesign of racial/ethnic categories, we should promote and support additional research in this area. For example, to learn about the existing biracial/multiracial population and how the public would respond to such "labels," a special survey might be added to the census's yearly surveys. Such information may shed some light on the direction of future changes in government data collection efforts.

National data on Latinos and other racial/ethnic groups who have been marginalized in the United States are crucial to our progress and must continue to be collected. While we work to integrate our perspectives into how these data are collected, we should, above all, seek to ensure a reliable count based on quality data, as well as on an accurate reflection of the nation's demographics.

A Single Census Question to Measure Race, Spanish Origin, and Ancestry

Reynolds Farley

The censuses of 1980 and 1990 asked distinct questions about race, Spanish origin, and ancestry. This permits us to describe the vibrant tessellation resulting from the many cultures, ethnicities, and linguistic groups now represented in the United States. We also have the detailed data required by the Voting Rights Act of 1965 to ensure equity in drawing up legislative districts down to the smallest local level. Nevertheless, the three questions seem overlapping and were, perhaps, confusing to many respondents. Furthermore, they produced an array of data many users immediately adjusted in order to separate non-Hispanic whites and non-Hispanic Blacks from Latinos.

How will the federal statistical system—especially the census—measure race and ethnicity in the future? We do not know, but we may confidently make several assumptions.

First, assimilation has effectively integrated whites of European origins and may now be effectively incorporating many Asians into the economic and social mainstream. But data from the 1990 census reveal that many Blacks, Native Americans, and both native and foreign-born Latinos are toward the bottom of the economic ladder. Spokespersons for these groups will insist upon obtaining data pertinent to addressing these substantial social and economic gaps.

Second, court rulings may strongly influence the federal statistical system. Courts could mandate an adjustment for undercount in the next census or could, in forthcoming redistricting decisions, place relatively great or relatively little weight upon racial and Spanish-origin data obtained from the census. Although there is no precedent for such a ruling, federal courts could conceivably mandate the race question for the census, including the specific categories to be listed.

Third, immigration from Asia and Latin America remains at very high levels, leading to the rapid growth of an increasingly diverse minority population. In addition, data from the 1990 census report sharp rises in racial intermarriage.

Fourth, as a society we are unlikely to develop a consensus about how to classify persons by race or ethnicity, so Congress and federal agencies will be subject to convincing but conflicting arguments, including suggestions to delete the race question, to make it open-ended, or to include many mixed-race categories. These challenges will undoubtedly increase as the number of people with parents from two racial groups or with a Spanish and a non-Spanish parent increases. Can a person be one-half Chinese and one-half white for purposes of redistricting a state legislature?

Fifth, if there is any consensus emerging, it is that for purposes of federal policy, persons may be members of only one major group and that almost all persons may reasonably be classified into one of the following five groups:

- Whites not Spanish in origin
- Blacks or African Americans not Spanish in origin
- Hispanic or Latino
- Asian or Pacific Islanders not Spanish in origin
- Native Americans not Spanish in origin

In view of this, it would be appropriate to test the question shown below. Each individual would be asked to identify with one, and only one, of the five major groups. Then individuals would have the opportunity to identify with a particular cultural, ethnic, or national origin group. The word "race" would not appear on the questions, just as it did not appear on the 1980 census enumeration schedule.

This proposed question has three advantages. First, rather than asking the current confusing array of three distinct questions about Spanish origin, race, and ancestry, only one question would be used. Second, the question is congruent with the actual practices of most of those who use 1980 and 1990 census data—including federal and state agencies, those working in litigation, and those investigating demographic trends. Third, this question would permit all respondents—not just a sample—to identify with an ethnicity, an ancestry, or a national origin.

PROPOSED QUESTION

Question to Simultaneously Obtain Race and Hispanic Identity

What is this person's primary identity?

Fill in only one circle and write appropriate term:

O WHITE

Write ethnicity or origin, such as English, German, Czech, or Irish:

O BLACK OR AFRICAN AMERICAN

Write ethnicity or origin, such as Jamaican, Nigerian, Ibo, or Ethiopian:

O HISPANIC OR LATINO

Write ethnicity or origin, such as Mexican, Cuban, Puerto Rican, or Argentinian:

O ASIAN OR PACIFIC ISLANDER

Write ethnicity or origin, such as Filipino, Chinese, Thai, or Japanese:

O NATIVE AMERICAN

Write ethnicity or origin, such as Cherokee, Navajo, Eskimo, Aleut, or Hawaiian:

On the Census Race and Ethnic Categories

Nathan Glazer

The responses on the question of whether and how the racial/ethnic categories in the census and other government statistics should be modified show the enormous problems involved in getting agreement on any set of categories. We have moved from the first census of 1790, and a situation in which we distinguished only between whites and Blacks—easy enough then, as the two categories were defined in law so that the line between the two races was absolutely clear—to one in which endless confusion prevails. More than 40 percent of the short census form, which every person must respond to, now consists of complicated questions on race and Hispanic origin, as if the chief business of government was to pigeonhole people by these categories. Why are they more important than questions on education, place of birth, citizenship, housing, income, occupation, and a host of other valuable items of information? This alone should embarrass us, and should lead us to consider seriously not only how we can improve these questions (whatever improvement means, which will be rather different, depending on whom you ask) but also how we can reduce the prominence of racial–ethnic assignment in our census. Do we want our census, whose origin was simply to permit the proper representation of the people in Congress, to be a document whose primary purpose is to assign the population to race and ethnic groups? Alas, the development of public policies, judged increasingly by their differential impact on various ethnic and racial groups, makes this development almost inevitable.

The categories we use should serve two purposes. One is to accurately reflect categories that are in fact socially significant—for politics, for social life, for culture, for personal identity—since one purpose of the census is to give a picture of the American people. The second is to serve public policy, by providing the numbers that politicians and people insist upon to judge our progress in fairness and equality. There are inevitable contradictions between the two objectives, as is clear in the rise of groups insisting on their mixed-race character, something that public policy does not recognize. People insist on defining themselves properly, from their personal point of view, but it is a point of view that does not cohere with the categories public policy has defined. For the census to take into account all the categories that are meaningful to people in defining themselves is of course impossible: the picture of the American people derived from the census and official statistics will always be crude, drawn in broad brush strokes, and will have to be supplemented by nonofficial social research based on small samples. A recent *Wall Street Journal* article describes the explosion of politically relevant categories in the local politics of tolerant San Francisco, where a Black male official challenges the appointment of a Black female lesbian to some post on the ground that she will be more sympathetic to lesbians than to Blacks, while the appointment is defended by a Hispanic lesbian. All the identities are relevant in San Francisco; only some should be relevant for the census.

Clearly, the key division in American society, from its origins and from the first census, has been between Black and other. It is still the basic division, and its centrality is indicated by the relatively low rates of intermarriage between Blacks and others, and the relatively high residential concentration of Blacks, compared with all other groups the census defines as "races." But when it comes to almost all other groups, intermarriage leads to an abundance of multiple ethnic ancestries, and to a declining significance for many individuals of ethnic ancestry. This means that non-Black groups are less sharply defined, less significant for American history and for the individuals identified with them, than are Blacks. The Voting Rights Act and other legislation try (quite wrongly) to assume an equivalence in the deprived status of all nonwhite racial groups and all Hispanic groups. The economic success of many Asian groups undermines this purely political assumption; the success of Cubans, politically and economically, and the differences in economic and educational achievement among Hispanic groups, also undermine it. Asians were once subject to a fierce legal discrimination, Mexican Americans were subject to political and social and (to some extent) legal discrimination, but there is no comparison between the status of Asian American and Hispanic groups and Blacks.

To have a lineup of races in the census that lists white, Black, Chinese, Japanese, Filipino, Asian Indian, and so on is false both to the limited scientific validity of racial difference and to the social significance of the varied groups. To distinguish specific Asian groups, considered separate "races" in the census, from European ethnic groups, considered all of one "race," makes no sense, except that for no good reason the voting rights of the former are given specific protection while those of the latter are not. The children of Greek or Irish immigrants, on the one hand, and of Korean and Asian Indian immigrants, on the other, are equally likely to intermarry, to go to college, and to get good jobs—except that the Asians will probably do better than the Europeans.

The two key distinctions should be, first, Black and other (whether white, Hispanic, or Asian); second, foreign-born (by country or birth) and native. One virtue of these two key distinctions is that they are less ambiguous and muddy than most others. The category of children of foreign-born is also a useful one. The effort by the new ancestry question to form a category of all persons of a specific ethnic ancestry including those of the third generation and beyond, is for the most part a failure, as Stanley Lieberson and Mary Waters have shown in their book *From Many Strands*. It is true that among the non-Black groups some are more insular and have sharper boundaries than others. Jews were once such, but with intermarriage rates today of 50 percent, the degree to which they can be separated out from the white group in general is declining—part-Jews will in a generation be relatively as numerous as part-Italians, and what the significance of this "partness" will be is something that should be left to social scientists, rather than something that should bother the census.

What then happens to various Hispanic groups, the Asian groups? The two questions—Black or other, foreign-born or other—will tell us who is foreign-born from various Latin American and Asian countries, just as we know who is foreign-born from various European countries. We will know the numbers of those who are the children of the foreign-born, who are generally married to the foreign-born of the same origin. For further generations, we will assume they are all Americans, of varied ethnic and racial backgrounds, which is increasingly the reality. This approach would abandon the Hispanic category and its variants (although presumably it is politically impossible to do so). Native Americans (American Indians) have a legal definition: it is not necessary to get their numbers from the census. It should be possible for them to distinguish themselves in responding to the census reports, but it is the legal count that should be relevant, not the inflated report of Native American or part–Native American identity.

Reynolds Farley, in his contribution to this symposium, has made a heroic effort to simplify the present blooming and buzzing confusion, and to take account of the political realities that have distinguished five categories, as used in present-day affirmative-action and antidiscrimination laws and regulations. His effort does not take account of the many who would not want to place themselves in one of the five categories he identifies. They are the "mixed," and insist on at least two identities from among these five. They should be given a sixth line to respond to. If that is done, I would consider his approach a reasonable middle ground between the present situation, which is unsatisfactory, and the approach I suggest, in which the census first would find out who is Black, by self-identity, then who is foreign-born and from what country, and perhaps go on to find out who is the child of foreign-born parents, from what country. The special prominence given to Asian groups (each presumed to be a "race") and to Hispanic groups (all presumed to be distinctively victimized) would be abandoned. We would not even have to ask who is "mixed"—we would assume they are simply numerous among all who do not define themselves as Black and/or foreign-born, for that is increasingly the reality of America.

Who Thought of Dropping Racial Categories, and Why?

john a. powell

The Office of Management and Budget is considering eliminating the racial and ethnic categories currently used by the Census Bureau in gathering data and compiling statistics. If the question is whether our government should continue to use categories of race and collect data based on racial and ethnic classifications, my answer is "Yes." So long as American society is organized around race—that is, racialized—our government should continue to compile statistics based on race.

The best thing to be said about our two-hundred-year experience with census statistics on race is that, almost inadvertently, it produced something truly important: a broad view of racial disparity. The statistics present an unsentimental education in American realities. Readers (reviewers, planners, demographers, lawyers, and politicians) have learned that poverty and wealth, residence and occupation, lifestyle and life expectancy have been, and are, fractured and uneven, rather than uniform. One fault line is race.

In our society, many institutions, interactions, and systems of distribution and power are racialized. Dropping racial categories from the census will not alleviate the racial hierarchy that supports the systems of resource distribution in American society. In fact, it would leave the systems of distribution of both public and private resources—and our notions of identity—intact but less visible. Modifying statistical categories to dilute or refract racial data is ineffectual, unless the desired effect is obscuring the reality of racial disparity.

The impetus for initiatives like e-race-ing the census count is generated in part by an awareness that race as a biological fact is problematic. However, the fact that race is socially constructed does not establish that race lacks meaning or force. Religion and nationality are also socially constructed. They are nonetheless, like race, social facts. Race certainly has meaning and force, in terms of individual identity and power as well as of social organization and domination. The use of purported genetic differences among races to justify subordination and exclusion is one example of the meaningfulness of race.

The social constructedness of race in America means that no one person controls it. The category I check on my census form is not determinative. Whether I see myself as Black, Negro, African American, multiracial, or other is only part of the equation. When I visit the suburbs to shop for a house, my race is important—to my realtor and potential neighbors, as well as to me. The taxi driver who passes me on the street is not concerned with what was put on my census form. Race is not simply a noun; race is a verb. It is what we do in ordering our society. It is not so simple to elect not to be "raced." This is not an option. Until this social reality shifts, we must be able to observe and chart race through statistics such as the census count.

Of course, racial identity and racial meaning have shifted over time. This, too, is part of what it means to say that race is socially constructed. Racial identity and meaning will likely continue to shift. There is, however, no indication that race as a societal organizing mechanism will disappear. In its current and future guises, race seems destined to contribute to our notions of identity and destined to direct resource distributions.

Without racial statistics, we will not know how distributions of resources affect racial and ethnic groups. Without them, racism, which is still very much a part of our society, will be that much harder to identify, that much more difficult to eradicate, and that much more likely to remain a societal norm. Dropping race categories will only strengthen our disturbing racial reality.

I wonder who thought of this change in the census, and why.

Part 3

Immigration

An International Perspective on Migration

Cathi Tactaquin

There are over 100 million migrants (immigrants and refugees) in the world today—an unprecedented level that has prompted widespread concern about the causes and consequences of international migration. Although migrant-sending countries have urged the United Nations General Assembly to convene an international conference on migration and development, migrant-receiving countries such as the United States are rapidly developing national immigration policies that may seriously jeopardize the basic human rights and economic survival of this growing population.

The United States receives less than 1 percent of the world's migrants each year. Nonetheless, it has responded to the international crisis in migration by cracking down on undocumented immigrants, tightening border controls, restricting access to political asylum, and threatening immigrant access to public assistance programs. Most policy makers are quick to pander to racist and xenophobic fears and claims that immigration has become a primary source of this country's economic instability.

However, despite the ever increasing volume of restrictions and resources devoted to controlling immigration, these measures have had little, if any, impact on the sources and patterns of international migration.

Sources of International Migration

Historically, some factors have consistently influenced migration flows, but dramatic political and economic changes over the last decade have produced new migrant populations and patterns that defy "traditional" immigration controls and have led to a widespread belief that international migration has indeed reached crisis proportions. Many experts consider it one of the most significant global issues of our time, reflecting economic and societal failures to provide adequate jobs and shelter, environmental protection, and the preservation of basic human rights.

The root causes of international migration are several and often intertwined, so that categories such as labor migration, family reunification, or asylum-seeking are no longer clear-cut:

- *Economic:* While economics is a major cause of displacement, migrants who come from impoverished conditions are likely to have been affected by other factors, including political and social unrest, not formally acknowledged as endangering human rights conditions.
- *Political:* Most of today's refugees—over 20 million people—are fleeing conditions of generalized violence and hostilities rather than individual persecution. Most current conflicts are taking place within countries rather than between them.
- *Environmental:* Millions of people have been displaced because the land they live on has become toxic or is unable to support them. While some conditions are the result of natural disasters, much environmental degradation is caused by humans—national and multinational business interests that disregard protections or purposely ravage natural resources.
- *Ethnic tensions:* Many of the highly publicized refugee flows today have been traced to ethnic tensions unleashed by national instabilities and conflicts or fomented by political adversaries. In the process of national consolidation, some minority groups may be viewed as obstacles, breaking up a country's national identity or dividing political loyalties.

The destinations of migrants have also shifted significantly over the last thirty years. Migration patterns have always been affected by such factors as geographic proximity, historical and political ties, culture, language, and so forth. But the dominant flow is south to north, a trend that has significantly increased in the last few decades, and with the United States as a particular magnet for migrants from developing countries. However, there is still considerable migration among Northern countries, and even more so among countries in the South. Obviously, 99 percent of the world's migrants do not come to the United States, despite current national fears that the country is being overrun by "hordes" of the foreign-born.

Who Are the Migrants?

The International Organization for Migration estimates there may be about 30 million "irregular" migrant workers—those who are undocumented or without legal permission to remain in countries where they live. The United States receives an estimated two hundred thousand to three hundred thousand undocumented immigrants annually.

About 20 million migrants are displaced within their own countries and have not crossed international boundaries.

The refugee population has more than doubled over the last decade and a half: over 20 million today, compared with an estimated 8.5 million in 1980. Seventy-five percent of these refugees have moved to bordering countries in developing regions, which are most hard-pressed to accept new and often rapid increases in population. Refugees are the most numerous within Asia—about 10 million people—with about 5.5 million in Africa and 4.5 million in Europe. By contrast, advanced countries such as the United States and Canada together receive just over 1 million refugees.

Because migration has become such an important issue, recent international forums, such as the United Nations' September 1994 International Conference on Population and Development (ICPD), held in Cairo, have been strongly criticized for their insufficient treatment of the migration question.

Sending countries were especially frustrated at the ICPD by the attitudes of Western nations, typically the receiving countries. A particularly heated debate broke out over the issue of "family reunification," which sending countries felt should be preserved in the official conference document as a "right" of migrant people. However, Canada, the United States, and European nations opposed the language, offering a compromise that merely "encouraged" nations to consider family reunification in determining their immigration policies—an action that the sending countries, predominantly composed of people of color, felt was just one more example of the racial hostility of the predominantly white receiving nations.

While the conference made gains in asserting the centrality of the empowerment of women in addressing resolutions to rapidly escalating population growth, the ICPD did not make any headway in confronting the impact of international development policies on population and consequent pressures toward increased migration. Of course, such gross omissions served the political and economic interests of the Western nations that continue to dominate these international gatherings and that resist fetters on their development policies and practices. The debate over family reunification, however, stirred sending country delegates to press for an international conference on migration and development, a controversial proposal now under consideration at the United Nations.

Such a conference is intended to address long-range measures to alleviate migration pressures, including economic growth, investment, and cooperative aid programs; easing the developing countries' tremendous debt burdens; promoting fair trade policies; education, health care access, and economic opportunities, especially for women in developing countries; and, generally, developing more stable economic environments.

Migration, Development, and Trade

There is strong feeling among developing countries that as trade and development policies and agreements are forged, the question of migration must also be put on the table. This was an especially sore point in the negotiations over NAFTA, which essentially redefined the international border between the United States and Mexico by allowing for the free flow of goods, resources, and capital, but which omitted discussion of the obvious flow of labor across borders—a permanent and essential element of the global economy.

In the meantime, as the scope of international migration in the new global economy continues to broaden, considerable concern has arisen for rights protections for migrants—and for foreign nationals residing temporarily in new countries. Most receiving countries are taking steps to restrict immigration in ways that have little impact on migration pressures, but that will severely limit the rights and mobility of immigrants already residing in those countries.

Many countries around the world—not just the major receiving nations—have growing percentages of foreign nationals living within their boundaries, and in many instances, migrants, whether documented or undocumented, have few, if any, rights protections.

Pursuing International Protections

The United Nations' 1990 Convention on the Protection of the Rights of All Migrant Workers and Members of Their Families was created to augment existing covenants, further delineating the growing classes of people not residing in their countries of origin. The Convention faces an uphill battle before it "comes into force" (it requires full ratification by twenty countries, and only six have ratified or acceded to it thus far). Even when it gains recognition, its provisions are still subject to the civil laws of each country. However, it does set the basis for promoting international rights standards in this era of the global work-force, and provides a framework for evaluating national proposals dealing with immigration. California's anti-immigrant initiative, Prop-osition 187, for example, certainly violates the spirit and intent of international migrants' rights protections. (Proposition 187 was passed in November 1994, but was ruled largely unconstitutional. It awaits further court action.)

The tendency of countries to build higher walls in an attempt to block immigration in no way addresses the complexities of migration, but is a simplistic response to heightening ignorance, racial intoler-ance, and xenophobia. Migration—not just immigration into any one country—is an international issue, a manifestation of uneven social, political, and economic development and conflict that requires cooper-ation and collective action among countries and regions.

Changing Relations
Newcomers and Established Residents in U.S. Communities

Robert Bach

Not since the turn of the century has America faced the diversity of cultures, nationalities, languages, and religions brought by immigrants during the last two decades. According to the 1990 census, there are nearly 20 million foreign-born residents in America, the most in the country's history. Changes in immigration laws in the 1960s shifted both the magnitude and the composition of new immigrant popula-tions, opening the gates to immigration from Asia and the Pacific, and

Robert Bach's "Changing Relations: Newcomers and Established Residents in U.S. Communities" (excerpts) is an April 1993 report to the Ford Foundation by the Na-tional Board of the Changing Relations Project.

stabilizing flows from Latin America and the Caribbean. The share of European immigrants declined. This new mix of diverse newcomers became an essential ingredient in the transformation of community life, recasting relations among groups, ethnic identities, community associations, and political alliances. Once again, America is changing.

Changing Relations: Newcomers and Established Residents in U.S. Communities reports on the findings and recommendations of the national board of the Ford Foundation's Changing Relations Project. In 1987 the board, a multidisciplinary group of scholars, launched a project to examine the everyday interactions and relations among new immigrants and established residents in six diverse U.S. communities: Albany Park (Chicago), IL; Garden City, KS; Houston, TX; Miami, FL; Monterey Park, CA; Philadelphia, PA. From the outset, the board was concerned about popular reports of unrest and conflict between members of immigrant and established resident groups. Spectacular incidents, such as conflict between Korean shopkeepers and African Americans or Southeast Asian refugees and Texas shrimp farmers, had been highlighted in the press and even become the subject of movies. Invidious comparisons of immigrant success stories with impoverished minorities also fueled a widespread mythology about intergroup tensions and job competition. Did these incidents represent what was to become of the nation's increasingly diverse communities?

The project was initiated during a highly charged national debate over the reform of immigration policy. Throughout the debate, undercurrents of concern about the capacity of U.S. communities to absorb newcomers remained unsettled. The answers found in this study, from the rare and exceptional nature of incidents of open conflict to infrequent but promising efforts at intergroup coalition-building, respond to those undercurrents. The answers are not only about immigrants. They demand that attention be given to community conditions that newcomers and established residents face and struggle to overcome together.

The research teams sought to answer five questions that guided the project:

- What is the nature of relations between native-born or longer-resident Americans and new immigrants? What are the primary settings for interactions among these groups, and what brings them together or keeps them apart?

- What are the cultural conceptions of American identity and life, and how do they take shape through intergroup interactions?
- What sources of conflict, distance, tolerance, accommodation, and competition exist among these groups, and what factors promote or inhibit their presence?
- To what extent have large-scale, long-term changes in the economy, population, structure, and policy influenced the way in which immigrants and established residents interact?
- What situations, actions, and strategies promote communications, understanding, accommodations, and accord when multigroup interactions occur?

Findings

Collective Change, Not Assimilation

The traditional view of immigrant history is that it is characterized by a process of assimilation. Such a perspective examines only the immigrants themselves, assuming that newcomers will adapt completely to established U.S. life. The Changing Relations Project research focuses on accommodation, a process by which all sides in a multifaceted situation, including established residents and groups at different stages of settlement, find ways of adjusting to and supporting each other. Accommodation embraces an entire community in collective change. America's story, then, is no longer simply one of "coming to America." It is also an account of the places where immigrants settle and how those already there change.

Economic Restructuring and Opportunities for Interaction

Where people live, and what brings them together, create opportunities for newcomers to interact with established residents. For example, family reunification connects successive waves of immigrants to already settled kinfolk and concentrates them in particular neighborhoods. In addition, American employers generate immigrant flows to fill particular jobs. The federal government resettles refugees with the help of local residents and agencies.

During the last two decades, a broad restructuring of work, family, and politics has shaped the opportunities for interaction among new-comers and established residents. Economic restructuring has changed the role that particular regions play in the national or international economy and has generated a new set of demands and services that affect newcomers and established residents. Increases in the volume and diversity of immigration were both a response and a further stimulus to this restructuring.

The communities studied in the project all exhibited the effects of political and economic restructuring. Each has experienced an accelerated pace of change that has disrupted personal and social connections. In each site, transformation of the American political economy has rekindled fears of social disorder, disorganization, and conflict among newcomers and established groups, and fragmentation of the entire social fabric. Yet, within each locality, researchers discovered a stable social order that newcomers and established residents have been able to create and maintain through a wide-ranging set of activities.

New Ethnic Diversity

Immigration has changed the racial and ethnic composition of community authority and power, giving old problems a new identity. Although established inequities of race and wealth persist, immigrants' diverse linguistic, cultural, and class backgrounds have changed perceptions of the source of group differences. For example, immigration had added new complexity to inequality, exposing sharp class differences within established racial and ethnic groups. Immigration by itself does not create these divisions. But it can add to and sometimes exacerbate them.

Separation, Tension, and Conflict

Newcomers and established residents coexist primarily by maintaining distance from each other. Separation—both residential and institutional—characterizes their divided world. While few opportunities for intergroup interaction exist, overt incidents of conflict among groups are rare.

The occasions and places for group interaction, including schools, workplaces, and playgrounds, are special and must absorb the strains of new demographic and social differences. Tensions may turn into conflict where the informal connections between groups are few. If a single source of conflict stands out, it involves the use of different languages.

The concentration of groups in different and unequal positions stimulates comparisons between winners and losers. Economic, social, and political opportunities exclude large subgroups, whether newcomer or established resident. Much of this exclusion results from well-established sources of division in America, including wealth, income, ethnicity, gender, and primarily race. The media often play an ambivalent, if not counterproductive, role in paying attention to diversity only when groups become involved in conflict.

Common Tasks in Building Community

Active engagement in common tasks most frequently brings about accommodation. When groups come together to participate in a shared task, the inspiration is usually a desire to improve specific community conditions—to secure better social services or housing, or to battle neighborhood crime and deterioration. The groups are not searching consciously for cross-cultural means to improve an abstract sense of "quality of life." Rather, in these situations, they are struggling together over a loss of control in the face of dramatic changes in their standard of living. Shared activities reduce tension and competition, and build bonds of trust among groups. Other community activities, like sports and recreational clubs, also provide opportunities for positive interaction among groups. When given the opportunity, occasion, and shared project, newcomers and established residents show a willingness to work together.

Local Organizations and Leadership

Although local organizations and institutions, such as schools, create opportunities for interaction because of their control of resources and shared values, many have not incorporated the full implications of the changes that have accompanied immigration into their communities. Institutions that are organized around small geographical units, such as schools and neighborhood associations, have advantages over other organizations. Yet, the individuals who will lead the way in encouraging full participation across group lines may be more important. In the communities studied, these individuals are often teachers, clergy, social workers, or police, not the elite cadre of institutional organizers. Through the day-to-day interaction and encounters, these "community brokers," often women, forge ties and ease tension among groups.

Recommendations to Foster Positive Interactions

How does the nation promote the occasions and opportunities for newcomers to interact with established residents in ways that build meaningfully shared interests and common goals, while recognizing the value of distinct group identities? The answer requires expanding capacities for accommodation among diverse local people and their institutions. It demands mobilization of joint efforts by newcomers and established residents, and decisive public strategies to encourage them:

• A primary rule of policy should be to avoid actions that worsen relations among newcomers and established residents. In the research sites, anti-immigrant reactions exacerbated community problems. Aggressive "get-tough" policies on immigration seldom work. Increasingly, federal policy that draws legal distinctions among groups of newcomers is part of the problem.

• Policies, such as the legalization program under the Immigration Reform and Control Act of 1986, should foster inclusion and participation of newcomers. The legalization program, particularly, should be extended beyond current limits.

• Newcomers with permanent residency status should be enabled and encouraged to participate in local elections, reinforcing efforts of coalition building through local electoral participation.

• Federal budgetary problems and the uniqueness of local combinations of groups require a renewed focus on community building. Grassroots organizing is a useful approach in promoting opportunities for interaction among groups at the local level. "Bottom-up" processes often work better than "top-down" ones. Leadership training for community members should be encouraged, particularly for teenagers and women, who have already forged interpersonal and intergroup relations in many communities.

• Local activities should encourage participation and mobilization across group lines. Attention should be focused on producing unified activities that require the energy of diverse people to reach a shared goal. It is not enough to simply try to negotiate group differences.

These common projects should address community conditions, such as housing, education, and recreation.

• Existing organizations are not necessarily responsive to the new demographic, social, and economic diversity in today's communities. They should consciously seek ways to cross group boundaries and identify common projects. Reexamination of and innovation in membership and approach in all organizations are needed to build cooperation and encourage inclusion of diverse participants.

• Efforts should be expanded to provide newcomers with access to English-language programs, and established residents should be encouraged to learn other languages. Although language differences cause major divisions, development of language skills can be a focal point around which people can rally and seek accommodation.

• Established residents need more and better information about newcomers. Such information could be provided through creative use of community newspapers, library resources, and outreach programs. In schools, efforts to promote better understanding and cooperation among newcomers and established residents should be expanded to include the whole family.

• Media reporting often misrepresents the range of interactions and the complexities of relations, especially in crises. Coverage should be continued until such incidents are resolved. There is currently too little media follow-up. Positive intergroup activities should be examined and reported, as well.

• Special events and public festivals can create a more tolerant tone in communities and are particularly effective when they involve face-to-face collaboration among groups in planning the events. Such efforts must lead to continued opportunities for inclusion and full participation. One-time efforts often exacerbate rather than resolve tensions.

The challenge for America may be less in harmonizing relations among groups than in mobilizing intergroup cooperation into strategies for economic and political advancement. Attention must focus on participation and membership, on opportunities to pursue shared concrete tasks, and on building organizations in local neighborhoods. If our goal is to create and ensure harmony, then the struggle must not be just for social peace but for opportunity and equality.

Commentary

Cathi Tactaquin

The Changing Relations Project report's emphasis on "intergroup cooperation" versus just "harmonizing" relations that never really addresses the sources of conflict between new and old residents is a good, basic approach to social change. At the same time, I was disappointed that the report, based on research launched in 1987, could not capture the incredible surge of tension and antagonism surrounding the issue of immigration today. In particular, the report does not adequately deal with the overt political maneuvering taking place among various forces over this issue—the rising influence of conservative, racist, and restrictionist voices, through the media and directly with policy makers, and "official" scapegoating of immigrants for local, state, and national economic problems. Any attempt to foster intergroup relations today will face a dangerous tide of racially motivated nativism and official policies further delineating "us" from "them."

The main thrust of the report—that we need more opportunities for positive interaction between new and established residents—is very important and, indeed, bears on public opinion. Most surveys have shown that when established residents are asked questions about immigration in the abstract, the answers appear much harsher than when people are asked questions concerning their own interaction with immigrants in their communities. I would emphasize or introduce to the listed opportunities for shared interaction a few more important areas: unions, ethnicity-based political and community organizations, churches, and civil rights organizations.

A significant vehicle for advancing intergroup relations should be unions, where historically people of various races and nationalities have come together for their common good. Of course, unions today have declined in members and influence, and many are not very well integrated racially. But it is also true that some unions have increased their organizing among immigrant workers, and in many areas, workplaces and unions are about the only places where people come into contact with someone of a different race or nationality. The potential certainly exists for unions to be an important source of interaction and common empowerment, where the common economic interests of immigrants and established residents are on the table.

The report seems to imply that in talking about "established residents" we are generally talking about the established white or non-immigrant-community residents. For the most part, however, the established residents whom many newcomers encounter are people of the same national or ethnic heritage, especially as newcomers move into or near established neighborhoods.

An important bridge between new and established residents is the more established immigrants and the second- and third-generation U.S.-born members of immigrant-based communities. They often still live in the same neighborhoods and attend the same schools and churches. They may interact in the same community organizations, although in some communities new immigrants are not included in these groups or may be excluded. These organizations should be encouraged to be inclusive in their membership, to adapt to new populations, to be bilingual and biculturally sensitive. They can be key to easing transitions, to articulating new community needs and concerns, and to working to empower future members of the community. Similarly, churches may be vehicles for encouraging intergroup relations.

The relative silence of civil rights organizations about attacks on immigrants today may bespeak a particular problem within the civil rights community itself—that these organizations themselves are still "separate," representing the established but not the new residents. There have certainly already been tensions, particularly over perceived conflicts between African Americans and new immigrants over job opportunities. Anti-immigrant organizations such as the Federation for American Immigration Reform have sought to exploit this issue with radio ad campaigns appealing to the African American community to support a moratorium on immigration. But there certainly seems to be a willingness to address the tensions. The NAACP, after considerable debate, agreed to support repeal of employer sanctions, the controversial 1986 provision outlawing the hiring of undocumented immigrants, noting that any discrimination is intolerable. Aggressive leadership is needed to help unify—not just mediate—constituencies that are a target of the renewed nativist campaign.

I certainly endorse the Changing Relations Project recommendations against "get tough" immigration policies, for an extension of legalization, and for consideration of local voting rights for permanent residents (all residents, regardless of status, may already vote in some school district and other local elections). But these recommendations are, in the end, hotly contested political issues and will need much more than public festivals if they are ever to gain credibility even as a proposal. We will have to fight for opportunity and equality in many spheres. We will need bold political leadership, common commitment, and resources. The Changing Relations Project has made some sound recommendations, and I hope that the philanthropic community is listening. We need to build bridges, and to unify our population on the basis of opportunity and equality for all in this global era of unparalleled economic change and democratization.

Immigration and the
Civil Rights Movement

William R. Tamayo

The civil rights movement in the United States is currently confronted by numerous social issues of unprecedented complexity: concerted attacks on affirmative action, increasing racial violence and hatred, questions about the "genetic ability" of African Americans to excel, and the lack of political leadership in government to address these issues.

Passage of California's Proposition 187 (the "Save our State" initiative) in November 1994 drove home a message that immigrants, like many others in America, are a drain on society. The public's perception of this community—nonwhite, undocumented, criminally bent, welfare abusers—was fueled by public officials and the media. Not surprisingly, while African Americans, Latinos, and Asian Americans voted against 187, whites voted for it 2–1.

The general alignment of all civil rights groups in California against Proposition 187 was positive. However, that alignment does not yet reflect a common view on the broader questions of undocumented immigration, immigrants' rights, and immigration policy overall.

As recently as the spring of 1990, the NAACP supported the employer sanctions provisions of the Immigration Reform and Control Act (IRCA) of 1986, which bars the hiring of undocumented persons and requires some verification of work authorization. While IRCA was being debated in Congress, Latinos, Asians, and members of the Congressional Black and Hispanic Caucuses condemned the measure as discriminatory. But the NAACP's Washington lobbyist in 1985 asserted that because of job competition between the undocumented and African Americans, the organization supported sanctions. And the Leadership Conference on Civil Rights—the nation's premier coordinating mechanism for civil rights advocacy before Congress and the executive branch, representing some 185 national organizations—did not oppose employer sanctions because of sharp division in its ranks.

A General Accounting Office study confirmed the predictions of discrimination and found that nearly 20 percent of employers admitted discriminating against Asians and Latinos (citizens and lawful permanent residents) because of IRCA. Armed with this evidence, Latinos and Asians, joined by the Lawyers' Committee for Civil Rights Under Law and the NAACP Legal Defense and Educational Fund (LDEF) and many others, convinced the NAACP to revisit the question. NAACP director Benjamin Hooks successfully urged his membership to reverse its position. The Leadership Conference eventually came around, but only after Latino groups publicly voiced their consideration of withdrawing membership.

Immigrant-Bashing = Racism

Racism has dominated and continues to dominate immigration policies in the United States and other Western nations. As recently as 1993, in response to a World Bank report that over 100 million people have left their home countries and to a United Nations High Commissioner for Refugees report that there are over 44 million refugees in the world, the G-7 countries (United States, Germany, France, Italy, Canada, Japan, and Great Britain) adopted policies to restrict immigration and deny quick access to asylum. These efforts were designed to stem immigration from Africa, Latin America, and Asia. The racial component of these policies was vividly illustrated as immigrants from Turkey, the Middle East, Africa, and Asia were victims of racial violence throughout Western Europe in 1992.

In the United States, these policies translated into proposed curbs on the political asylum process, rapid deportation, increased border enforcement (without provisions for oversight), and efforts to deny undocumented immigrants public services, à la Proposition 187. In 1993, California governor Pete Wilson proposed denial of citizenship to U.S.-born children whose parents were undocumented. Wilson chose to turn back the clock to an era when U.S.-born African Americans and Native Americans were denied citizenship by law. While this effort was unsuccessful, Wilson touched an extremely hot button and realized that fanning the flames of xenophobia was not only popular but provided the key element for his reelection.

The welfare reform bill President Clinton signed in 1996 severely restricts various programs to assist most low-income *legal* immigrants, those presently in the country as well as those entering in future years.

The Task for Civil Rights Groups

What should the civil rights movement do amidst this cacophony of hate, racism, and nativism? Foremost, the movement must draw out the commonalities among the communities it seeks to represent and on whose behalf it is advocating. Allowing to go unchallenged the pattern of blaming similarly situated victims of racism for one's plight would be a striking setback. If anything, the current heightened racialized climate serves as a painful reminder that many of us are in the same boat and need not blame each other for being there. Even perceptions that nonwhite but non-Black minorities who may or may not be citizens should not be at the table of civil rights debate do an injustice to the vision of civil rights leaders like Dr. Martin Luther King, Malcolm X, and others who approached the issue of civil and human rights with a global and internationalist perspective.

While the history of the movement has been inconsistent on the issue of immigrants' rights, there have been proud moments. The ACLU was formed out of challenges to the roundups and deportations of immigrant labor activists during the Palmer Raids of 1919–20 and continues to represent immigrants in civil rights matters. In 1915, the NAACP successfully defeated a Senate amendment to deny admission to persons of African descent, and in 1952 argued for defeat of the dangerous McCarran–Walter Act, which maintained the racist national origins quotas in our immigration laws. During the Proposition 187 campaign, the Urban League, NAACP LDEF, Mexican American Legal Defense & Educational Fund, and Asian organizations vociferously opposed the measure. These experiences laid the foundation for a more concerted effort to protect the rights of immigrants and beat back the racism that underlies anti-immigrant measures. More important, that joint practice serves to build a common vision about who is responsible for this climate of hate and racism, and leads to a decrease in interethnic hostilities.

Civil rights groups have an important mission in this period. They must be able to more forcefully articulate the issues of the immigrant population, including the undocumented, and assert that this community is part of the civil rights community. They must assert that working together and drawing the lessons are the main ways in which we can survive this period of vitriolic scapegoating and "racialized patriotism" in which nonwhites and noncitizens are being jointly demonized without mercy.

Job Competition Between Immigrants and African Americans

Paul Ong and Abel Valenzuela, Jr.

On the question of whether immigrants are taking jobs away from African Americans, one is tempted to deny the existence of this competition, based on findings from studies done in the 1980s on the effects of immigration during the 1970s, which show very little or no adverse impact. However, the validity of these studies has been called into question on methodological grounds, and furthermore, there is no reason to believe that the impacts during the 1980s were identical to

Paul Ong and Abel Valenzuela, Jr.'s, "Job Competition Between Immigrants and African Americans" is an earlier version of a chapter in *Ethnic Los Angeles,* ed. Roger Waldinger and Mehdi Bozorgmehr. © 1996 Russell Sage Foundation, New York, New York. Used with permission.

those in the 1970s. We find adverse effects for African Americans, with the impacts coming from the presence of low-skilled Latino immigrants. However, our findings should not be interpreted as blaming the poor labor market outcomes of African Americans on immigrants. Our findings, rather, should be placed in a context of continuing structural and labor market discrimination.

Our analysis focuses on the impact of immigration on the joblessness and earnings among Black males between the ages of eighteen and twenty-four, and those between the ages of eighteen and sixty-four with no more than a high school education. These populations were chosen because they are the most susceptible to job competition, primarily due to their concentration in the low-pay and high-turnover secondary sector. The analysis of joblessness and earnings is based on a comparison of outcomes in Los Angeles County with those in fifty-five other metropolitan statistical areas (MSAs). Through the use of multivariate techniques, we attempt to estimate how immigration has disadvantaged Blacks in Los Angeles relative to their counterparts in other metropolitan areas, after taking into account both individual and regional factors. Our findings indicate that immigration increases joblessness among African Americans, with a larger net impact coming from the presence of Latino immigrants with limited education. On the other hand, there is no detectable net impact on earnings.

While Los Angeles has a relatively small percentage of the African American labor force, it has a very large percentage of the immigrant labor force. Immigrant–Black ratios are very high in Los Angeles, and in the case of Latino immigrants, the ratios are about ten times higher than the average for the other fifty-five MSAs. Consequently, whatever immigrant impacts are found for Los Angeles should be higher than in other parts of the United States.

We estimate that there is a small positive impact of Latino immigration on earnings, which is produced by two offsetting effects. The presence of immigrants appears to have a direct complementary effect in increasing the earnings of African Americans who are employed, but on the other hand, the larger flow of immigrants works indirectly, through joblessness, to depress earnings.

We argue that immigrants have a complementary effect for African Americans in public sector employment due to the increased demand for public services and agencies as a result of the growth of legal and illegal immigration. As the demand for public services, programs, and personnel has grown due to the population growth, a large part of which comes from immigration, African American employment in this sector has increased.

While the above findings indicate measurable impacts of Latino immigration in Los Angeles, this is not the same as saying that all aspects of immigration are bad for African Americans. There are at least three other factors at work here. First, our own analysis indicates that other immigrants appear to have a positive, or net complementary, effect on African Americans. The presence of Asian and other (non-Hispanic and non-Asian) immigrants is not related to higher Black joblessness, but is positively related to higher Black earnings. Second, other native minority populations are likely to be affected by immigration. And finally, immigrants generate benefits for many segments of society by providing cheap goods and services. For many professionals and better-paid workers, Latino immigrants are a major source of nannies and other domestic support workers.

Moreover, the impact of Latino immigrants on African Americans should be placed in the context of racism in the labor market. Indeed, we find sizable racial effects on joblessness and earnings. These disparities hold for both 1970, which was prior to the massive influx of immigrants, and 1990.

The analyses of Latino immigrant impact and racism show that both factors play significant roles in disadvantaging African Americans in terms of joblessness and earnings. The estimates suggest that racial discrimination and segmentation are relatively more important in both areas. The additional joblessness associated with racial disparity is three to four times greater than that associated with immigration, and all of the adverse impacts on earnings come from racial disparity. However, the impacts of racism and immigration are not unrelated. The differences we report between young adults and less-educated adults support our contention. The higher concentration of Blacks in the secondary labor market, where the bulk of low-skilled Latino immigrants have been incorporated, exposes Blacks to greater job competition and perhaps contributes to their increased joblessness rates and to their lack of progress in earnings relative to non-Hispanic whites. Last, in an issue we did not analyze, the interaction between racism (discriminatory practices and segmentation) and immigration may be further compounded by interacting with imports. George Borjas argues that immigration and imports are highly correlated, and may produce the same impacts on native workers. Consequently, some of the substitution effect associated with immigration is also caused by growing imports. Moreover, immigrant workers are most likely to be incorporated into the domestic sectors that are under import pressures. In other words, these jobs would have been lost even if there had been no immigrants.

Policy Implications and Conclusion

Our study shows that the impacts of Latino immigrants on African Americans should be placed in the context of racism in the labor market. The finding of a persistent Black–white differential is consistent with a national pattern of higher joblessness and lower earnings for African Americans than for non-Hispanic whites, even after controlling for schooling and age. In this regard, African Americans in Los Angeles are no different from African Americans in other regions of the country, many of whom live in areas with very little immigration. The explanation for our findings is complex. African Americans start off being disadvantaged by having less education, a product of a biased and ineffective educational system. This racial bias is magnified in the labor market, which concentrates African Americans in the secondary sector. Consequently, our findings suggest that being African American increases the likelihood of being confined to jobs in the secondary sector. Our study shows that increased joblessness for African Americans is connected to increases in Latino immigration, but it also shows that endemic racism plays a central role.

Our findings present a serious challenge to the simultaneous pursuit of civil rights for African Americans and upholding our heritage as a nation of immigrants. The existence of job competition between Latino immigrants and African Americans (and possibly other U.S.-born minorities and more established immigrants) has been seized by some as a rationale for stopping immigration. This position—that immigrants hurt Blacks and the poor—is at best incomplete. In part, there is evidence that some types of immigration can be beneficial. To generalize about all immigration is an exercise in misleading polemics. Furthermore, to truly fight for Black equality in this country, a sound policy must include efforts to eradicate endemic racism. To focus only on immigrants as the source disadvantaging African Americans would, in our opinion, constitute scapegoating an already vulnerable group and miss the point of our study—that other factors, such as labor market discrimination and segmentation, are more important in explaining African American inequality. Even worse, focusing solely on immigration brings out a form of nativism that ultimately reinforces racially based prejudices.

Rhetorical anti-immigrant arguments may be easily dismissed, but the political movements for minority rights can also fall into an ideological trap. Some political activists would dismiss this form of conflict (e.g., job competition) as a strategy of divide-and-conquer perpetuated by those in power or one based on cultural misunderstandings. One could argue that, with experience and education, those at the bottom would come to see their shared plight and unite in a common struggle. This position, however, flies against the material reality and an emerging political nationalist sentiment within minority communities. It would be unfair to insist on "Third World solidarity" while ignoring a real cost of immigration for African Americans. There is a fundamental problem of racism that not only seriously disadvantages minorities but also magnifies the impact of immigration on some communities, but this retort does little to address the immediate harsh reality. Indeed, there is a rising anti-immigrant sentiment among native-born minorities. Much of this has taken the form of growing resentment toward undocumented aliens, who are almost always seen as Latinos. This resentment became vividly clear in a pre- and postelection poll on minority voter support for the 1994 California Proposition 187. Indeed, statewide exit polls showed that 47 percent of African American and Asian voters and 23 percent of Latino voters supported passage of this proposition. Other polls showed strong minority support, including among Latinos, for more stringent immigration laws. But, as stated earlier, anti-immigrant politics is not easily confined to attacks on illegal immigration, for it easily spills over as a nativist attack on all immigrants.

Xenophobic reactions, which are heavily tinged with racial overtones, have the potential to mute the struggle for civil rights and racial justice. As California has changed from a mostly white population to a mostly Latino, Asian, and African American population, the politics of fear and uncertainty has resurfaced. Anti-immigrant political rhetoric, unconstitutional propositions, and increased violence are as much targeted against undocumented and legal immigrants as they are against dissatisfaction with California's deteriorated lifestyle and poor economic status. Indeed, placing the blame for California's fallen economy on immigrants and, by extension, on minority communities distracts attention from the ineptitude of current and former state and local government officials and bad public policy.

We must engage in a conscious effort to formulate a new civil rights agenda if we are to attack racial inequality and the scapegoating of immigrants. We should start by recognizing the uniqueness of Los Angeles. Based on our analysis, the impact of Latino immigration throughout the rest of the nation is only one-tenth as great. The effects may be even smaller, since the ability to absorb immigration need not be linear—that is, smaller flows over longer periods may be incorporated without the adverse impacts documented in our study. National immigration policy should not be dictated by this region's concerns. We should also recognize, as we pointed out earlier and as is documented in countless studies, that immigration also generates positive outcomes often felt on an aggregate or national level. Newcomers add to the dynamism and vitality of this nation. They bring skills that will prove invaluable to our country in an increasingly competitive global economy.

The task before us, then, is finding ways to lower the uncomfortable trade-off imposed by job competition. In part, this means that we should seriously consider enforcing border policies and increasing the role of economic objectives in formulating immigration policy. The weak enforcement of border policies creates a large undocumented population that is at the heart of the immigration debate. While stringent enforcement will not cease undocumented immigration, it can stem the flow to some degree and thus lessen the supply of less-skilled workers. However, controlling the border is not the same as attacking those already in the United States. It is important that the rights of those already here in the United States be protected, especially since they are the product of lax enforcement policies and an implicit policy that supports employers who have become accustomed to and even dependent on cheap immigrant labor. By establishing roots in Los Angeles and participating in economic activities including the labor market, consumerism, and tax outlays, undocumented immigrants have rightful claim to being a part of this society. In addition to enforcing the border, we must have fair levels of legal immigration to fulfill our obligations as an "immigrant" country and to meet our labor demand. In doing so, we must be careful not to reintroduce race and nationality quotas into laws governing immigration. Immigration laws have legitimacy from a civil rights perspective only when they are nondiscriminatory.

We should be equally concerned about attacking the underlying racism that unfairly concentrates African Americans into the very sector that is being adversely affected by immigration. Civil rights policy needs to continue to amend past and present injustices in the educational, political, and economic areas with an explicit realization that immigrants also belong to America and, by extension, to the civil rights family.

Latino Immigrants in Los Angeles
A Portrait from the 1990 Census

David Hayes-Bautista, Werner Schink, and Gregory Rodriguez

Reasoned analysis of authoritative data sources has been in short supply in recent debates over immigration. Skewed estimates and dubious extrapolations have been bandied about in a discourse that has become, at times, increasingly illogical. While this country has every reason to consider its immigration policies carefully, the current climate of blame, fear, and hyperbole has not afforded the issue of immigration the proper consideration it deserves.

Recently released data from the 1990 census, the Public Use Microdata Samples (PUMS), finally allow for a comprehensive analysis of Latino immigrants. Unlike small area surveys, or extrapolations taken from small, segmented subpopulations (e.g., construction workers, border crossing detainees, day laborers, etc.), the census data provide the most reliable overview of the Latino immigrant population.

While census PUMS data are not flawless, because of the sheer volume of people enumerated (over 440,000 respondents in Los Angeles County alone) and the attempts at completeness, these data form the "gold standard" in population matters.

David Hayes-Bautista, Werner Schink, and Gregory Rodriguez's "Latino Immigrants in Los Angeles: A Portrait from the 1990 Census" (excerpts) appeared first as a report published by the Alta California Policy Research Center.

Latino Immigrants: How Many?

The 1990 census counted a total of 3,306,116 Latinos in Los Angeles County. Of these, 1,511,744 were Latinos born in the United States. Thus, the U.S.-born Latinos were slightly under half (45.7 percent) the total Latino population.

There were 1,794,372 immigrant Latinos in the county in 1990. They were predominantly of Mexican origin, although 315,798 Central Americans were included in that figure. Immigrant Latinos account for slightly over half (54.3 percent) of the total Latino population of Los Angeles County.

Estimating the Undocumented

The PUMS data offer a new opportunity to estimate the size of the undocumented population, in that they are based on an actual enumeration of people residing in the county, with information about birthplace and date of arrival in the United States included. By a process of elimination, in which those Latinos who are not likely to be undocumented are eliminated from the total census figure, we can approximate the size of the undocumented population.

Of the total number of Latino immigrants in the county (1.794 million), 1,072,825 had arrived prior to 1982. Thus, they would have either arrived with full documentation, or should have applied for the amnesty provision of the Immigration Reform and Control Act of 1986: there is no reason why any significant portion of this pre-1982 group should, by 1990, still have been undocumented.

Of the remaining number, data from the Immigration and Naturalization Service provide a basis for refining the census data. Between 1982 and 1990, the INS reported 273,282 Latinos admitted to the United States with documents who indicated their intention to ultimately reside in the Los Angeles–Long Beach metropolitan region. In addition, the INS reported a total of 190,983 special agricultural worker (SAW) applicants (a post-1982 amnesty program for agricultural workers) from the Los Angeles–Long Beach region.

Of the total 3,306,116 Latinos enumerated in the 1990 census, a total of 257,280 cannot be accounted for as U.S.-born or presumably documented immigrants, and hence may be assumed to be undocumented. This figure indicates that approximately 7 percent of the total Latino population might be undocumented in 1990.

Because the PUMS data do not distinguish between documented and undocumented immigrants, the rest of this report will present data on all immigrant Latinos.

Labor Force Participation

High Labor Force Participation

Latino male immigrants are the most active participants in the Los Angeles workforce: their participation rate far exceeds that of Anglo, Black, Asian, or U.S.-born Latino males. Fully 86 percent of immigrant Latino males age sixteen and older participate in the labor force, compared with 77.8 percent for Anglo, 76.2 percent for U.S.-born Latino, 69.7 percent for Black, and 75.3 percent for Asian males of the same age.

Low Rates of "Not in Labor Force"

Latino immigrant males are the least likely to leave the labor force: only 14 percent occupied the status of "not in labor force" for 1990, much lower than the 22.2 percent of Anglo, 23.8 percent of U.S.-born Latino, 30.8 percent of Black, and 24.7 percent of Asian males age sixteen and older.

Hours Worked

Labor force activity is also measured in hours worked per week. A higher percentage of immigrant Latino males worked thirty-five or more hours per week than did males of any other group: 67.5 percent of such males worked thirty-five or more hours per week, compared with 62.5 percent of Anglo males, 56.8 percent of U.S.-born Latino males, 50.2 percent of Black males, and 60.5 percent of Asian males.

Private Sector

The private sector of the economy is the engine of economic growth. Immigrant Latino males are, by far, much more likely to be employed in the private sector than any other group: 76.8 percent worked in the private sector, compared with 59 percent of Anglo, 64.2 percent of U.S.-born Latinos, 51.7 percent of Black males, and 66.2 percent of Asian males.

Public Sector

Immigrant Latino males were by far the least likely to work in public sector jobs, at the federal, state, county, city, or special district level.

Only 3.2 percent of Latino immigrant males worked in government jobs, much lower than the 9.2 percent of Anglo, 11.1 percent of U.S.-born Latino, 17.7 percent of Black, and 9 percent of Asian males.

Female Labor Force Participation

Although policy makers tend to focus exclusively on male labor force status, female labor force activity should also be considered. Females of all groups have lower labor force participation rates than males. While the rates for male participation varied quite a bit (ranging from a high of 86 percent to a low of 69.7 percent), female rates are grouped more closely together. Latina immigrant females had the lowest rate of labor force participation, but their 49.2 percent rate was only slightly lower than the 54.8 percent of Anglo, 53.7 percent of U.S.-born Latina, 51.5 percent of Black, and 54.8 percent of Asian females.

Even though the immigrant Latina rate is the lowest, it should be borne in mind that immigrant Latina females are many times more likely to be married with children than Anglo, U.S.-born Latina, or Black females, and somewhat more likely to be married with children than Asian females. From that perspective, immigrant Latina participation rates are extraordinary.

Income, Poverty, and Public Assistance

Low Income

For all their activity in the labor force and economy, immigrant Latinos are poorly rewarded. Their average household income of $29,989 was much lower than that of any other group: $52,375 for Anglo, $43,777 for U.S.-born Latino, $32,813 for Black, and $49,042 for Asian households.

High Poverty

Once again, despite being the most active element in the labor force, immigrant Latinos have the highest poverty rate of any group: 24.2 percent of immigrant Latino adults live in poverty. By way of contrast, only 7.8 percent of Anglo adults, 13.2 percent of U.S.-born Latino adults, 19.2 percent of Black adults, and 13.5 percent of Asian adults live in poverty.

Low Public Assistance

While there is a widely disseminated image that immigrant Latinos are welfare abusers, the 1990 census PUMS data show a different profile. Immigrant Latinos were by far the least likely to receive public assistance: immigrant Latino adults receiving public assistance represented only 16.9 percent of immigrant Latino adults in poverty. By contrast, Anglo adults receiving public assistance represented 41.7 percent of Anglo adults in poverty; U.S.-born Latino adults receiving public assistance represented 50.4 percent of such adults in poverty; Black adults receiving public assistance were 64.6 percent of Black adults in poverty; and Asian adults receiving public assistance represented 48.8 percent of such adults in poverty.

Immigrant Latino adults receive the least income, yet have the least propensity, by far, to utilize public assistance programs.

Family

Couples with Children

Immigrant Latino households are, by far, more likely to be composed of the classic nuclear family—a couple with children—than are households from any other group. Fully 49.6 percent of immigrant Latino households are made up of couples with children. This is much higher than the 18.4 percent of Anglo, 30.7 percent of U.S.-born Latino, 16.8 percent of Black, and 38.4 percent of Asian households.

Nonfamily and Primary Single

In part because of their propensity to form couple with children households, immigrant Latinos are the least likely to form a household composed of nonfamily (unrelated adults in the same housing unit) or primary single (adult living alone). Only 19.5 percent of immigrant Latino households were of the nonfamily and primary single type. By contrast, 48.1 percent of Anglo, 31.9 percent of U.S.-born Latino, 45.1 percent of Black, and 30.4 percent of Asian households were composed of the nonfamily or primary single type.

Divorced Households

Immigrant Latino households were the least likely to be composed of a divorced householder. Only 3.7 percent of immigrant Latino households consisted of a divorced householder. This is much lower than the 11.2 percent of Anglo, 8.1 percent of U.S.-born Latino, 13.6 percent of Black, and 4.4 percent of Asian households.

Education

Adult High School Noncompletion

Immigrant Latino adults, age twenty-five and older, usually come from the rural areas of Mexico and Latin America, where elementary school education is often all that is available. Thus, when enumerated in the 1990 census, immigrant Latino adults had the highest percentage of high school noncompletion: 70.5 percent of immigrant Latino adults did not complete high school. This is a much higher percentage than among Anglo adults (14.4 percent), U.S.-born Latino adults (35.3 percent), Black adults (25.4 percent), or Asian adults (20.7 percent).

Immigrant Latinos and In-migrant Anglos: A Comparison

California's metamorphosis into a virtual nation-state was a product of people meeting resources: the values, dreams, and hard work of millions of individuals woven into policy. From 1940 to 1970, the in-migrants who nearly tripled the state's population were considered an essential asset. To accommodate them, the state built roads, aqueducts, freeways, schools, and the world's premier public university system.

The foundation of post–World War II California was laid with civic money and a broadly shared civic consensus to invest in the new population and the future. The in-migrant population, and its children, were provided with resources for commerce, development, and research, which, when combined with their vigor and character, created wealth.

The Anglo population was, at the start of World War II, very similar to the immigrant Latino population of 1990 in its income, education, work ethic, and family structure. Some comparison may be instructive. The Anglo data are taken from the 1940 census PUMS for the state of California.

Recent Arrivals

California has long had a very mobile population. Since its incorporation as a state in 1850, California's growth has been largely a product of people moving into the state from other areas. This is true for the

Anglo population as well as for the Latino. In 1940, 64.9 percent of the Anglo population had moved into the state from another area. In 1990, a similar percentage of Latinos were also in-migrants: 54.3 percent moved in, this time from another country.

High Labor Force Participation

Anglo males in 1940 had a high rate of participation in the labor force: 81.5 percent were active in the workforce. In 1990, immigrant Latino males had a similar, and slightly higher, rate of participation: 86 percent.

High Poverty

Poverty data were not available for 1940, but even in 1950, with the post–World War II economic boom well under way, 25.5 percent of the Anglo population lived in poverty. Forty years later, in 1990, a nearly identical, but slightly lower, percentage of immigrant Latinos live in poverty: 24.2 percent.

Strong Families

In 1940, 32.9 percent of Anglo households were composed of couples with children. Immigrant Latino households in 1990 are more likely to be composed of couples with children: 49.6 percent of immigrant Latino households are so composed.

High School Noncompletion

A fact often forgotten is that in 1940, 61.5 percent of Anglo adults did not graduate from high school. While the rate for immigrant Latinos in 1990 is higher, 70.5 percent, the two rates are surprisingly close.

A Final Word

Today's immigrant Latinos are, in their values and behaviors, very much like the earlier generation of in-migrating Anglos who benefited from an exuberant civic spirit. Investing in a youthful, hardworking, forward-looking population was a wise decision in the 1940s and 1950s, and is still the wisest approach to a more prosperous future for all.

The Immigration Quiz

Applied Research Center

1. In the last four years, the poorest immigrants arriving in the U.S. came from:
   A. Africa
   B. Asia
   C. Central America
   D. Former Soviet Union

2. The area with the highest percentage of immigrants to the United States who are high school graduates is:
   A. Europe
   B. Central America
   C. Africa
   D. Asia

3. In 1910, the U.S. population was 15 percent foreign-born. In 1990, the foreign-born percentage of the population was:
   A. 8 percent
   B. 10 percent
   C. 18 percent
   D. 22 percent

4. Studies by the Urban Institute show that for every one hundred new immigrants:
   A. Employment decreases by sixty-two jobs
   B. The number of jobs stays the same
   C. Employment increases by forty-six jobs
   D. It's impossible to tell how the job market reacts

5. Nationally, immigrants receive about $5 billion annually in welfare benefits. Approximately how much do they earn and pay in taxes?
   A. Earn $10 billion, pay $1.3 billion in taxes
   B. Earn $15 billion, pay $3 billion in taxes

   C. Earn $100 billion, pay $15 billion in taxes
   D. Earn $240 billion, pay $85 billion in taxes

6. In northern California, undocumented immigrants and refugees seeking political and economic asylum may be jailed and (true/false):

A. Not be accused of any crime	T	F
B. Are allowed bail	T	F
C. Are allowed a public defender	T	F
D. Are not allowed trial by jury	T	F
E. May be placed in maximum security	T	F
F. Women may be locked down for up to 22 hours/day	T	F

Answers to the Immigration Quiz are on page 237.

Part 4

"The Underclass"

American Apartheid
Segregation and the Making of the Underclass

Douglas S. Massey

During the 1970s, Black poverty became more persistent and geographically concentrated in American cities. Many observers explained these trends by pointing to the class-specific effects of government welfare policies, industrial restructuring, changing sexual mores, the breakdown of the family, and the departure of the middle class from inner-city neighborhoods. While not denying the importance of these trends, I contend that racial segregation was the key factor responsible for the social transformation of the Black community and the concentration of poverty during the 1970s. A pernicious interaction between rising poverty rates and high levels of segregation created the population we know as the urban underclass.

Illustrating my general theoretical arguments with a simulated experiment, I have shown how racial segregation shapes, and to a large extent determines, the socioeconomic environment experienced by poor minority families. Racial segregation concentrates deprivation in Black neighborhoods by restricting the poverty created by economic downturns to a small number of minority neighborhoods. To the extent that cities are also segregated by class, increases in poverty are confined largely to poor minority neighborhoods. Simulations demonstrate that under conditions of high class and racial segregation, poor Black neighborhoods rapidly move to high concentrations of poverty following an overall rise in Black poverty rates.

Using empirically derived equations to predict neighborhood socio-

Douglas Massey's "American Apartheid: Segregation and the Making of the Underclass" (excerpts) appeared in the *American Journal of Sociology* 96, no. 2 (September 1990): 329–57, published by the University of Chicago. © 1990 by the University of Chicago. All rights reserved. Used by permission of the University of Chicago and the author.

economic outcomes from poverty concentrations, I have also shown how racial segregation acts to undermine the socioeconomic environment faced by poor Blacks and leaves their communities extremely vulnerable to any downturn in the economy. Under conditions of high racial segregation, a rise in Black poverty rates produces a dramatic loss in potential demand in poor Black neighborhoods, leading to the withdrawal, deterioration, and outright elimination of goods and services distributed through the market. Moreover, to the extent that public services are dependent on local tax revenues or user fees, they also disappear or suffer declines in quality.

The Transforming Power of Segregation

Because segregation concentrates disadvantages, shifts in Black poverty rates comparable with those observed during the 1970s have the power to transform the socioeconomic character of poor Black neighborhoods very rapidly and dramatically, changing a low-income Black community from a place where welfare-dependent, female-headed families are a minority to one where they are the norm, producing high rates of crime, property abandonment, mortality, and educational failure. All of these deleterious conditions occur through the joint effect of rising poverty and high levels of racial segregation. They can be produced at any time through a simple increase in Black poverty rates under conditions prevailing in most large U.S. cities. They can be generated for any fixed level of class segregation, and they do not require out-migration of middle-class Blacks from the ghetto. Thus, racial segregation is crucial to understanding and explaining the existence of America's urban underclass.

The way that segregation concentrates poverty and creates disadvantaged minority neighborhoods provides a succinct, comprehensive explanation that resolves several issues in the underclass debate. First, it explains why the urban underclass, however one defines it, is so disproportionately composed of Blacks and Puerto Ricans. In the nation's largest urban areas, these groups are the only ones that have simultaneously experienced high levels of racial segregation and sharp increases in poverty. Black–white dissimilarity indices representing the percentage of Blacks who would have to change neighborhoods in order to achieve an even or integrated pattern generally exceed .700; in the largest urban areas, they are usually above .800. Likewise, Puerto

Ricans are the only Hispanic group whose segregation indices are routinely above .700. During the 1970s, other minority groups, such as Mexicans and Asians, experienced lower levels of segregation, smaller increases in poverty, or both.

Segregation's role in concentrating poverty also explains why the urban underclass is confined primarily to the Northeast and Midwest, and mostly to a small number of large metropolitan areas, such as New York, Chicago, Philadelphia, and Baltimore. During the 1970s, older industrial cities in these regions not only experienced the sharpest economic reversals but also exhibited the highest levels of racial segregation in the United States. Thus, industrial restructuring drove minority poverty rates upward most sharply in cities where Blacks and Puerto Ricans were most segregated.

Explaining the "Underclass" Phenomenon

Explaining the origins of the underclass in terms of continuing racial segregation is also consistent with earlier research showing that upper-income Blacks remain highly segregated from whites, that this pattern has not changed over time, and that the degree of class segregation among Blacks is actually lower than that among other minority groups. Segregation, therefore, provides a more cogent and plausible explanation for the concentration of Black poverty than the out-migration of the middle class from the ghetto. The latter hypothesis does not explain why Blacks are overrepresented in the underclass or why geographic mobility should concentrate poverty among Blacks but not other groups. In the United States, spatial mobility has always accompanied social mobility, and middle-class families have always moved out of racial and ethnic enclaves into residentially integrated neighborhoods. Middle-class Blacks are not unique in seeking to put distance between themselves and the poor; rather, they stand out because they are less able to do so than the middle class of other groups.

The role that segregation plays in the creation of the underclass also explains the recent empirical findings of other researchers. Thomas LaVeist, for example, has shown that the level of Black residential segregation is the strongest predictor of Black infant mortality rates and that, whereas racial segregation sharply increases mortality among Blacks, it strongly reduces it among whites. My simulations show clearly how whites gain and Blacks lose through the imposition of racial segregation. By confining Blacks to a small number of segregated neighborhoods, whites insulate themselves from the higher rates of Black poverty and the problems associated with it; and as segregation rises, the total income of white neighborhoods grows while that of Black neighborhoods falls, so that whites are in a better position to support hospitals, clinics, and other medical facilities.

Another set of empirical results has recently been generated by George Galster and Mark Keeney, using a simultaneous-equations model of segregation in forty U.S. metropolitan areas. They uncovered a very significant and dynamic feedback relationship among segregation, Black socioeconomic status, and discrimination, whereby rising segregation increased Black–white occupational differences, which in turn increased the level of Black–white segregation through a negative relationship with Black income. At the same time, falling Black socioeconomic status raised the level of discrimination in the housing market, which, in turn, increased segregation, further reducing Black incomes and occupational status, leading to additional discrimination and segregation, and so on.

This sort of dynamic relationship is interpretable in terms of the model of segregation and poverty concentration I have developed. Whites benefit from segregation because it isolates higher rates of Black poverty within Black neighborhoods. These higher concentrations of Black poverty then reinforce the connection, in whites' minds, between Black race and behaviors associated with poverty, such as crime, family disruption, and dependency. Segregation heightens and reinforces negative racial stereotypes by concentrating people who fit those stereotypes in a small number of highly visible minority neighborhoods—a sectoral version of "blaming the victim"—thereby hardening prejudice, making discrimination more likely, and maintaining the motivation for segregation. The persistence of segregation, in turn, worsens the concentration of poverty, putting additional downward pressure on Black socioeconomic status, making further segregation and discrimination more likely, and so on. In short, the feedback loop identified by Galster and Keeney could very well operate through a close connection between racial segregation and Black poverty concentration.

Needed Policies

Finally, an appreciation of the role that segregation plays in generating and perpetuating the underclass points to the need for a very different set of policies toward poverty and the underclass. In recent years, a variety of initiatives have been proposed or enacted to address class-based problems within the Black community, such as joblessness, family disruption, drug abuse, low levels of education, alcoholism, and crime. These serious social problems clearly must be addressed, but I argue that, unless the issue of race is simultaneously addressed, these class-related problems cannot be solved.

The issue for public policy is not whether race or class is responsible for the current plight of Blacks in the United States, but how race and class interact to undermine the well-being of this group. Arguments about the declining significance of race, debates on the effect of government welfare policies, and disputes about trends in the concentration of poverty have largely ignored the continuing reality of segregation imposed on Blacks because of their race.

Race affects the social and economic well-being of Blacks primarily through the housing market. Two decades after passage of the Fair Housing Act, levels of Black segregation remain exceedingly high in large urban areas where the concentration of poverty is more severe (New York, Chicago, Philadelphia, Newark, and Detroit). This high level of Black segregation cannot be explained by Blacks' objective socioeconomic characteristics, their housing preferences, or their limited knowledge of white housing markets. Rather, it is linked empirically to the persistence of discrimination in housing markets and to continuing anti-Black prejudice. Ironically, Puerto Ricans are the exception that proves the rule, since the high degree of segregation they experience is clearly attributable to the persistence of a Black racial identity among them.

In short, my explication of segregation's role in concentrating urban poverty and creating the underclass strongly suggests that class-based policies will not succeed by themselves. As long as racial discrimination and prejudice are translated so directly into economic disadvantage through housing markets, and as long as racial segregation persists at such high levels in American cities, Blacks and Puerto Ricans will remain vulnerable groups whose basis for community life and socioeconomic well-being can be systematically undermined by the closing of a factory or the onset of a recession. This vulnerability stems from the fact that segregation intensifies and magnifies any economic setback these groups suffer and builds deprivation structurally into their social and economic environments.

Fighting the Biases Embedded in Social Concepts of the Poor

Herbert J. Gans

One of the ways that America and its policy makers avoid dealing with poverty is to label some of the poor as morally deficient or undeserving, and therefore not worthy of help. This line of reasoning presumes that everyone can rise out of poverty and become middle-class (there being lots of well-paying jobs for them), if they only make the effort.

This is ironic, since most poor people want to be as middle-class as everyone else and wish that their efforts enabled them to escape poverty. This is also true of the minority of poor people who drop out of school; do not work; become unmarried mothers; engage in mugging, robbery, or other criminal activities; or wind up as alcoholics or drug addicts. Most people who behave in such ways do so primarily for poverty-related reasons stemming from a sheer lack of resources and the stresses of coping with poverty.

Crime is immoral, whether carried out by the poor or by Wall Street millionaires, but no one has ever supplied data showing that the poor, as a class, are less moral than the middle class or the rich. (The news, media currently are filled with stories of rising middle-class unemployment, but no one ever suggests that the middle-class jobless are lazy.)

Labeling the Poor

Labeling the poor as undeserving does nothing to reduce poverty or poverty-related behavior, including the crime rate. While there are continuing scholarly—and ideological—debates about the interplay of different economic, social, cultural, and psychological factors that contribute to keeping people poor, consensus is fairly widespread that only when the poor lose the struggle to escape poverty do they give up mainstream behavior. For example, a major reason for the formation of single-parent families among the poor is the high rate of male unemployment, which makes poor men—of any color—bad marital risks.

Herbert J. Gans's "Fighting the Biases Embedded in Social Concepts of the Poor" appeared in the January 8, 1992, *Chronicle of Higher Education.*

Social scientists have played a part in labeling the poor as lazy and undeserving. Their predecessors in medieval times and the early industrial period helped to invent, codify, and apply various conceptions of undeservingness to the poor, and today social science concepts are still being used in harmful ways.

In the 1950s, the anthropologist Oscar Lewis developed the concept of the "culture of poverty," which claimed that some of the poor belonged to a special culture, passed on from generation to generation, that adapted them so well to poverty that they did not even want to try to escape it. Policy makers in the 1960s used Lewis's thesis to argue that the poor were culturally disadvantaged and to justify their claim that low-income people needed cultural uplift before they could make proper use of jobs and higher incomes.

The current conceptual equivalent of Lewis's culture of poverty is the term "the underclass." Gunnar Myrdal, the famous Swedish political economist, first used this term in 1962 as an economic concept, to describe the people he thought were being made unemployable by what we now call the postindustrial economy. Myrdal said nothing about the race or gender of his underclass; he was writing about economic victims.

Myrdal's concept never made it into policy-making circles and also was virtually ignored by academics when it was first published. Then, in the late 1970s, the word surfaced again—in the news media and with a totally new meaning—as a behavioral concept that described poor people whose actions violated the law or did not fit mainstream values. "Underclass" had become the latest label for the undeserving poor, and it continues to be used that way today.

Underclass: A Pejorative Label

"Underclass" is a particularly nasty label, however. Earlier terms such as "pauper," "vagrant," and "tramp" were openly pejorative, but "underclass" is a technical-sounding word that hides its pejorative meaning. Moreover, once people are labeled as underclass, they are often treated accordingly. Teachers decide that they cannot learn, the police and the courts think that they must be incorrigible, and welfare agencies feel justified in administering harsh policies. Such treatment sets in motion a self-fulfilling prophecy: If the poor are treated like an underclass, their ability to escape poverty is blocked further. In addition, the term is turning into a racial code word, since by now it is increasingly applied solely to Blacks. The public expression of racial prejudice being no longer respectable, "underclass" becomes an acceptable euphemism.

Journalists played the main role in transforming the meaning of Myrdal's concept, and if any publications were central, they were a series of 1981 articles by Ken Auletta in the *New Yorker* and in his 1982 book, *The Underclass*. However, by then the term had already appeared on a 1977 *Time* magazine cover and was being used by other popular media. If Auletta had not made it famous, someone else would have done so. Writers for the commercial media have to use words that will grab their audiences, and "underclass" graphically lumps together, into one scientific-sounding stereotype, images of sinister-looking and promiscuous young Blacks (and Hispanics) whom the white population fears and disapproves of.

In the late 1970s, social scientists finally had begun to use the terms as Myrdal had, as an economic concept. Subsequently, William J. Wilson elaborated the term as a sociological concept, looking, in *The Truly Disadvantaged* (1987), at the way social changes such as the increasing concentration of the very poor in the inner cities had exacerbated the economic problems of poverty. But other scholars, particularly those of conservative or nonpolitical bents, stayed with the behavioral concept.

By the mid-1980s, the term "underclass" had become so popular in scholarly circles that—either in its Myrdal form, in its Wilson form, or in its behavioral version—social scientists, like journalists, began using the term to grab their audiences (for example, by using the term in the titles of journal articles). Some foundation officials found the word helpful with boards of trustees who had been reluctant to finance research on poverty but who became enthusiastic when it was called research on the underclass. In fact, the anthropologist Mercer Sullivan once described "underclass" as basically a marketing term.

Social scientists have the same right as anyone else to use marketing terms. They are also free to use pejorative concepts, but if they intend to be judgmental, I wish that they would be so openly—and talk about the undeserving poor rather than hide behind euphemisms. In their role as scientists, however, they should be especially sensitive to the biases and unexamined assumptions that too often wander into scientific concepts. They should try especially hard to frame concepts and hypotheses that make no overt a priori value judgments about what or whom they analyze.

Research Needed on Causes of Poverty

Equally important, I wish that social scientists would decrease their study of the victims of poverty and devote more research to its causes—the economic, political, and other processes by which America has developed by far the highest rate of poverty in the "first world" of highly developed nations.

Once social scientists have done their scholarly duty, they have the right to preach the same duty to others, including journalists. The media now regularly consult social scientists as experts, and their quotes are used to give a scientific imprimatur to all kinds of news stories. Thus, when they are being consulted, social scientists have a right to suggest that journalists be more thoughtful about the definitions they use, that they supply supporting evidence if they want to write about the moral condition of the poor, and that they do more exposés on the myth of the undeserving poor.

In the end, the real evil is poverty. Less bias and more thoughtfulness in the choice of concepts and topics will help a little, but only a little. The simple fact that young middle-class men do not mug people—and that some poor men do—carries a potent message. The only really effective solution to poverty-related behavior is the elimination of poverty itself. Scholars must use their insights and their research to cut through ideological obstacles and focus the attention of the general public and policy makers on achieving this goal.

The Welfare Quiz

World Hunger Year

1. The AFDC program consumes _____ percent of the federal budget and _____ percent of the average state budget.

2. In 1970, 4.1 percent of the population received AFDC; in 1992, at the height of the recession, _____ percent received AFDC.
   A. 9
   B. 5.3
   C. 1.4
   D. 14.2

3. In 1969, the average number of children in an AFDC family was three. In 1992, it was _____.

4. _____ percent of AFDC claims are fraudulent.
   A. 9
   B. 5.3
   C. 1.4
   D. 14.2

5. _____ families who receive benefits from AFDC leave the program within one year.
   A. Only a few
   B. More than half of all
   C. Almost all
   D. About one-fourth of all

6. The median state AFDC maximum benefit for a family of three in 1994 was _____ a month.
   A. $745
   B. $624
   C. $254
   D. $366

7. In 1994, the median AFDC maximum benefit was _____ per-
cent of the poverty line.
   A. 10
   B. 82
   C. 36
   D. 100

8. After adjusting for inflation, AFDC benefits increased _____
percent from 1970 to 1994.
   A. 62
   B. 0
   C. 45
   D. –47

9. Some welfare proposals, including the Personal Responsibility
Act proposed in the Republican Contract with America, would
require AFDC recipients to work full-time in order to receive
benefits. Based on a thirty-five-hour workweek and the median
annual state benefit for a family of three, what would be the
average wage under this proposal?
   A. $5.12/hour
   B. $2.42/hour
   C. $4.25/hour
   D. $3.68/hour

Answers to the Welfare Quiz are on page 237.

The Income and Jobs Quiz

World Hunger Year

1. The "jobless rate" includes unemployed workers, involuntary part-time workers, "discouraged" workers, and all others who want to work but do not have a job. In June 1995, when the "official" unemployment rate was 5.6 percent, how many Americans were jobless?
   A. Fewer than 2 million
   B. 5 million
   C. 11 million
   D. More than 17 million

2. If one were to rank all countries according to average hourly wages paid to workers (highest to lowest), where would the United States rank?
   A. 20th
   B. 3rd
   C. 5th
   D. 14th

3. _____ Americans who either work full-time or are dependent on someone who works full-time have no health insurance coverage.
   A. Fewer than 1 million
   B. 26 million
   C. 14 million
   D. 3 million

4. In the twenty years from 1973 to 1993, average weekly inflation-adjusted earnings:
   A. Declined 19 percent
   B. Increased 73 percent
   C. Increased 32 percent
   D. Increased 14 percent

5. From 1979 to 1993, the real value of the minimum wage:
   A. Decreased 24.9 percent
   B. Decreased 12.4 percent
   C. Stayed the same
   D. Increased 8.7 percent

6. In 1994, _____ percent of all year-round, full-time individual workers did not make enough money to keep a family of four out of poverty.
   A. 5
   B. 11
   C. 17
   D. 23

7. In 1991, government tax and transfer systems in Canada lifted about 20 percent of single-parent families out of poverty; in West Germany, about 33 percent; in France, about 50 percent; and in the Netherlands, Sweden, and the U.K., at least 75 percent. In the United States, government tax and transfer systems (AFDC, food stamps, etc.) lifted _____ of single-parent families out of poverty.
   A. Fewer than 5 percent
   B. 10 percent
   C. More than half
   D. Nearly 40 percent

8. In 1994, _____ percent of all female-headed households with children under eighteen lived below the federal poverty line.
   A. 22
   B. 35
   C. 44
   D. 57

Answers to the Income and Jobs Quiz are on page 238.

Part 5

Multiculturalism

Racism and Multicultural Democracy

Manning Marable

What is racism? How does the system of racial discrimination that people of color experience today differ from the type of discrimination that existed in the period of Jim Crow, or legal racial segregation? How is the rich spectrum of cultural groups affected by practices of discrimination within America's "democratic society" today? What parallels can be drawn between sexism, racism, and other types of intolerance, such as anti-Semitism, anti-Arabism, homophobia, and handicapism? What kinds of national and international strategies are needed for a multicultural democracy in the whole of American society and throughout the Western world? And finally, what do we need to do to not just see beyond our differences, but to realize our commonalities and deepen each other's efforts to seize our full freedom and transform the nature of society?

Let's begin with point one: Racism is the system of ignorance, exploitation, and power used to oppress African Americans, Latinos, Asians, Pacific Americans, Native Americans, and other people on the basis of ethnicity, culture, mannerisms, and color. Point two: When we try to articulate an agenda of multicultural democracy, we run immediately into the stumbling block of stereotypes—the device at the heart of every form of racism today. Stereotypes are at work when people are not viewed as individuals with unique cultural and social backgrounds, with different religious traditions and ethnic identities, but as two-dimensional characters bred from the preconceived attitudes, half-truths, ignorance, and fear of closed minds. When seen through a stereotype, a person isn't viewed as a bona fide human being, but as an object onto which myths and half-truths are projected.

There are many ways that we see stereotypes degrade people, but perhaps most insidious is the manner in which stereotypes deny people their own history. In a racist society like our own, people of color are not viewed as having their own history or culture. Everything must

Manning Marable's "Racism and Multicultural Democracy" (excerpts) appeared in the Open Magazine Pamphlet Series as "Black America: Multicultural Democracy in the Age of Clarence Thomas, David Duke and the LA Uprising" (June 1992).

conform to the so-called standards of white bourgeois society. Nothing generated by people of color is accepted as historically original, dynamic, or creative. This even applies to the way in which people of color are miseducated about their own history. Indeed, the most insidious element of stereotypes is how people who are oppressed themselves begin to lose touch with their own traditions of history, community, love, celebration, struggle, and change.

In the 1980s we saw a proliferation of racist violence, most disturbingly on college campuses. Why the upsurge of racism? Why was it occurring in the 1980s, and why does this disease continue to spread into the 1990s? How is it complicit with other systemic crises we now face within the political, economic, and social structures of our society?

First, we need to be clear about how we recognize racism. Racism is never accidental within a social structure or institution. It is the systematic exploitation of people of color in the process of production and labor, the attempt to subordinate our cultural, social, educational, and political life. The key concepts here are subordinate and systemic. The dynamics of racism attempt to inflict a subordinate position for people of color.

Racism in the 1990s means lower pay for equal work. It means a process that sustains inequality within the income structure of this country. Institutional racism in America's economic system today means that the rhetoric of equal opportunity in the marketplace remains, in effect, a hoax for most people of color. Between 1973 and 1993, the real average earnings for young Hispanic males age eighteen to twenty-nine declined by 27 percent. For African American males in this age group, the decline was a devastating 48 percent.

Pushing Drugs

What else intensifies racism and inequality in the 1990s? Drugs. We are witnessing the complete disintegration of America's inner cities, the home of millions of Latinos and Blacks. We see the daily destructive impact of gang violence inside our neighborhoods and communities, which is directly attributable to the fact that for twenty years the federal government has done little to address the crisis of drugs inside the ghetto and the inner city. For people of color, crack addiction has become part of the new urban slavery, a method of disrupting lives and regulating masses of young people who would otherwise be demanding jobs, adequate health care, better schools, and control of their own communities. Is it accidental that this insidious cancer has been unleashed within the very poorest urban neighborhoods, and that the police concentrate on petty street dealers rather than on those who actually control and profit from the drug traffic? How is it possible that thousands and thousands of pounds of illegal drugs can be transported throughout the country, in airplanes, trucks, and automobiles, to hundreds of central distribution centers with thousands of employees, given the ultra-high-tech surveillance and intelligence capacity of law enforcement officers? How, unless crack presents a systemic form of social control?

The struggle we have now is not simply against the system. It's against the kind of insidious violence and oppressive behavior that people of color carry out against each other. What I'm talking about is the convergence between the utility of a certain type of commodity—addictive narcotics—and economic and social problems that are confronting the system. That is, the redundancy, the unemployment of millions of people of color, young women and men, living in our urban centers. The criminal justice system represents one type of social control. Crack and addictive narcotics represent another. If you're doing organizing within the Black community, it becomes impossible to get people and families to come out to your community center when there are crack houses all around the building. It becomes impossible to continue political organizing when people are afraid for their own lives. This is the new manifestation of racism in which we see a form of social control existing in our communities, the destruction of social institutions, and the erosion of people's ability to fight against the forms of domination that continuously try to oppress them.

Women's Freedom

How do we locate the connections between racism and sexism? There are many direct parallels, both in theory and in practice, between these two systems of domination. A good working definition of sexism is the subordination of women's social, cultural, political, and educational rights as human beings and the unequal distribution of power and resources between women and men based on gender. Sexism is a sub-social dynamic, like racism, in that the dynamic is used to subordinate one part of the population to another.

How does sexism function in the economic system? Women experience it through the lack of pay equity—the absence of equal pay for comparable work performed by women and men on the job. Sexism exists in the stratification of the vocational hierarchy by gender, which keeps women disproportionately at the bottom. The upper levels of the corporations are dominated by white wealthy males, as is the ownership of productive forces and property. Women consequently have less income mobility and frequently are defined as "homemakers," a vocation for which there is absolutely no financial compensation, despite sixty to eighty hours of work per week.

Sexism within cultural and social institutions means the domination of males in decision-making positions. Males control the majority of newspapers, the film industry, radio, and television. Sexist stereotypes of both males and females are thus perpetuated through the dominant cultural institutions, advertising and broadcast media.

In political institutions, sexism translates into an unequal voice and influence within the government. The overwhelming majority of seats in the Congress, state legislatures, courts, and city councils are controlled by white men. The United States has one of the lowest percentages of women represented within its national legislature among Western democratic societies.

And finally, like racism, the wire that knots sexist mechanisms together, that perpetuates women's inequality within the fabric of the social institution, is violence. Rape, spouse abuse, and sexual harassment on the job are all essential to the perpetuation of a sexist society. For the sexist, violence is the necessary and logical part of an unequal, exploitative relationship. Rape and sexual harassment are therefore not accidental to the structure of gender relations within a sexist order. This is why progressives must first target the issue of violence against women, in the struggle for human equality and a nonsexist environment. This is why we must fight for women's right to control their own bodies.

Sexism and racism combine with class exploitation to produce a three-edged mode of oppression for women of color. Economically, African American, Latina, and Native American women are far below white women in terms of income, job security, and job mobility. The median income of a Black woman who is also a single parent with children is below twelve thousand dollars annually. One-third of all Black people live below the federal government's poverty line. And more than three-quarters of that number are Black women and their children.

Black and Latina women own virtually no sizable property; they head no major corporations; they only rarely are the heads of colleges and universities; they possess no massive real estate holdings; they are not on the Supreme Court; few are in the federal court system; they are barely represented in Congress; and they represent tiny minorities in state legislatures or in the leadership of both major parties. Only a fractional percentage of the attorneys and those involved in the criminal justice system are African American women. It is women of color, not white women, who are overwhelmingly harassed by police, arrested without cause, and who are the chief victims of all types of crimes.

Sexism and racism are not perpetuated biologically like a disease or drug addiction; both behaviors are learned within a social framework and have absolutely no ground in hereditary biology. They are perpetuated by stereotypes, myths, and irrational fears that are rooted in a false sense of superiority. Both sexism and racism involve acts of systemic coercion—job discrimination, legal domination, and political under-representation. And both sexism and racism may culminate in acts of physical violence.

Education

What are some other characteristics of the new racism we are now encountering? What we see in general is a duplicitous pattern that argues that African Americans and other people of color are moving forward, whereas their actual material conditions are being pushed back. Look at America's education system. The number of doctoral degrees being granted to Blacks, for example, is falling. The Reagan administration initiated budget cuts in education, replacing government grants with loans, and deliberately escalated unemployment for low-income people, making it difficult to afford tuition at professional schools. Between 1981 and 1995, the actual percentage of young African American adults between the ages eighteen and twenty-six enrolled in colleges and universities declined by more than 20 percent. A similar crisis is occurring in our public school systems. In many cities, the dropout rate for nonwhite high school students exceeds 40 percent. Across the United States, more than fifteen hundred teenagers of color drop out of school every day. And many of those who stay in school do not receive adequate training to prepare them for the realities of today's high-tech labor market.

Despite the curricular reforms of the 1970s and 1980s, American education retains a character of elitism and cultural exclusivity. The overwhelming majority of faculty at American colleges are white males: less than 5 percent of all college faculty today are African Americans. The basic pattern of elitism and racism in colleges conforms to the dynamics of Third World colonialism. At nearly all white academic institutions, the power relationship between whites as a group and people of color is unequal. Authority is invested in the hands of a core of largely white male administrators, bureaucrats, and influential senior faculty. The board of trustees or regents is dominated by white, conservative, affluent males. Despite the presence of academic courses on minorities, the vast majority of white students take few or no classes that explore the heritage or cultures of non-Western peoples or domestic minorities. Most courses in the humanities and social sciences focus narrowly on topics or issues from the Western capitalist experience and minimize the centrality and importance of non-Western perspectives. Finally, the university or college divorces itself from the pressing concerns, problems, and debates that relate to Blacks, Hispanics, or even white working-class people. Given this structure and guiding philosophy, it shouldn't surprise us that many talented nonwhite students fail to achieve in such a hostile environment.

The Color of Our Prisons

The racial oppression that defines U.S. society today is most dramatically apparent in the criminal justice system and the prisons. Today, about half the inmates in prisons and jails, more than 750,000 people, are African Americans. One-quarter of all African American males in their twenties today are in prison, on probation or parole, or awaiting trial. According to a 1991 survey, about one-third of all prisoners were unemployed at the time of their arrest, while two-thirds of all prisoners have less than a high-school-level education and few marketable skills. The prisons of our country have become vast warehouses for the poor and unemployed, for low-wage workers and the poorly educated, and, most especially, for Latino and African American males.

Toward a Multicultural Democracy

So what do we need in this country? How do we begin to redefine the nature of democracy? Not as a thing, but as a process. Democracy is a dynamic concept. African Americans twenty-five years ago did not have the right to eat in many restaurants, we couldn't sit down in the front seats of buses or planes, we couldn't vote in the South, we weren't allowed to use public toilets or drink from water fountains marked "For Whites Only." All of that changed through struggle, commitment, and an understanding that democracy is not something you do once every four years when you vote. It's something that you live every single day.

What can we do to create a more pluralistic, democratic society in America? Before the end of this decade, the majority of California's total population will consist of people of color. And not long after the midpoint of the next century, no later than 2056, we will live in a country in which people of color will be the numerical majority. Over the next fifty years, there will be a transition from a white majority society to a society that is far more pluralistic and diverse, where multilingualism is increasingly the norm, where different cultures, different spiritualities, and different philosophies are a beautiful mosaic of human exchange and interaction. This is the emerging multicultural majority.

People of color are radically redefining the nature of democracy. We assert that democratic government is empty and meaningless without active social justice and cultural diversity. Multicultural political democracy means that this country was not built by and for only one group—Western Europeans; that our country does not have only one language—English; or only one religion—Christianity; or only one economic philosophy—corporate capitalism. Multicultural democracy means that the leadership within our society should reflect the richness, colors, and diversity expressed in the lives of all of our people. Multicultural democracy demands new types of power-sharing and the reallocation of resources necessary to create economic and social development for those who have been systematically excluded and denied. Multicultural democracy enables all women and men to achieve full self-determination, which may include territorial and geographic restructuring, if that is the desire of an indigenous group, community, or oppressed nation. Native Americans can no longer be denied their legitimate claims of sovereignty as an oppressed nation, and we must fight for their right to self-determination as a central principle of democracy.

Multicultural democracy articulates a vision of society that is feminist. The patterns of subordination and exploitation of women of color—including job discrimination rooted in gender, race, and class; rape and sexual abuse; forced sterilizations; harassment and abuse within the criminal justice system; housing discrimination against single mothers with children; the absence of pay equity for comparable work; political underrepresentation and legal disfranchisement—combine to perpetuate a subordinate status for women within society. No progressive struggles have ever been won for people of color throughout history without the courage, contributions, sacrifices, and leadership of women. No political agenda of emancipation is possible unless one begins with the central principle of empowerment and full liberation for all women, at every level of organization and society. Men must learn from the experiences and insights of women if we are to liberate ourselves from the political, cultural, and ideological restraints that deny us our rights as Americans and free human beings.

What else is multicultural democracy? Multicultural democracy includes a powerful economic vision that is centered on the needs of human beings. We each need to go out into the community and begin hammering out an economic vision of empowerment that grassroots people can grasp and understand and use. We need to break the media monologues that talk at us through the TV and begin talking with each other in the terms of our practical life experiences.

What kinds of questions should we raise? Is it right for a government to spend billions and billions for bailing out fat cats who profited from the savings and loan scam while millions of jobless Americans stand in unemployment lines, desperate for work? Is it fair that billions of our dollars are allocated for the Pentagon's permanent war economy, to obliterate the lives of millions of poor people from Panama to Iraq to Grenada to Vietnam, while 2 million Americans sleep in the streets and 37 million Americans lack any form of medical coverage? Is it a democracy that we have when we have the right to vote but no right to a job? Is it a democracy when people of color have the freedom to starve, the freedom to live in housing without adequate heating facilities, the freedom to attend substandard schools? Democracy without social justice, without human rights, without human dignity is no democracy at all.

We can unite by pooling our resources and energies around progressive projects designed to promote greater awareness and protest among national communities of people of color. We can initiate "Freedom

Schools," liberation academies that identify and nurture young women and men with an interest in community-based struggles—a curriculum that teaches young people about their own protest leaders, that reinforces their identification with our collective cultures of resistance, and that deepens our solidarity by celebrating rather than stifling our cultural differences. The new majority must build progressive research institutes, bridging the distance between activists, community organizers, and progressive intellectuals who provide the policies and theoretical tools useful in the empowerment of grassroots constituencies and national communities.

Finally, we must infuse our definition of politics with a common sense of ethics and spirituality that challenges the structures of oppression, power, and privilege within the dominant social order. Part of the historic strength of the Black freedom movement was the deep connections between political objectives and ethical prerogatives. This connection gave the rhetoric of Frederick Douglass, Sojourner Truth, W.E.B. Du Bois, Paul Robeson, and Fannie Lou Hamer a clear vision of the moral ground that was simultaneously particular and universal. It spoke to the uplifting of African Americans, but its humanistic imperative continues to reach far further.

Multicultural democracy must perceive itself in this historic tradition, as a critical project that transforms the larger society. We must place humanity at the center of our politics. It is not sufficient that we assert what we are against; we must affirm what we are for. It is not sufficient that we declare what we want to overturn, but what we are seeking to rebuild, in the sense of restoring humanity and humanistic values to a system that is materialistic, destructive to the environment, and abusive to fellow human beings. We need to enact policies that say that the people who actually produce society's wealth should control how it is used.

The moral bankruptcy of contemporary American society is found, in part, in the vast chasm that separates the conditions of material well-being, affluence, power, and privilege of a small elite from the whole spectrum of America's communities. The evil in our world is politically and socially engineered, and its products are poverty, homelessness, illiteracy, political subservience, race discrimination, and gender discrimination. The old saying from the 1960s—we either are part of the solution or part of the problem—is simultaneously moral, cultural, economic, and political. We cannot be disinterested observers as the physical and spiritual beings of millions of people are collectively crushed.

Can we believe in certain inalienable rights that go beyond Jefferson's terminology of "life, liberty, and the pursuit of happiness"? What about the inalienable right not to go hungry in a land of agricultural abundance? The right to decent housing? The human right to free public medical care for all? The human right to an adequate income in one's old age?

If we can achieve such a democracy, if we can believe in the vision of dynamic democracy in which all human beings, women and men, Latinos, Asian Americans, Native Americans, come to terms with one another, we can perhaps begin to achieve Martin Luther King, Jr.'s, vision when he said, "We shall overcome."

The Debate on Multiculturalism

john a. powell

Today's headlines indicate that the United States is facing a race relations crisis of a magnitude not seen in a generation. One issue around which passions are surging is multiculturalism. Minorities are demanding that our schools provide young people with a more accurate and inclusive picture of American and world history.

Arguing that our society's diversity is a positive source of individual and institutional enrichment, multiculturalism's advocates call for an end to overemphasis on the European influences in American culture to the neglect of the contributions made by minorities. Among other changes around the country, this demand has led to textbook revisions, new curriculum guidelines for the public schools in New York state, and the creation of a "cultures, ideas, and values" track for undergraduates at Stanford University.

Those who take exception to this demand complain that such changes

---

john a. powell's "The Debate on Multiculturalism" appeared originally as one of his "You Have the Right" columns, syndicated nationally to the Black press.

threaten the dominance of "Western civilization" in the content of American education. Opponents of multiculturalism see any deviation from the educational "norms" set by white Americans as a threat to our society's purported "European" heritage and identity. They also claim that the concept does not accommodate any standards.

False Assumptions

The false assumptions underlying such criticisms of the multicultural approach are precisely what educators who support it want to see corrected: the assumption that American culture is basically European, and that greater ethnic and racial inclusiveness automatically means "no standards."

First of all, from the beginning, the culture of the United States has been a mixture of ingredients from different cultures. Indeed, most cultures throughout the world are amalgamations of ingredients from several cultures. At this juncture in our history, it should be clear that diversity itself is the essence of American culture. It has been predicted that by the year 2056, no one racial group of Americans will be in the majority. Contributions from different racial and ethnic backgrounds have intersected at various points, over several hundred years, to form an indivisible cultural entity that is uniquely American. Moreover, our culture is always evolving and changing.

Second, multiculturalists know full well that standards are important. They merely contend that standards reflecting a European perspective are not universal; they are not the only standards. It would be absurd to presume that the Japanese or Tanzanians don't have standards just because their standards are not the same as those of Europeans. Of course, one way to justify the exclusive application of one set of standards would be to say: I am the most powerful; therefore, I set the standards. But that stance obviously lacks legitimacy.

Multiculturalism's opponents are not the only ones who have staked out some wrongheaded positions. Some of its supporters have, too. For example, their belief that each racial or ethnic group should concentrate on its own history and culture, without learning much about other groups, or about the historical interaction between different groups and cultures, is counterproductive. Among other things, that approach could contribute to perpetuating the racial and ethnic hostilities that fragment society. Young people must learn about, and learn to appreciate, humanity as a whole.

Assimilation or Cultural Integrity?

Inevitably, when we talk about our cultural diversity, the question arises whether we Americans can or should melt—the word most often used is "assimilate"—into one homogeneous mass.

Whatever the answer is to that question, it has to be said that some white Americans who press the case for assimilation do so out of fear of, and prejudice toward, people whose backgrounds are non-European. One result of such fear and prejudice is passage of English-only laws.

The 1960s civil rights movement, in its drive for integration, indirectly addressed the assimilation question and answered it in a particular way. Many integrationists believed that ending segregation and the oppression of Blacks would trigger an assimilation process that would eventually smooth out the differences between people. Others argued that the cost of such a process was too high: People of color were expected to abandon the distinctive features of their identities and assimilate into the "white" or "European" norm, while white Americans would not have to assimilate into anything.

In the context of the present, such theoretical considerations are irrelevant. Today, instead of being mostly integrated, our society is more racially polarized and segregated than it was twenty years ago. And we know now that the "neutral" and "universal" values our society purportedly inherited from Europe, which we were all supposed to accept without question, were really part of a cultural game plan for keeping some people up and others down.

In short, the "neutral values" claim was often a ruse used to disguise racism and domination.

Is Multiculturalism Enough?

Does multiculturalism promise an end to racism in education? No. Educators warn that while revamping curricula along multicultural lines can go a long way toward correcting the false assumptions that have afflicted our educational system, multiculturalism is not by itself an adequate response to racism. In addition to learning about American culture, our young people must also study the history of American race relations. American society cannot be understood without a sense of the role of race and racism.

The issues in the current debate on multiculturalism are complicated, but one thing is clear: To prepare our children for the future, we must educate them about the true nature of American culture and society, celebrate our many-splendored American heritage, and work harder—together—to defeat racism.

Social History
Our Rudder in the Midst of Storms

Henry Hampton

I like to remind audiences and colleagues of the vision that drives most of us. It is not ideology, but the belief in a nation that welcomes diversity and insists on opportunity. However, there are many competing visions of America, and in difficult times, when resources are short, the differences grow more painful and the risks more dangerous.

Our nation is at a critical juncture, probably not unlike those years during Reconstruction, during the turmoil of the 1930s, during the years after the *Brown* decision. Such moments open up America to the possibility of real change, and that adds even more pressure for good, truthful history.

History may seem to be a luxury that can await calmer times, but I fear not. History is our rudder that can keep us on track in the midst of storms.

Most of my work is designed to try to empower the users of our programs and materials, to present viewers with the messy, difficult business of social history, to try to illuminate lives today with choices made in the past.

At the center of all this work are two basic questions: What is the responsibility of our government to its citizens, and of the citizens to the government? Why is a television series on the War on Poverty

Henry Hampton's "Social History: Our Rudder in the Midst of Storms" was a speech given in October 1992 in Boston to the Neighborhood Funders Group.

important? From almost any perspective, I think most agree that our nation and the national idea are about to be greatly tested. And our greatest failure as a nation remains our inability to deal with racism and poverty. It is under pressure that the weaknesses can destroy the whole. We are at great risk and need to move quickly toward cures.

What do we hope to accomplish in revisiting these times and events? We believe it is important to deliver stories that confirm the enormous human potential and the ways of leadership development that came out of the War on Poverty. Probably the most important untold story is that of the thousands of grassroots leaders, people who have made a difference in their communities, people who have been elected to the wide spectrum of political offices. Peruvian novelist Mario Vargas Llosa has a wonderful line that goes simply, "Memory is a snare, pure and simple. It alters, it subtly rearranges the past to fit the present."

Memory is a snare. Nothing highlights this better than having watched President Bush's press secretary, Marlin Fitzwater, pull forth the War on Poverty as the major cause of the Los Angeles riots. The war was not an unqualified success, but even its failures had many positive benefits. And more often than not, when failure occurred, it was due to a lack of readiness and the conscious hostile objections of those who disagreed with its intent.

We need to talk of a highly responsible activist government that attempted to highlight the problems of poverty and race and move those issues to a higher priority for the nation.

We must tell of powerful individuals and institutions that resisted change and often caused failures that did not have to be.

We must treat fairly not just the many successes that got labeled as failures, but those that failed for the good reasons of poor direction, political infighting, and sometimes outright theft.

We hope to gather insights from communities that have generated workable programs; to see what worked and what didn't; to track how national policy found its way into the neighborhood; to tie the events of Los Angeles to earlier times and focus on solutions that really worked in the postriot environment; and to put poverty, especially in the urban centers, front and center for America, with viable, credible solutions included.

G.K. Chesterton tells us that good history is the ability to walk to the top of a tall hill. From there we can see not only the past but the future. Americans are bad at visiting history and making it available, especially to those whose lives have been severely damaged by poverty and racism.

But one of the great benefits of revisiting such times can be finding strength and a freshened belief that something can be done. For example, it seems clear that we are faced with a situation that threatens our future because of the problems of racism, drug abuse, poor education, unemployment, crime, horrific violence. These problems seem insurmountable, but for anyone who watched and resonated to the history of the American civil rights movement, it is clear that challenges faced in the segregated South were equally daunting, and that success was gained through discipline, creativity, courage, intelligence, and faith. It does not happen immediately, but stories well and often told tie the past to a people who may seem adrift and dangerously without roots.

If we look at today's landscape, I have great hope that much knowledge and many solutions can be found. These are just some of the key elements in one of the most successful movements in world history—lessons that changed the nation.

Also, the recapturing of the history gives us the opportunity to see the difficulties faced by those who conceptualized and implemented the early War on Poverty. It will allow us to watch idea and policy become program, and then to see the results and consequences of that action.

These are powerful lessons, and instruction can be taken from the miracle of the civil rights movement that is directly applicable to the problems of today. Lessons like the impact of coalitions. The role that government—municipal, state, federal—can appropriately play. The role of the law. Political options that can be used to propel a movement forward. The multiple strategies—people seem to think the movement was almost a single act of impulse to stand up and move into the streets. They ignore the intelligence and the strategic awareness that were in play, which allowed the movement to succeed.

Why did it work? It worked because it was accessible: you could go to your church, you could go someplace and get into the movement. It had achievable objectives: you didn't have to wait for the whole thing to come down to find some wins. And it cut across class lines, in part because the jeopardy was common to all Blacks.

There were vanguard movements, critically important things like the Black Panther Party and SNCC, that shook up the basically conservative civil rights movement and moved it forward. There were independent community financial sources and foundations and churches and businesses and individuals keeping open the traditional money linkages from the local community, which could be controlled and controlling. And people need to learn how to recognize victory and defeat. It's amazing how many of us fight, fight, fight, and then somebody has to tap us on the shoulder and say, "By the way, you won."

There are bad lessons we taught our children, which perhaps we have not fully incorporated ourselves. Sometimes people believe the only way to get something done is through confrontation, while the arts of negotiation and compromise need to be elevated as successful weapons as well.

We have strong organizations, political and church-based, that surely can serve as successful models. And finally, the role of the media, which could be, in the years of the movement, either friend or foe. Often in the beginning it was very much a friend, transmitting what was basically a regional event out to the nation and making it an international phenomenon. Media were the prism that gave the leverage that made the civil rights story work. And there was brilliance in the quick recognition of the potential of the media. The dramatic and moral power of marchers petitioning hostile governments for their constitutional rights helped create the television news industry and was fired into our memories.

Media, particularly television, which has played such an important role, need to be understood and carefully followed, because they are your prism as well for much of what you are doing, both within your neighborhood and in the world at large.

Now that media system, which often served as the single prism, is changing greatly and can no longer be relied on the way it was. The technology has expanded, as well as the number of broadcast options. There has been an enormous capacity increase. The audience has become fractionalized, which means that it's no longer possible to have major national events—I call them "water cooler programs"—that will allow people to stand around and react to something they've seen. You see it now and then—*The Civil War* series was one, I think; *Eyes on the Prize* was one, especially among African Americans—and I believe that we intend to make our programs the types of events around which we can generate enormous support, programs that will elevate themselves out of the clutter of conventional broadcasting and of the technology.

Outrage has been overused. There's little left to shock. Even the death of starving children in Somalia—you have to shake yourself to remind yourself that this is real, that it's happening at that moment. But TV has a unique capacity to focus. It can also do it around positive ventures, and I think we all need to think of ways to manipulate it so that we can use it for our own agenda.

I have gone into such great detail on the lessons of the civil rights movement and the shifting landscape of media because I believe much of what we have learned can be applied to our time. And as we go about the business of rebuilding our urban neighborhoods, we must minimize the mistakes of the past and focus hard on the successes, for circumstances may not allow another opportunity. Unless we confront these issues, we may find ourselves in a flawed democracy of high walls and private security guards.

As surely as I stand here, I know that there will be uprisings that threaten the public good. I have held these words of Frederick Douglass close:

> Those who profess to favor freedom and deprecate agitation are men who want crops without plowing up the ground, they want rain without thunder and lightning. They want the ocean without the awful roar of its many waters. This struggle may be a moral one or it may be a physical one, and it may be both moral and physical, but it must be a struggle. Power concedes nothing without a demand—it never had and it never will. Find out just what any people will quietly submit to and you have found out the exact measure of injustice and wrong which will be imposed upon them, and these will continue till they are resisted with either words or blows or with both. The limits of tyrants are prescribed by the endurance of those whom they oppress.

Douglass was speaking of the Civil War, but those of you on the front lines know that there is a dangerous quality of resistance and frustration in neighborhoods abandoned too long, in places of too little hope, places where young men and police stare at each other across bloody streets and justice is defined as getting home safely at night.

But you have in your successes created that most powerful of human weapons, a spirit that will not be stilled, an intent to change the world. While memories can trap us, revitalized dreams can empower the poor far beyond the barriers that now hold them and will hold us all prisoners.

Just two final thoughts. Even while we struggle with our own belief in the nation's future, we must help rebuild the public trust of all Americans, but particularly the poor. They must have some faith and trust that they can claim some part of the American promise for themselves and their children.

That trust is now in jeopardy, and it jeopardizes us all. People without hope are dangerous people, and we must renew our commitment to see that all have opportunity and access. Many will be surprised that out of a sustained assault on poverty and racism we will free America and truly make it the powerful, humane, prosperous country we know it can be.

The writer Roberto de Roberto said that among all human constructions, the only ones that withstand the dissolving hands of time are the castles in the air. Those castles are the dreams that drive us forward, the dreams that give us courage to meet the challenges of a time such as this. Most of us understand the diagnosis of what ails our nation; the issue now is to chart a course and a vision, for shared dreams are at the very core of rebuilding public trust.

Graham Greene says eloquently that there is a moment in childhood when life opens up and lets the future in. For America, this is such a moment, and we must seize the day.

Part 6

Affirmative Action

Affirmative Action
The Questions to Be Asked

William L. Taylor

The questions to be asked include the following: Has affirmative action worked? Is affirmative action still needed? Is affirmative action unfair to others; does it undermine the merit principle? Are the social costs of affirmative action too high? What would be the cost to society of abandoning affirmative action?

Has Affirmative Action Worked?

Much evidence shows that affirmative action is one of a cluster of national policies that enabled minorities and women to make substantial economic and educational gains during the 1970s and 1980s. These gains have occurred across the spectrum of occupations—in police and fire departments and other public service occupations, in manufacturing and trucking, in the construction trades, in service occupations, in managerial positions, and in the professions.

For example, in police departments, the number of Black officers went from 23,796 in 1970 to 63,855 in 1990. Black representation in fire departments rose from 2.5 percent in 1960 to 11.5 percent in 1990.

Black representation also increased dramatically in other key industries during the period 1970–90. For example, the number of electricians went from 14,145 to 43,276; bank tellers, from 10,633 to 46,332; health officials, from 3,914 to 13,125; and pharmacists, from 2,501 to 7,011.

There can also be little question that affirmative-action policies of colleges and universities and the creation of more minority scholarship opportunities, along with federal programs providing greater access for low-income students to institutions of higher education through loans and Pell grants, have played a large role in the major increases in minority college enrollment that occurred during the 1970s and 1980s.

William L. Taylor's "Affirmative Action: The Questions to Be Asked" (excerpts) was testimony he gave on April 3, 1995, before the House Subcommittee on the Constitution.

A 1994 RAND Corporation study—*Student Achievement and the Changing American Family*—reports that the largest gains in student performance in elementary and secondary schools from 1970 to 1990 were made by minority students. Indeed, according to this study and others, 40 percent or more of the academic gap between Black and white youngsters was closed during this period.

That is remarkable progress. Among the contributing factors, according to the RAND study, is the fact that the numbers of Black parents with college degrees or experience quadrupled during the two decades, so that now about 25 percent of Black parents have college degrees or experience. (Hispanic American parents have made similar, although less dramatic, educational gains.) The occupational and income gains made by Black parents during this period have also contributed to the formation of stable, middle-class families and to the achievement gains of children. Affirmative action has played an important role in all this.

We should not fail to note that the RAND study and others like it provide powerful evidence that affirmative-action policies do not dilute the merit principle. As the achievement gap between minorities and whites is closed, what we are witnessing is increased productivity for individuals and for the nation.

Is Affirmative Action Still Needed?

While affirmative action has contributed significantly to closing the gap attributable to discrimination, minorities and women still face barriers in seeking jobs, education, and housing. Evidence of the continuing legacy of discrimination can be seen in the number of employment discrimination complaints filed at the Equal Employment Opportunity Commission (over ninety-one thousand in 1994); the litany of Justice Department cases cited by Assistant Attorney General Deval Patrick in his testimony before the House Subcommittee on Employer–Employee Relations; the testing studies conducted by the Urban Institute and the Fair Employment Council of Greater Washington summarizing the overall prevalence of discrimination encountered by minority job seekers; and the conclusions of the Federal Glass Ceiling Commission's report, which include, among other things, finding that 97 percent of senior managers at Fortune 1000 industrial corporations are white

males, and that only 5 percent of senior management at industrial and
service companies are women, virtually all of them white.

Is Affirmative Action Unfair to Others?

The notion that affirmative action somehow constitutes "reverse discrimination" ignores the fact that courts have taken pains to balance
competing interests in shaping affirmative-action remedies. The rules
of affirmative action have been worked out over two decades, and the
parameters of the policy have been set by the Burger and Rehnquist
courts.

Evidence of misapplication of the policy is minimal (as is demonstrated by the Equal Employment Opportunity Commission's data that
only 1.7 percent of race-based charges received by the EEOC are made
by white males filing on the basis of race, as well as by the recent
study of court cases and other data conducted by Professor Alfred
Blumrosen of Rutgers, which found that "reverse discrimination" cases
accounted for a tiny percentage of some three thousand reported employment discrimination cases between 1990 and 1994), and certainly
is not cause to junk the policy.

What Would Be the Cost to Society of
Abandoning Affirmative Action?

Abandoning affirmative-action policy is bound to do damage to the
economic status of minorities and women. Abandoning affirmative
action would also likely divide us even more into a society of "haves"
and "have-nots."

Certainly we all aspire to become a "color-blind" society in which
judgments are made, in Dr. King's memorable phrase, on the content
of one's character rather than the color of one's skin. But who in
Congress or in this nation can say with a straight face that we have
reached the point in our society where the great bulk of our citizens are
color-blind, where race does not matter, where children do not suffer
disadvantage because of their race or national origin?

If we cannot truthfully make these statements, then abolishing or
curtailing affirmative action would be akin to throwing away one of
the major cures while allowing the disease to continue unchecked.

Racism Has Its Privileges

Roger Wilkins

Affirmative action, as I understand it, was not designed to punish anyone; it was, rather—as a result of a clear-eyed look at how America actually works—an attempt to enlarge opportunity for everybody. As amply documented in the 1968 Kerner Commission report on racial disorders, when left to their own devices, American institutions in such areas as college admissions, hiring decisions, and loan approvals had been making choices that discriminated against Blacks. That discrimination, which flowed from doing what came naturally, hurt more than Blacks: It hurt the entire nation, as the riots of the late 1960s demonstrated. Though the Kerner report focused on Blacks, similar findings could have been made about other minorities and women.

Affirmative action required institutions to develop plans enabling them to go beyond business as usual and search for qualified people in places where they did not ordinarily conduct their searches or their business. Affirmative-action programs generally require some proof that there have been a good-faith effort to follow the plan and numerical guidelines against which to judge the sincerity and the success of the effort. The idea of affirmative action is *not* to force people into positions for which they are unqualified, but to encourage institutions to develop realistic criteria for the enterprise at hand and then to find a reasonably diverse mix of people qualified to be engaged in it. Without the requirements calling for plans, good-faith efforts, and the setting of broad numerical goals, many institutions would do what they had always done: assert that they had looked but "couldn't find anyone qualified," and then go out and hire the white man they wanted to hire in the first place.

Affirmative action has done wonderful things for the United States by enlarging opportunity, and developing and utilizing a far broader array of the skills available in the American population than in the past. It has not outlived its usefulness. It was never designed to be a

Roger Wilkins's "Racism Has Its Privileges" (excerpts) appeared in the March 27, 1995, *The Nation* magazine. © 1995 by The Nation Company, Inc. Reprinted with permission.

program to eliminate poverty. It has not always been used wisely, and some of its permutations do have to be reconsidered, refined, or, in some cases, abandoned. It is not a quota program, and those cases where rigid numbers are used (except under a court or administrative order after a specific finding of discrimination) are a bastardization of an otherwise highly beneficial set of public policies.

President Clinton is right to review what is being done under present laws and to express a willingness to eliminate activities that either don't work or are unfair. Any program that has been in place for thirty years should be reviewed. Getting rid of what doesn't work is both good government and good politics. Gross abuses of affirmative action provide ammunition for its opponents and undercut the moral authority of the entire effort. But the president should retain—and strengthen where required—those programs necessary to enlarge social justice.

Uses of the Past

It goes without saying that Blacks and whites remember America differently. The past is hugely important, since we argue a lot about who we are on the basis of who we think we have been, and we derive much of our sense of the future from how we think we've done in the past. In a nation in which few people know much history, these are perilous arguments, because in such a vacuum, people tend to weave historical fables tailored to their political or psychic needs.

Blacks are still recovering the story of their role in America, which so many white historians simply ignored or told in ways that made Black people ashamed. But in a culture that batters us, learning the real history is vital in helping Blacks feel fully human. It also helps us understand just how deeply American we are, how richly we have given, how much has been taken from us, and how much has yet to be restored. Supporters of affirmative action believe that broad and deep damage has been done to American culture by racism and sexism over the whole course of American history, and that they are still powerful forces today. We believe that minorities and women are still disadvantaged in our highly competitive society and that affirmative action is absolutely necessary to level the playing field.

The Politics of Denial

The fact is that the successful public relations assault on affirmative action flows on a river of racism that is as broad, powerful, and American as the Mississippi. And, like the Mississippi, racism can be violent and deadly, and is a permanent feature of American life. But while nobody who is sane denies the reality of the Mississippi, millions of Americans who are deemed sane—some of whom are powerful and some even thought wise—deny, wholly or in part, that racism exists.

One of the best examples of denial was provided not too long ago by the nation's most famous former history professor, House Speaker Newt Gingrich. According to the *Washington Post,* "Gingrich dismissed the argument that the beneficiaries of affirmative action, commonly African Americans, have been subjected to discrimination over a period of centuries. 'That is true of virtually every American,' Gingrich said, noting that the Irish were discriminated against by the English, for example."

That is breathtaking stuff coming from somebody who should know that Blacks have been on this North American continent for 375 years and that for 245 the country permitted slavery. Gingrich should also know that for the next hundred years we had legalized subordination of Blacks, under a suffocating blanket of condescension and frequently enforced by night-riding terrorists. We've had only thirty years of something else. For a historian to assert that "virtually every American" shares the history I have just outlined comes very close to lying.

Denial of racism is much like the denials that accompany addictions to alcohol, drugs, or gambling. It is probably not stretching the analogy too much to suggest that many racist whites are so addicted to their unwarranted privileges and so threatened by the prospect of losing them that all kinds of defenses become acceptable, including insistent distortions of reality in the form of hypocrisy, lying, or the most outrageous political demagoguery.

The United States is not now, and probably never will be, a color-blind society. It is the most color-conscious society on earth. Over the course of 375 years, whites have given Blacks absolutely no reason to believe that they can behave in a color-blind manner.

While I don't hold the view that all Blacks who behave badly are blameless victims of a brutal system, I do believe that many poor Blacks have, indeed, been brutalized by our culture, and I know of *no* Blacks, rich or poor, who haven't been hurt in some measure by the racism in this country. The current mood (and, in some cases like the Speaker's, the cultivated ignorance) completely ignores the fact that some Blacks never escaped the straight line of oppression that ran from slavery through the semislavery of sharecropping to the late mid-century migration from Southern farms into isolated pockets of urban poverty. Their families have always been excluded, poor, and without skills, and so they were utterly defenseless when the enormous American economic dislocations that began in the mid-1970s slammed into their communities, followed closely by deadly waves of crack cocaine. One would think that the double-digit unemployment suffered consistently over the past two decades by Blacks who were *looking for work* would be a permanent feature of the discussions about race, responsibility, welfare, and rights.

Angry White Males

But a discussion of the huge numbers of Black workers who are becoming economically redundant would raise difficult questions about the efficiency of the economy at a time when millions of white men feel insecure. Any honest appraisal of unemployment would reveal that millions of low-skilled white men are being severely damaged by corporate and Federal Reserve decisions; it might also refocus the anger of those whites in the middle ranks whose careers have been shattered by the corporate downsizing fad.

In a society that, from the beginning of the Republic, has been taught that skin color is destiny and that whiteness is to be revered, it is understandable that white males would take their preferences as a matter of natural right and consider any alteration of that a primal offense. But a nation that operates in that way abandons its soul and its economic strength, and will remain mired in ugliness and moral squalor because so many people are excluded from the possibility of decent lives and from forming any sense of community with the rest of society.

Though the centuries of cultural preference enjoyed by white males still overwhelmingly skew power and wealth their way, we have in fact achieved a more meritocratic society as a result of affirmative action than we have ever previously enjoyed in this country.

If we want to continue making things better in this society, we'd better figure out ways to protect and defend affirmative action against the confused, the frightened, the manipulators, and, yes, the liars in politics, journalism, education, and wherever else they may be found. In the name of long-standing American prejudice and myths, and in the service of their own narrow interests, power lusts, or blindness, they are truly victimizing the rest of us, perverting the ideals they claim to stand for, and destroying the nation they pretend to serve.

Scapegoating

Maxine Waters

The California anti–affirmative action initiative is a product of a climate that has nothing to do with affirmative action per se. Unemployment is still high in California. Many manufacturing jobs have fled to Third World countries in search of cheap labor. We've been buffeted by fires and floods and quakes.

Governor Pete Wilson and others are telling white males who are working people that Blacks, Latinos, women, and the like are taking away their jobs, their businesses, their admissions to higher education.

That's easier than explaining to working people about economic policies that have shifted good-paying American jobs overseas, rewarded financial speculation over real investment in jobs, and caused working people's incomes to stagnate or decline. There's a word for this. It's called scapegoating.

White males make up one-third of America. Yet, white males constitute 80 percent of the membership in the House of Representatives, 92 percent of the Senate, 92 percent of the Fortune 500 senior executives, 67 percent of the Supreme Court, 80 percent of tenured university faculty, and 90 percent of newspaper editors. Given these numbers, can anyone tell me how white males are being put upon by affirmative action?

In fact, even *white males* have a stake in affirmative action. They have wives, daughters, mothers, and others who are in the workforce, making money to pay the mortgage. Without affirmative action, those women would have *less* opportunity and bring home *less* pay.

Maxine Waters's "Scapegoating" (excerpts) was a talk she gave on March 16, 1995, before the Congressional Black Caucus Brown Bag on Affirmative Action.

There is already too much political posturing in the debate about affirmative action. I do not support wide-ranging, ill-defined reviews. All this talk about "reviews" signals that perhaps something is wrong and needs to be "fixed." I do not want people starting with the idea something is wrong before first understanding what affirmative action is and is not.

Affirmative Action
Why Bosses Like It

The Economist

Corning, a small town in upstate New York, used to be about as multicultural as an episode of *I Love Lucy*. In the past decade, however, it has made enormous efforts to immerse itself in the melting pot, getting hooked up to a Black-oriented cable channel, bringing in a Black hairdressing business (which has recently decamped), and instituting a "diversity awareness" program in the local schools.

All this was the work of the town's biggest employer, the eponymously named Corning, a technology company. When James Houghton became chairman in 1983, he made workforce diversity one of the company's top three priorities (the other two were total quality and a higher return on equity). The company has made every effort to recruit people from minority groups, forming close relations with organizations such as the National Black MBA Association and even linking managers' bonuses to diversity targets.

But it has discovered that affirmative action is not enough if the people you have carefully hired and expensively trained decide to leave. So the company has also gone out of its way to make minorities feel at home, providing them with "mentors," putting all managers through "sensitivity training" (one and a half days for gender awareness, two and a half for racial awareness), and celebrating diversity in its in-house newspaper.

Corning is not alone in its enthusiasm for such things. Avon Products, a cosmetics company, has set up a "multicultural participation council" to encourage diversity among employees. Xerox Corporation, an office equipment maker, regards affirmative action as "a corporate value, a management priority, and a formal business objective" (in the words of its former chairman, David Kearns) and has set employment targets for women and minorities throughout the company.

Digital Equipment, a computer company, has established a Valuing Differences program, which sponsors cultural events, such as Black History Month, and encourages workers to form small discussion groups to help them "confront their prejudices." Many companies send employees to the American Institute for Managing Diversity, based at Morehouse College in Atlanta, to have their consciences raised on matters multicultural.

Even Wall Street is catching political correctness. Firms that win Department of Labor awards for their success in implementing affirmative action are rewarded with a boost in their share price within ten days of the announcement, according to a recent article in the *Academy of Management Journal*. Press disclosures that firms discriminate against women or minorities soon result in a fall in the share price.

So far as many businesses are concerned, multiculturalism is not just a moral matter. White males already make up a minority of the workforce, and 85 percent of new recruits between now and 2000 will be women or nonwhite men. So firms with a good track record of producing nonwhite managers and managing people from different backgrounds will enjoy a growing advantage in recruiting and motivating workers. They may also be more attuned to an increasingly diverse population of customers. Equally, firms that continue to favor white men will find themselves fishing in a shrinking pool of potential employees.

Most intriguingly, ethnic diversity may help American firms outperform their rivals abroad. In particular, it is becoming an article of faith in American business schools that heterogeneous firms will be better placed to form global alliances and strike international deals than the Japanese, who tend to reserve real power for themselves, or the Europeans, with their history of colonial entanglements.

The Presumption of Stupidity
Affirmative Action, Occupational Apartheid

Brent Staples

It is absurd to argue, as many critics do, that affirmative action has placed African Americans under suspicion of incompetence by propelling them into positions they do not rightly deserve. Bred into this country's bones, the presumption that Blacks are inherently less "qualified" would be a driving force in any case. An alternative view of affirmative action is that it breaks down occupational apartheid, the notion that elite jobs are for white folks only. The process is wrenching, but how could it be otherwise?

In high school, I was an average student, with no plans for college. Providence appeared in the form of a professor from Widener University who talked me into going to college one afternoon on a street corner. I was accepted without SATs, but took them for ceremonial purposes. My scores were unimpressive, and the college was right not to care. Often the scores tell more about privilege than about "merit" or potential to succeed. I graduated twenty-sixth in a class of 370 at Widener, well ahead of many white prep-school kids who had done well on the SATs. This Black boy who was "not college material" went on to earn a Ph.D. at the University of Chicago.

There are thousands of stories like this one. But in the Reaganaut 1980s, many African Americans who could tell those stories became converts to the gospel of Horatio Alger, suddenly claiming that success had been earned through hard work and rectitude alone. Poverty, they said, stems from sloth and moral laxness. The convert's role I will never play.

When I was seventeen, the society spotted me a few points on the SATs and changed my life. I became a writer—and a middle-class taxpayer—as many other Black men went on to prisons, cemeteries, and homeless shelters. Sounds like a smart investment to me. The country would be wise to keep making it.

Brent Staples's "The Presumption of Stupidity: Affirmative Action, Occupational Apartheid" (excerpts) appeared in the March 5, 1995, *New York Times*.

Reaffirm the Affirmative

Max Frankel

To reward people for something beyond merit is as American as apple pie. Universities routinely bend a bit to admit the children of alumni, acknowledging with a wink that this fosters loyalty and annual contributions. Few objected when "diversity" in a Northern college meant saving a few places for Southern or Western students. If Californians don't watch the language of their amendments, they could end up sinking their best college teams; how else but by "affirmative action" do they recruit so many Black athletes and favor them with "set-aside" scholarships?

Many enterprises, including this newspaper [*New York Times*], favor the rapid rise of the boss's kids, tapping their devotion to the business. Immigrants have always acted affirmatively to help their own advance in certain lines of work—Irish cops, Italian truckers, Jewish peddlers, Portuguese fishermen, Chinese launderers, Korean grocers. And politicians practiced affirmative action long before they had a name for it; no Voting Rights Act was needed fifty years ago to persuade New York Democrats to nominate Vincent Impellitteri and Lazarus Joseph to share the ticket with William O'Dwyer.

Affirmative Action
The Army's Success

Charles Moskos

There is an institution where affirmative action works and works well—the U.S. Army. Not that the Army is a racial utopia by any

Max Frankel's "Reaffirm the Affirmative" (excerpts) appeared in the February 26, 1995, *New York Times Magazine*.

Charles Moskos's "Affirmative Action: The Army's Success" (excerpts) appeared in the March 15, 1995, *Washington Post.* © The Washington Post. Used with permission.

means. But nowhere else in American society has racial integration gone as far or has Black achievement been so pronounced. Indeed, the Army is the only institution in America where whites are routinely bossed around by Blacks.

Affirmative action has been crucial in bringing about this positive state of affairs. It has also been key in our military's unquestioned effectiveness. What, then, can we learn from the Army's affirmative-action program?

The first lesson is that affirmative action in the Army eschews quotas but does have goals. Guidelines for Army promotion boards are to select minority members equivalent to the percentage in the promotion pool. This means that the Army promotion process is based not on the number of minority members in the Army but on the number of minority members in the pool of potential promotees to the next higher rank. Very important, there are no "timetables" to meet goals.

The process goes like this. The board takes into consideration past assignments, evaluation ratings, education, and promotability to the next higher level after the one under consideration. The strongest candidates are eliminated quickly; so are the weakest ones. In reality, goals become operative only in the gray middle. As one well-informed white officer said: "Only fully qualified people are promoted, but not necessarily the best-qualified. But don't forget, we are talking micromillimeter differences in these cases."

There is no denying that pressure to meet the goals is strong. If the goal is not met, the board must defend its decisions. If this looks like a quota by another name, think again. The number of Blacks who are promoted from captain to major, a virtual prerequisite for an officer seeking an Army career, is usually below the goal. Why this is so is a matter of debate and Army heartburn. The most plausible explanation for the shortfall is that a disproportionate number of Black officers do not possess the writing and communication skills for promotion to staff jobs. In all other ranks, including colonel through general officers, promotions show little racial difference.

One other remark on the "goals vs. quota" distinction. The military has no hint of two promotion lists, whites being compared only with whites, Blacks with Blacks. All candidates are held to the same standards.

Maintenance of standards may cause short-term turmoil, as it did in the Army in the 1970s, but it also means that those who attain senior positions are fully qualified. Also important, those Blacks promoted have self-confidence that makes them the strongest defenders of standards for their own Black subordinates. The Army, by taking the heat early on, reduced its troubles later. An organization that promotes less highly qualified people to buy temporary peace only invites long-term disaffection.

Although affirmative action in the Army is not without its tensions, it is not a prescription for loss of self-esteem by Blacks or resentment by whites. No identifiable group of underqualified minority members occupies positions of authority in the Army. The military does not elaborately disguise its goals or its methods of attaining them because it does not have to deal with the situation that drives quota systems in civilian institutions: a dearth of qualified Blacks.

This brings us to another lesson: A level playing field is not always enough. The Army shows how youths from diverse backgrounds can be made to meet uniform and demanding standards. The Army has successfully introduced programs to bring young people up to enlistment standards, to raise enlisted soldiers up to noncommissioned officer standards, to bring Black undergraduates up to officer commissioning standards, and to raise high school graduates up to West Point admission standards. These programs are not exclusively targeted on minority soldiers, but they are disproportionately Afro-American. These programs cost money and require a significant commitment of resources.

The objective should always be to prepare members of a historically disadvantaged population to compete on an equal footing with the more privileged. Good affirmative action acknowledges that compensatory action may be needed to help members of disadvantaged groups to meet the standards of competition. Bad affirmative action suspends those standards.

So what, finally, can be transferred from the Army? Maybe a broad lesson: Affirmative action can do what it is supposed to do when there are an unambiguous guarantee of equal opportunity, clear standards of performance, and a commitment to raise people to meet those standards.

Affirmative Action, R.I.P.

Salim Muwakkil

Affirmative action, as we have known it, is probably dead. Good riddance. For the past quarter of a century, many Blacks have looked to affirmative action, despite its shortcomings, as a symbol of America's long-denied promise of racial equity.

But its original purpose, as a means to help compensate African Americans for slavery and its racist legacy, has long since been lost. With affirmative action's racial aspects toned down for the consumption of white voters, it has become less a hand up for poor Blacks than a stepladder to the middle class for many white American families.

The original purpose of affirmative-action policies was to chip away at race-specific disparities between Black and white Americans. But according to most studies, the major beneficiaries of these policies have been white women.

By de-emphasizing affirmative action's racial aspects, liberals succeeded in making the programs more palatable but less effective. The raging right-wingers who have seized control of Congress have no intention of making it either more effective or more palatable; they have targeted it for death.

The notion of legislative recompense for racial injustice was never wildly popular in a land so steeped in traditions of white supremacy, but national leaders thirty years ago at least understood the need for compensatory justice. Of course, their motives were not entirely pure.

During the 1960s, when federal programs were first designed to "take affirmative action to overcome the effects of prior discrimination," American cities were going up in smoke. From 1964 to 1969, some sixty-five U.S. cities exploded in violent upheavals. Aside from the toll in lives and property, the situation was bad for business. Studies assessing the violence found that racist hiring policies had been a precipitating factor. Affirmative action was born in that smoke-charred climate.

The policy's Democratic architects were praised for devising a relatively innocuous way to redistribute some of the United States'

Salim Muwakkil's "Affirmative Action, R.I.P" (excerpts) appeared in the March 20, 1995, *In These Times*.

maldistributed wealth. Support for the policies was bipartisan; during a time of economic expansion, most Americans thought the measures deserved a try.

The concept of affirmative action essentially is a euphemism for reparations, and this point is lost when its advocates urge its expansion across race lines. African Americans were deeply damaged by the institution of slavery; indeed, they were created by slavery.

Until this society understands the need to devote itself to repairing that damage, it seems certain that we will continue to drift from crisis to crisis, until we reach one too many.

The Affirmative Action Quiz

Fred Pincus

Questions 1 through 5 pertain to federal affirmative-action guidelines administered by the Office of Federal Contract Compliance Programs (OFCCP) of the U.S. Department of Labor.

1. Who is legally required to have a written affirmative-action plan?
   A. All employers with at least twenty-five employees
   B. All federal contractors, regardless of size
   C. Federal nonconstruction contractors with fifty or more employees and $50,000 or more in contracts
   D. Federal construction contractors with one hundred or more employees and $100,000 or more in federal contracts

2. Affirmative-action plans must include "goals and timetables." This means that by a specific date, employers who are covered by affirmative-action guidelines and whose labor force falls below a specified percentage of women and/or minorities must:
   A. Actually hire a certain number of women and minorities, whether they are qualified or not
   B. Actually hire a certain number of women and minorities, but only if they are qualified
   C. Try to hire a certain number of women and minorities, whether they are qualified or not
   D. Try to hire a certain number of women and minorities, but only if they are qualified

The Affirmative Action Quiz was prepared by Fred L. Pincus and appeared in the April 1996 *Current World Leaders: International Issues.* Used by permission of International Academy at Santa Barbara, 800 Garden Street, Suite D, Santa Barbara, Calif. 93101–1552; phone (805) 965–5010; (800) 530–2682; fax (805) 965–6071; E-mail ias@igc.org

3. After formulating their affirmative-action plans, employers are required to:
   A. Submit them to the OFCCP for approval
   B. Keep them on file in their own offices and be ready to submit them to OFCCP upon request
   C. Have a majority of their women and minority employees approve the plan
   D. All of the above

4. The OFCCP conducts "compliance reviews" where they investigate employers who they believe may be violating affirmative-action guidelines. In any given year, what percentage of employers covered by affirmative-action guidelines undergo compliance reviews?
   A. Less than 5 percent
   B. 11 percent
   C. 24 percent
   D. More than 50 percent

5. Employers who violate affirmative-action guidelines and fail to take corrective action can lose their existing federal contracts and be declared ineligible to receive others. This is known as being "debarred." Between 1972 and 1995, how many employers have been debarred?
   A. 0
   B. 39
   C. 197
   D. More than 1,000

Questions 6 through 8 are based on federal law and U.S. Supreme Court decisions as of January 1, 1996.

6. Which of the following policies may *any* employer legally use for hiring and promotion decisions without first getting the approval of a federal court?
   A. Decide to hire or promote a Black or Hispanic for a particular position even though a white is clearly better qualified
   B. Decide to hire or promote a woman for a particular position even though a man is clearly better qualified

   C. Use race or gender as one of many factors in considering hiring and promotion

   D. All of the above are legal

7. In order to attract more Black and Hispanic students, *any* college or professional school may legally:

   A. Offer special minority scholarships that whites cannot apply for

   B. Set aside or reserve a certain number of places for Black and Hispanic students

   C. Require the admissions office to visit all predominantly Black high schools in a fifty-mile radius to talk about the college

   D. None of the above are legal

8. According to the U.S. Supreme Court, under what conditions can a lower federal court require an employer to hire and/or promote a certain number of qualified women and minority group members?

   A. The proportion of minorities and women employees is lower than the proportion of minorities and women in the United States

   B. The judge suspects that the employer has discriminated in the past

   C. Either A or B would be sufficient

   D. None of the above would be sufficient

Questions 9 through 11 are based on the results of national public opinion polls that were administered in 1995.

9. National public opinion polls of white Americans show that:

   A. More than 90 percent are opposed to affirmative action

   B. They have different feelings about different kinds of affirmative-action policies

   C. They are surprisingly supportive of affirmative action

   D. None of the above

10. National public opinion polls show that Black Americans:

   A. Generally support affirmative action

    B. Are neutral toward affirmative action
    C. Are opposed to affirmative action

11. National public opinion polls show that women have:
    A. More positive attitudes toward affirmative action than men
    B. The same attitudes toward affirmative action as men
    C. More negative attitudes toward affirmative action than men

12. Two studies of lawsuits by white males, which allege reverse discrimination, show that these suits:
    A. Are becoming almost as common as discrimination suits brought by minorities and women
    B. Are less likely to be successful than suits brought by minorities and women
    C. Are more likely to involve charges of race discrimination than sex discrimination
    D. All of the above

13. In considering whether or not to admit students, elite universities like Harvard, Yale, and Princeton:
    A. Consider only measures of academic skills such as grades, class rank, Scholastic Assessment Test (SAT) scores, and teacher recommendations
    B. Give special preference to the children of parents who graduated from that university
    C. Have never discriminated against Blacks, Jews, or Asians
    D. None of the above

14. After fifteen years of affirmative action, Blacks received _____ percent of the medical degrees and _____ percent of the law degrees during the 1992–93 academic year.
    A. 5.8 and 5.7
    B. 9.8 and 10.5
    C. 19.2 and 21.7
    D. 30.2 and 28.3

Answers to the Affirmative-Action Quiz are on page 238.

Reparations

The issue of reparations for slavery is a deeply felt strand of thought and strategic thinking in at least a portion of the Black community, and among some whites as well. There is of course precedent for righting historic racially inflicted wrongs in this manner: U.S. government payments made to Japanese Americans interned during World War II; payments made by the German government to Jewish Holocaust survivors; various federal payments/land returns/tribal recognition for Native Americans; a recent state of Florida payment to survivors of racial violence against a Black town in the 1920s.

Profound and difficult moral, legal, fiscal, political, and practical issues are raised in this discussion, not unrelated to the affirmative-action debate. A bill to establish a national commission to study reparations proposals has been introduced several times, since 1989, by Rep. John Conyers (D-MI), but has never made it out of committee.

The PRRAC newsletter has run four symposia on the subject of reparations. The following are excerpts from salient points made by various contributors to these symposia.

john a. powell

It is important to reframe the issue of reparations so as not to focus solely on slavery. We must also examine the aftermath of slavery and the institutions and distributional structures it created, including an analysis of the numerous ways in which the American government and the larger society have economically subordinated and disenfranchised African Americans.

The debate cannot center on an empirical evaluation of whether whites today are individually responsible for the ills suffered by African Americans today. It must center instead on exposing how the wrongs exacted by whites in the past continue to privilege and benefit whites today and how those structures that benefit whites still operate to disadvantage persons of color. When one looks seriously at how racial hierarchy has distributed resources, it becomes apparent that nonracism (color-blindness) or even affirmative action is insufficient to the task of addressing the inequities of the postslavery structure. Instead, we must be *anti*racist and structurally oriented.

Reparations, in and of itself, may not produce the forty acres and a mule promised to freed slaves, nor may it compensate for the trillions of dollars African Americans may be owed for their exploited labor and cultural uprooting. Nonetheless, these cannot be reasons not to consider reparations seriously. Nor is the argument that all former slaves are dead and therefore will not themselves receive compensation a reason not to consider reparations. The structure that creates and distributes wealth in the United States continues to be based on a racial hierarchy that was established by the slave system.

Sharon Parker

Racism is so deeply embedded in the dominant American culture that we fail to see that it continues to affect all of us: every person, male or female; every immigrant, every refugee; every race, every age group; and every religious, social, legal, artistic, business, educational, governmental institution in the country. Many Americans want to believe that racism has been overcome and that white Americans have no responsibility for slavery because it ended a century and a quarter ago. Such an attitude is consistent with American historical perspective: we are shortsighted, unilateral, and vainglorious. As rugged individualists, we are conditioned to believe that we can fix any problem and overcome any challenge that tarnishes the idealist image of America. But we have not yet "fixed" the problem of racism, and we cannot even hope to do so until we, as a nation, are willing to look beyond the utopian image to the root causes. The legacy of slavery is definitely a root cause of the persistence of racism in today's society.

The cost to all of us is demonstrated in the local, state, and federal budget priorities on funds for security and punishment rather than education and employment; education systems that cannot address their purpose because of overcrowding, understaffing, inadequate facilities and supplies; health care systems responding to the crisis needs of assaults and drug-related accidents rather than disease prevention and treatment; substandard services and goods because workers are not literate, are under great stress, or are malnourished and weak. Incalculable is the loss of human dignity and potential.

Theodore M. Shaw

The issue of reparations is not a useless discussion. Its value may be in the light it sheds on the way we as a nation have dealt with the issue of race, and how we continue to deal with it. When a wrong has been committed, the first step in "righting" it is acknowledgment. Only then can those involved move to heal the effects of the injury. This is no less true for groups than it is for individuals. When Germany compensated Jewish Holocaust survivors, and the United States compensated Japanese Americans wrongfully interned during World War II, money was not significant beyond its symbolic value; mere money could not heal the scars of those experiences. The true value of reparations is in the acknowledgment of the wrong.

The United States government and the state governments that sanctioned the practice of slavery have never formally apologized to African Americans for slavery or acknowledged that it was wrong. The Thirteenth, Fourteenth, and Fifteenth Amendments were enacted to put Black Americans on equal footing with white citizens; however, nowhere do they acknowledge the wrongs of slavery. Nineteenth- and twentieth-century civil rights legislation aimed to enforce the Civil War amendments and eliminate continuing racial discrimination, but nowhere do these statutes contain an official apology. While individual legislators and government officials have acknowledged the wrongs of the past, there has been no official recognition or apology. Thus, a great psychological wound remains unhealed, haunting our national psyche.

The reparations discussion is valuable not because of any expectation it creates with respect to monetary compensation. Its real value is that it places America's discourse about race in a different context—one in which affirmative action is a modest remedy and in which the historical disconnection of present-day disparities in Black and white achievement, wealth, and status from America's undeniable history of racial discrimination will be impossible to maintain.

Howard Winant

There are two parts to the reparations issue. There has to be a very substantial redistribution of resources to address the real subsidy slavery provided. It is important to recognize that reverse reparations have been paid for centuries by Black people to white people in this country, not only in slavery times but right up until the present. Black people subsidize white people's employment by absorbing higher levels of unemployment. They subsidize white people's wages by accepting, however reluctantly, very much lower wages for doing the same kind of work, and so on.

So on a material level, the question is, How do you reverse some of those kinds of subsidies, how do you equalize them in the future? I think that means some kind of massive redistribution of wealth and income toward low-income communities, in particular Black communities and urban communities.

The practical problem is that we have to do this while not at the same time exacerbating very real racial conflicts and racial tensions that we're attempting to resolve. And that means looking at who pays, looking at the way this redistribution would be financed.

How would we actually finance the kind of redistribution I'm talking about? If we just did it as a straight payment for social programs or perhaps paying individuals, there would be tremendous resentment, tremendous reaction, opposition, and exacerbation of racial conflict. But suppose it were framed differently. Suppose it were framed in terms of a system of finance that the wealthy paid and did not simply draw from general tax revenues. Say, a wealth tax, based on the fact that Black labor has created so much of the capital, so much of the wealth in this country. For example, a very high, loophole-free tax on the transfer of wealth above a certain level at the point of death, above one million dollars or something like that. Or a tax on excess profits.

There might be resentment, there's certainly a tremendous antitax feeling in this country. But the kind of educational work we could do around that might lead us as a nation to an understanding that Black people and white people have some interests in common in this kind of redistribution. That redistributing wealth from the very wealthy to the less wealthy and the very poor would have a lot of positive consequences for this nation as a whole, not just for Black people, and it wouldn't be coming out of the hides of working white people.

It seems much more morally sound to organize not whites to pay reparations, but rather the state to undertake egalitarian and redistributive policies in a racially conscious manner.

Richard America

The real question is, what is the present value and distribution of the stream of income that has been coercively and wrongfully diverted from Blacks to whites through slavery and discrimination to produce lopsided income and wealth distributions by race, and, in doing so, has robbed too many Blacks of skills they need to perform effectively?

Whites owe Blacks $5 to $10 trillion. It should be repaid primarily through investment in human capital—education and training over two to three generations. It should also be repaid through investments in targeted housing, capital formation, and business creation.

Most of the reparations investment should go to those in the bottom 30 percent. Some should go to institution building. These institutions, including higher education and business, would have grown up except they were consciously hindered in order to benefit competing white institutions and businesses.

Civil rights is, or ought to be, about how to make median Black income roughly the same as median white income by the year 2020. The concept of reparations is an inescapable public policy tool for reaching that objective.

David McReynolds

Reparations has, of course, certain logical problems. Does the funding go to all African Americans, including those who came here from the West Indies after my own ancestors? And how do you separate out the issue of funding owed to the Chinese who were brought here as virtual slaves to build our railroads and then left on their own? Does the reparations movement separate itself from the Native American community, which in some serious ways has a prior claim to the whole shebang? I don't exempt myself from feeling an irritation that the burdens of the dead are suddenly on my shoulders. The reparations issue will prove divisive, and I do not see it leading us toward the grander and broader coalitions we need to build.

Kalonji Olusegun

We didn't *come* here to be part of a New World or a New World Order. We lost a "War of Enslavement" and, unlike those European families who came so willingly to America, members of African families were captured, kidnapped, inhumanly crated in sailing tombs, and then the surviving brother and mother were dropped in Brazil, a sister and maybe father dropped off in the Caribbean for rum, and the remaining family members brought to the high-bidding settlers of the United States to work until they just dropped. Upon manumission, this country abandoned the freed Africans left destitute on the land of our incarceration; abandoned us without food, clothing, shelter, or the means to get back home. As refugees of a "War of Enslavement," we were left defenseless to survive the terror of hostile communities, while those who enslaved and brutally forced us to labor from sunup to sundown were paid for the loss of "their chattel property," now freed.

Reparations is not simply about "the enslavement of blacks a century ago," but about finally terminating the illegal and oppressive slave–master relationship perpetuated against them and their descendants, us; about recognition of the injury inflicted on generations of Africans in America; about respect and restoration of our basic human rights; about obtaining the complete and unconditional control of our resources, those resources stolen from us, of which we were deprived; and last but not least, about ending the continuing oppression in the form of political and economic subjugation, illegal taxation, and the cold-spirited impending terror of mass imprisonment. Reparations are needed to elevate the pain, suffering, and rage, so that our people won't be dependent on the whims and racism of a hostile, mechanized system. This is not just a demand for money, this is a matter of fairness, justice, human rights, morality, equality, atonement, trust, and the God-given right to pursue our own destiny, unmolested. Reparations can provide some of the resources needed to accomplish the healing and strengthening of our self-determination.

Let me repeat, reparations has to do with the relationship between America and Africans in America. Reparations is our demand for an *apology,* and the self-determination necessary for us to pursue our *own destiny,* make our *own contribution* to the progress of this planet.

Howard Winant

It's an uphill battle, but every time this proposal has come up in the past and has been resisted or rejected, the cost has gone up. In other words, the consequences for society have gotten much worse. If the forty acres and a mule had happened—and it didn't happen only because it was vetoed by Andrew Johnson in 1866; it was passed by Congress—that would have been much more effective, not only effective but a morally justified effort to transform the situation in the country.

The reparations issue was brought up again by James Forman in 1969. He was talking at that point about $500 million. I believe he was calculating that on the basis of $15 per Black person in the United States, not to be given to individuals but to be used for social programs. Again, that was sneered at.

Unless we open this dialogue about the meaning of race in the United States and the continuing existence of white supremacy and racism, the cost continues to escalate. It's not enough to say, It's so hard, we can't deal with it.

At the same time, it's really important that we understand reparations or any attempt to deal with the systematic racism and white supremacy that has structured our society and our political, economic, and cultural order as a significant class issue. Until you can finance this kind of program in a way that does not punish one group of relatively low-income people to aid another, until you can make the point really clearly that efforts to overcome racial inequality will in fact benefit white folks not only economically but also morally and spiritually, reparations will be a losing cause.

Ronald Trosper

The experience of American Indians in obtaining reparations from the federal government should interest those who seek similar actions with respect to Black Americans. American Indians have received three types of reparations: (1) cash payments, through the operation of the Indian Claims Commission and the U.S. Court of Claims; (2) land, through an occasional action of Congress to return control over land to particular tribes; and (3) tribal recognition, by either Congress or the Bureau of Indian Affairs.

The majority of tribes that received payments distributed them on a per capita basis among the members enrolled in the tribe at the time of the award. This dissipation of jointly held capital to one generation of recipients has meant that their descendants' benefits depend solely on the private action of parents to their children and grandchildren. In many cases, people on welfare had their welfare payments suspended until they had used up their per capita share of the tribal award. Some tribes developed traditions of per capita payments, which continue to inhibit community development.

Recognition of tribal sovereignty and the implementation of self-government have achieved the most significant results. Economic development tends to follow assertion of governing powers. The creation of casinos is the best-known example of this phenomenon; but the success of casinos over the long term is not assured. While other tribes have established economic development with other industries, many tribes have not yet been able to assert enough sovereignty to build solid economies.

What are the analogies to tribal self-government among Black

Americans? Perhaps a Marshall Plan for cities has an element of political institution building similar to the reconstruction of tribal governments. The narrow definition of reparations as investment in human and business capital does not. The Native American example would recommend investment in political capital, in institutions of community organization similar to tribal governments. Money cannot buy such institutions, and some kinds of reparation payments undermine them.

John Tateishi

The lessons drawn from the Japanese American redress issue are varied and numerous. Whether those can serve African American reparations remains to be seen. The World War II internment was a singular event at a given moment in the history of this nation, and while the victims were traumatized by being dishonored as Americans, they somehow found the means to put the episode aside and get on with their lives.

One is inevitably left wondering how African American reparations can possibly rectify the inhumanity of slavery and the legacy of injustice left in its wake. For Japanese Americans, the symbolic payment of $20,000 for the loss of freedom precludes forever any future claims for redressing the wrongs of the internment. The damage done to African Americans over many generations cannot be swept away by a simple clearing of the collective conscience of a nation. Promises are too easily broken, and promises will no longer suffice to address the profundity and lasting effects of slavery.

john a. powell

White society may decline to pay for slavery and its aftermath. My guess is that it probably will. Just raising the claim that African Americans should receive reparations will anger some whites. Even without raising reparations, conservative whites have been able to generate racial hostility and polarization. For the most part, at least on the level of individual operation of daily interactions with African Americans, many whites are not explicitly racially exclusionary or supremacist. They are in a sense "innocent." However, on a deeper level, reliance on this narrow concept of innocence is fraudulent and moves the debate away from analysis of the distributional structure that drives our society. It allows for a debate as to whether individual whites or individual African Americans are morally superior or morally blameworthy. It also creates a disjuncture between seeing how the country has benefited from slavery and how individuals still benefit from the structure. It allows whites to admit that discrimination is wrong, but in the same breath argue for the continuing benefit of this wrong.

Mainstream approaches, such as affirmative action, will not, regardless of how well they are applied, begin to address the underlying inequalities confronting African Americans in our dominant white society. Playing fair now is not enough to put African Americans in a comparable position to accumulate wealth today. At some point it may be necessary to forget the past, but not until we have remembered. I believe that far too many have forgotten without ever remembering.

Part 7

Democracy/Equality

Race, Wealth, and Inequality in America

Melvin L. Oliver and Thomas M. Shapiro

The distribution of wealth depends, not wholly, indeed, but largely, on [a society's] institutions; and the character of [a society's] institutions is determined, not by immutable economic laws, but by the values, preferences, interests, and ideals which rule at any moment in a given society.
— *R.H. Tawney*, Equality

African Americans have not shared equally in the nation's prosperity. They earn less than whites, and they possess far less wealth, whatever measure one may use. Table 1 presents data on income along with median wealth figures. The Black-to-white median income ratio has hovered in the mid-50 to mid-60 percentage range for the past twenty years or so. Fluctuations have been relatively minor, and in many ways American society became accustomed to this standard of inequality. Results from the Census Bureau's 1988 Survey of Income and Program Participation (SIPP) showed that for every dollar earned by white households, Black households earned sixty-two cents.

The median wealth data expose even deeper inequalities. Whites possess nearly twelve times as much median net worth as Blacks, $43,800 versus $3,700. In an even starker contrast, perhaps, the median white household controls $6,999 in net financial assets (excluding equity accrued in a home or vehicle), while the median Black household retains no such assets whatsoever.

Access to Assets

The potential for assets to expand or inhibit choices, horizons, and opportunities for children emerged as the most consistent and strongest common theme in interviews we conducted with a small number of

Melvin L. Oliver and Thomas M. Shapiro's "Race, Wealth, and Inequality in America" (excerpts) is reprinted from *Black Wealth/White Wealth,* by Melvin L. Oliver and Thomas M. Shapiro (1995), by permission of the publisher, Routledge: New York and London.

Table 1

Wealth and Race

	Median income	Median NW[a]	Mean NW[a]	Median NFA[b]	Mean NFA[b]
White	$25,384	$43,800	$95,667	$6,999	$47,347
Black	15,630	3,700	23,818	0	5,209
Ratio	0.62	0.08	0.25	0.0	0.11

[a]Net worth (assets minus debts).
[b]Net financial assets (assets minus debts, excluding equity accrued in a home or vehicle).

Table 2

Who Is on the Edge?

Race	Households with 0 or negative NFA[a] (%)	Households without NFA[a] for 3 months[b] (%)	Households without NFA[a] for 6 months[b] (%)
White	25.3	38.1	43.2
Black	60.9	78.9	83.1
Hispanic	54.0	72.5	77.2

[a]Net financial assets (assets minus debts, excluding equity accrued in a home or vehicle).
[b]NFA reserves to survive the poverty line of $968 per month.

Black families in Los Angeles and white families in Boston. Since parents want to invest in their children, to give them whatever advantages they can, we wondered about the ability of the average American household to expend assets on its children. We found a strong relationship between the amount of wealth and the composition of assets. Households with large amounts of total net worth control wealth portfolios composed mostly of financial assets. Financial investments make up about four-fifths of the assets of the richest households. Conversely, home and vehicle equity represents over 70 percent of the asset portfolio among the poorest one-fifth of American households, one in three of which possesses zero or negative financial assets.

Table 2 reports households with zero or negative net financial assets by race. It shows that one-quarter of white households, 61 percent of Black households, and 54 percent of Hispanic households are without financial resources.

Besides looking at resource deprivation, Table 2 also sets criteria for "precarious-resource" circumstances. Households without enough net financial asset reserves to survive three months at the poverty line ($2,904) meet these criteria. Thirty-eight percent of white households and 79 percent of Black households live in precarious-resource circumstances.

Among our interviewees, parents with ample assets planned to use them to create a better world for their children. Those without them strategized about acquiring some and talked about their "wish list." Parents talked about ballet lessons, camp, trips for cultural enrichment or even to Disney World, staying home more often with the children, affording full-time day care, allowing a parent to be home after day care. The parents discussed using assets to provide better educational opportunities for their children.

Analysis of data on the percentage of children in resource-poor households by race discloses imposing and powerful racial and ethnic cleavages. For example, 40 percent of all white children grow up in households without financial resources, in comparison with 73 percent of all Black children. Most telling of all perhaps, only 11 percent of Black children grow up in households with enough net financial assets to weather three months of no income at the poverty level. Three times as many white kids live in such households.

Financial wealth is the buried fault line of the American social system: highly concentrated wealth at the top; steep resource inequality; the disproportionate asset reserves held by various demographic groups; the precarious economic foundation of middle-class life; and how few financial assets most American households can call upon. Substituting what is known about income inequality for what is not known about wealth inequality limits, and even biases, our understanding of inequality. A thorough understanding of inequality must therefore pay more attention to resources than has been paid in the past.

Income and Wealth

The Black middle class stands on very shaky footing, no matter how one determines middle-class status. Most significant, we believe, is that Blacks' claim to middle-class status is based on income and not assets. The net worth that middle-class Blacks command, ranging from $8,000 for white-collar workers to $17,000 for college graduates, largely represents housing equity, because neither the middle-income earners nor the well-educated nor the white-collar workers control anything other than petty net financial assets. Without wealth reserves, especially liquid assets, the Black middle class depends on income for its standard of living. Without the asset pillar, in particular, income and job security shoulder a greater part of the burden.

Theories of wealth accumulation emphasize income as the preeminent factor in wealth differentials. There is a clear relationship between income inequality and wealth accumulation: wealth accrues with increasing income. Since Black households earn less than two-thirds as much as the average white household, it only makes sense to ask, To what extent can the gross wealth disparities that we have noted be explained by the well-known income inequality between whites and Blacks? Examining Blacks' and whites' wealth at similar income levels provides a clear and direct way to respond to this question. Standardizing for income permits us to test whether the Black–white disparity in wealth holding emanates from income differences.

We standardized SIPP household wealth data into four income brackets: *Poverty*-level ($11,611 or less); *Moderate*-level ($11,612 to $24,999); *Middle*-level ($25,000 to $50,000); and *High*-income (over $50,000). These data represent only households headed by those under age sixty-five, because we did not want age effects to cloud the relationship between income, wealth, and race.

The data are very convincing in one simple respect: differences in observed income levels are not nearly sufficient to explain the large racial wealth gap. The Black-to-white wealth ratio comes closest to equality among households earning $50,000 or more. Even here, where the wealth gap is narrowest, however, Blacks possess barely one-half (0.52) the median net worth of their high-earning white counterparts. For net financial assets, the mean ratio ranges from 0.006 to 0.33. The highest-earning Black households possess twenty-three cents of median net financial assets for every dollar held by high-income white households. One startling comparison reveals that poverty-level whites control nearly as many mean net financial assets as the highest-earning Blacks, $26,683 to $28,310. For those surviving at or below the poverty level, poverty means one thing for whites and another for Blacks.

The general conclusion from these tabulations is that the long-term life prospects of Black households are substantially poorer than those of whites in similar income brackets. This analysis of wealth leaves no doubt regarding the serious misrepresentation of economic disparity that occurs when one relies exclusively on income data. Blacks and whites with equal incomes possess very unequal shares of wealth. More so than income, wealth-holding remains very sensitive to the historically sedimenting effects of race.

The Composition of Wealth

Closely scrutinizing the composition of wealth may yield additional insights that help explain why the wealth gap between Blacks and whites will increase. SIPP data on composition and distribution of assets for Black and white households who held wealth in 1988 show that consumable assets make up 73 percent of the value of all wealth held by Blacks. Conversely, whites invest over one-half (51 percent) of their aggregate wealth in income-producing assets, in comparison with 28 percent for Blacks. Refining asset categories further to include only liquid financial assets (stocks, mutual funds, bank deposits, IRAs, bonds, and income mortgages), we find that Blacks place only 13 percent of their wealth in direct income-producing assets. In sharp contrast, liquid financial assets account for almost one-third of the total white wealth package.

Race: The Key Variable

If Blacks were more like whites with regard to the pertinent demographic and human capital variables, then income parity would be close at hand. The average racial income difference would be reduced from $11,691 to $5,869. This robust reduction in income inequality is not repeated for wealth. A potent $43,143 difference in net worth remains, even when Blacks and whites have the same human capital and demographic characteristics. Nearly three-quarters (71 percent) of the difference is left unexplained. A little over three-quarters of the difference in net financial assets is also unaccounted for. Taking the average Black household and endowing it with the same income, age, occupational, educational, and other attributes as the average white household still leaves a $25,794 racial gap. Clearly, something other than human capital and identifiably important social characteristics is at work here. We cannot help but conclude that factors related to race are central to the racial wealth gap and that something like a racial wealth tax is at work.

The sharp critic could easily respond to these results, however, by pointing out that we have not included in our analysis a central factor that may very well account for a great deal of the unexplained variance—namely, marital status. The furor over marital status in relation to the economic condition of Black America rages daily. In both popular and scholarly discussions, the poor economic fortunes of Black families are consistently linked to the disproportionate share of Black female-headed households: if Black households are poor, it is because they are headed by single women who have not made the necessary human capital investments and who have not been active earning members of the labor force.

To demonstrate the relevance of these ideas for wealth, we conducted similar decomposition analyses for Black and white married and single households. For married heads, differences in wealth-related characteristics between whites and Blacks explain 25.8 percent and 23.1 percent of the net worth and net financial assets wealth differentials. Our results indicate that even if the barriers and disadvantages Blacks face were leveled tomorrow, about three-quarters of the net worth and net financial assets racial wealth differences would remain. In other words, if married Blacks shared income, educational, family, occupational, regional, and work experience characteristics with whites, they would still confront a deficit of $46,294 in net worth and $27,160 in net financial assets.

Conclusion

Racial inequality is still the unsolved American dilemma. The nation's character has been forged on the contradiction of the promise of equality and its systematic denial. For most of our nation's history we have allowed racial inequality to fester. But there are other choices. These choices represent a commitment to equality and to closing the gap as much as possible, and in so doing, redefine the values, preferences, interests, and ideals that define us.

To address these fundamental issues, to rejuvenate America's commitment to racial justice, we must first acknowledge the real nature of racial inequality in this country. We must turn away from explanations of Black disadvantage that focus exclusively on the supposed moral failings of the Black community and attempt to create the kinds of structural supports that will allow Blacks to live full and socially productive lives. The effort will require an avowedly egalitarian, antiracist stance that transcends our racist past and brings Blacks from the margin to the mainstream.

RESPECT!

S.M. Miller and Karen Marie Ferroggiaro

The ultimate test of a society is not only how well its citizens live but how they feel about themselves and others. The basic (though not exclusive) standard of a society is that people feel good about themselves, that they are respected, respect others, and have self-respect. Respect and self-respect shape what happens to people, politically and economically as well as socially.

Respect and self-respect are now burning questions of inequality, policy, and politics. They share the public spotlight with the distribution of income and wealth as our society's central stratification worries.

At a time of widespread unemployment, declining real wages, welfare state tightening, and profound fears about the economic future, it may appear strange to point to these terms of social appraisal and personal feelings as the cutting edge of policy and understanding inequality. But economic difficulties have fed rather than undermined the significance of respect. Emphasizing respect and self-respect as questions of inequality does not downgrade the importance of poverty and economic inequalities or concerns with the level and distribution of income and wealth, for the adverse consequences of these pressing issues are most manifest among those who are disrespected. Low respect leads to low income, as evidenced in many employers' reluctance to hire African Americans, and low incomes reinforce the lack of respect for particular groups, for then they can be, and often are, characterized as reluctant to work. Today, respect and self-respect are central components of an enlarged concept of citizenship. Furthermore, as we continuously relearn, economics is not all if we seek to redress the manifold injustices of society. Today, therefore, respect and self-respect are central components of an enlarged understanding of inequality in society.

Respect is not a minor question of politeness and niceties. While individuals may be told that they are "different" from the appraisals of their identity group or class, that does not change how the group is perceived and treated. Nor is it restricted to the personal irritations that afflict those who are disrespected because of their identity group or class standing. As a component of social capitals—the nonmonetary assets of cultural background, network connections, trust, and know-how—it influences these economic and political assets. Respect affects how we are treated, what help from others is likely, what economic arrangements others are willing to engage in with us, when reciprocity can be expected.

The desire for respect, then, is not a silly, empty game for prestige or status. It opens doors, invites communication, wins cooperation, breeds money and power. It is part of the competitive game, providing access, information, and responsiveness. In short, respect is a resource.

Disrespect has many benefits for those who seize for themselves the right to be judges: it gives them a feeling of superiority; it enhances their chances of capturing rewards in economic and political markets. Those who can authoritatively give or withhold respect have economic, political, and social power. As economic gaps widen, disrespect and revulsion toward the losers grow.

A sense of shame inhibits individual or group action. The consequence is to strengthen the position of those who already have power. Inflicting shame is a weapon. That is one of the reasons identity groups that are testing the economic, political, and/or social limits on them develop a history that corrects distorted or neglectful mainstream accounts and gives members of the group a more positive view of itself.

Public/Collective Respect

At issue here is not individual respect but what might be called public or collective respect—the respect that is generally allocated to a group as a whole, whether on the basis of social identity or of economic position.

The problem of public respect is not new; struggles about it have been occurring for a long time. What is new is understanding respect and disrespect as issues producing and maintaining inequalities and social stratification. Public respect and group self-respect affect not only the command over economic and political resources of marginalized groups, but the character of their daily lives as well. That is why the objective of greater economic and social equality has to be joined to the promotion of respect and self-respect. It is not better incomes and a better distribution versus lessened disrespect, but the pursuit of both, that is important.

While we often talk about rights, respect is less often the explicit topic of discussions about social justice. Rights are important. But it is also important to realize that rights and respect go hand in hand. Legally sanctioned and enforced rights are basic, but respect plays a crucial role in the development and implementation of rights. Whether and how rights are enforced (e.g., the behavior of the police) is affected by the respect accorded to a given group. Respect and rights are reciprocal: the emergence of rights contributes to or enforces respect; respect encourages the development and implementation of rights.

The United States is undergoing a not-so-silent revolution about respect. Many groups—such as women, gays and lesbians, African Americans, and Latinos—demand it. The growing significance of public respect and identity group self-respect is evident in the heightened public and personal sensitivity about harassment, racism, sexism, ageism, homophobia, and multiculturalism. The situation discomforts the many who do not understand ("Why are they making such a fuss?") or oppose ("They're going too far") the new demands for respect. The quest for respect is often met by irritation and counteraction.

Collective respect is unevenly distributed: Asians, Latinos, and African Americans know that in general, whites gain an automatic measure of respect because of the color of their skin; women are regularly accorded less respect than men; a construction worker applying to a bank for a housing loan is treated with less respect than a doctor or lawyer. Disrespected segments encounter distorting opportunities and obstacles. Their life chances are shaped by degrees and types of disrespect. It has deep effects on their daily life as well as on long-term prospects.

Survey Research Data

Survey data by the University of Chicago's National Opinion Research Center (NORC) confirm that white evaluations of Blacks and Latinos are strongly negative, especially when compared with white self-ratings. Almost one-third of whites surveyed thought Blacks and Latinos were unintelligent, while only one-fifth thought they were intelligent. (The rest rated them in a middle category.) By contrast, nearly three-fifths of whites rated their own racial group as intelligent, and only 6 percent rated them as unintelligent. On another question inquiring whether various identity groups were hardworking or lazy, whites again had a high opinion of their own work habits (57 percent hardworking, only 5 percent lazy), while denigrating Latinos and Blacks: for Latinos, whites' ratings were 26 percent hardworking, 37 percent lazy; for Blacks, whites' ratings were 18 percent hardworking, 47 percent lazy. While the NORC survey does not convey a completely negative assessment by whites, it does confirm the widespread feeling among African Americans and Latinos that the white community does not think of them with respect, and that this judgment carries over into behavior.

Class Disrespect

Disrespect has a class bias. As economic gaps widen, disrespect and revulsion toward the losers grow. In the contemporary United States, attitudes about poverty, especially that of African Americans, often condemn the sufferers rather than criticize the conditions that produce low incomes and marginalization. The pejorative term "underclass" indicts the inner-city poor, largely but not exclusively defined as African Americans, who are considered the authors of their poverty because of their presumed cultural practices.

Those whom we would exploit or dominate we first disrespect, and then attribute the subordination to the presumed disreputable condition or attributes of the dominated. Viewing a group as deficient in some human qualities or desirable social practice makes it easier to mistreat them. Slavery seemed acceptable when those enslaved were not regarded as fully human. Holocausts do not appear reprehensible when the victims are seen as threatening or lacking the positive qualities that the perpetrators believe they themselves possess. This is the social construction of the "other." Guilt is banished.

Constructing the "other" in a negative fashion simplifies the ability to oppress. It eases one's conscience to believe that exploited workers are dumb, depraved, and undeserving of respect. Those who are deemed "different" or "less worthy," be it because they are believed incompetent, improvident, work-shy, or as engaging in disapproved cultural styles, are regarded as undeserving and available for social and economic denigration.

The Golden Rule is reversed: treat "the others" as you would *not* have your group treated. Those who treat others with disrespect are according themselves the right to think and act as superior. Such outlooks and behaviors distort the self-assigned superiors as well as damage those who are disrespected.

Negative feelings about the "others" develop or intensify during difficult, strained times. For example, economic difficulties have fueled the fear of immigrants. Concern about "those Mexicans" has resulted not only in barriers to immigration but in physical and political attacks in many countries, including the United States.

Forms of Disrespect

Societal pressures and strains promote scapegoating and disrespect. One group can be played off against another, as in the long-time setting of poor whites against poor Blacks in the U.S. South. Right-wing hate groups such as the Aryan Nation and the KKK are current threats. Calls for "English only" and anti-immigration policies such as California's Proposition 187 reflect fears about demographic and social changes occurring in the United States.

Disrespect takes many forms: discrimination, physical action, prejudice, mocking, segregation, marginalizing, automatic relegation to subordinate positions, harassing, demonizing, stereotyping, overgeneralizing, and much more. Both stereotypes and institutional practices are essential processes of disrespect. Culturally, disrespect is produced by the media, in our schools, and in our everyday practice, such as language. Economically, disrespect is produced in institutional practices such as housing and school segregation and employment discrimination.

All too frequently, schools are prominent agencies for disrespect. They have labeled some classes and identity groups as having low educability and have made them feel that they are stupid in one way or another. They have, for example, convinced girls that they are not good in science and mathematics, though with increased awareness this disabling is now less frequent. African American students, especially those who come from one-parent families, are sometimes characterized as having "educational deficits" when they enter school and therefore as unable to learn. Many African American school and college students have teachers and peers who display open disdain for their competence and potential. For some, schools educate; for "the educational others," they often are made to feel and act dumb. Disrespect and low self-respect feed each other.

Yet schools contribute to the perpetuation of disrespect in other ways as well. Many examinations, especially the SAT, which is required for college entrance, are cited for racial bias against nonwhites. Further, elementary school books portray a United States that is homogeneous, that has only one history, and disrespected groups are often portrayed stereotypically and/or negatively, or omitted altogether.

Perhaps nowhere do we learn more about who we are and how we view ourselves than in the mass media. Television, by providing us with a mediated version of reality, has the potential to influence us into believing in that reality, and modifying our attitudes and behavior accordingly. A wealth of research conducted over more than three decades demonstrates that indeed television has become an important aspect of our social life, capable of influencing our attitudes, values, and behavior. When media portrayals of disrespected groups reinforce negative stereotypes, disrespect is perpetuated and ingrained.

Television news is no less complicit. Media accounts mainly report on African Americans when welfare, crime, or violence is involved. Latinos gain attention mainly when illegal immigration is the focus. The activities of those who are not poor or who are attempting to improve communities get much less attention (unless they are celebrities). The public's false impression is that most African Americans are poor and on welfare, and that underclass conditions are their usual way of life. Hollywood has contributed to the stereotyping of African Americans, especially the young, as mainly poor, hostile, and violent.

The Consequences

Disrespect and fear join to create a disturbing situation for young Black males. They are bitter about the disrespect shown by those white people and police who assume their presence means crime or violence will occur. For example, in a February 1993 Gallup Poll, 80 percent of Blacks surveyed said that the police treat suspects from low-income neighborhoods differently. Furthermore, when asked whether they felt the U.S. justice system is biased against Black people, 68 percent of

Blacks responded yes, compared with 33 percent among white respondents. Consequently, getting "respect" becomes an important goal. That concern may lead to a tough demeanor, which in turn may cause some whites and police to feel more threatened, and to respond with more disrespect and force. Thus, a vicious circle is created where the disrespected demand respect and are in turn disrespected even more.

The respect accorded to particular identity groups significantly affects their participation in the economy and the way that politics responds to their needs and interests. Respect determines, to a major extent, economic interactions and national attention and help. Two examples: the loss of tax revenues through the deductibility of mortgage interest and property tax payments is much greater than government spending on housing subsidies for low-income families, but the latter expenditure is frequently battered in Congress, while merely placing a cap on the deductibility of very high mortgage interest payments is difficult to pass; and crimes such as rape and murder in African American neighborhoods receive much less police attention than rape and murder in white areas.

Respect is part of the competitive game. Well-respected identity groups have an easier time than those low in respect in gaining information, access, and responsiveness. In short, respect pays off. When a figure like Richard Whitney, the head of both the New York Stock Exchange and a prominent brokerage firm, was jailed for misappropriating customers' funds, the event was treated as an aberration, not as an indictment of his identity group. That is not the fate for the member of a less-respected identity group accused of criminal activity. Then, the response is more likely to be "What can you expect from those people?"

Respect has political payoffs that may also contribute to economic gain. Useful networks and connections are constructed by and for respected identity groups. Their members are in positions to help one another, and do so—although they may think of the reciprocity as simply the way business is done: you do business with people you know. They have access to political leaders and the media, are consulted on issues important to them, are treated seriously, and are often considered disinterested voices for "the national interest." By contrast, those identity groups marked by low respect are derided as "self-seeking" or "special interests." They are often unflatteringly described as "strident," "unruly," or "loud," making it easy to discount their views.

At the policy level, contrast the way that farmers, students, and AFDC recipients are treated. Farmers receive enormous subsidies that maintain high prices, which burdens us all. They are not described as "on welfare" or attacked as "chiselers" suffering from "the culture of dependency." Reduced tuition fees and below-market-rate loans for some less advantaged college students are not criticized as encouraging irresponsibility or regarded as a welfare handout. Former college students who do not repay their loans are often treated lightly. Welfare recipients, however, are not accorded similar latitude.

A Vicious Cycle

The result is a vicious cycle: members of disrespected groups and classes stand a substantial chance of needing public assistance because of the obstacles they encounter in trying to achieve a decent outcome; a negative view of welfare recipients reinforces the lack of respect for them, which results in low benefits; inadequate income leads to a difficult existence that reinforces not only low collective respect but often low self-respect as well.

Where we live is largely determined by how much money we have. Those who are relegated to low-status, low-paying jobs oftentimes live in low-income neighborhoods or ghettos that are neglected by the municipality, dirty, and unsafe. Thus, disrespect has consequences of immediate personal safety as well. This can be seen in the fact that there has been a rise in TB cases among low-income persons, as well as a high infant mortality rate among disrespected groups.

Thus, what is needed is not limited to quantitative and qualitative economic improvements. Changes in the social fabric, in people's daily experiences, and in their relationships are imperative. If powerlessness, disconnection, disrespect, and hierarchy at home, at work, and in the community are obstacles to a healthy, functioning society, then genuine participation and the promotion of respect and collective respect would contribute to a healthy society.

Solidarity

"Solidarity," a word much more widely used in Europe than here, is a broader term than "community." "Solidarity" implies mutual concern and responsibility on the part of people who may be socially or geographically distant. More specifically, "solidarity"—at least in European discourse—signifies concern among those who are doing well for those who are faring poorly. For example, the Swedish solidarity wage policy followed by unions, with membership and government support, improved the wages of low-level workers more than those of higher-paid employees, thus reducing the income gap. The animating spirit was that of "one nation."

The keys to building a sense of solidarity, then, are the narrowing of social distance and the involvement of diverse people in common pursuits. Widening the scope of local decision-making is likely to encourage more people to participate in community affairs. Federal- and state-funded programs could require broader-based local participation and self-determination. Community service programs to which individuals could voluntarily contribute for the good of the locality or nation could make a difference. Simply put, inducements to community solidarity can call forth latent desires for mutual aid.

Ending discrimination and disrespect is central, but how to design policies to accomplish this is a difficult task. How can public policy bolster group respect and self-respect while reducing disrespect? There is a need for programs that go beyond promoting individual self-esteem to influence how social identity groups are viewed and treated.

Lessening economic inequalities is crucial, but their decline does not assure that disrespected identity and class groups will automatically experience fewer disturbing daily experiences. Contrary to the childhood taunt that only sticks and stones hurt, words and deeds do damage, resulting in anger or repression and in blocked access to important economic, social, and political resources. Dollars count, but so do group respect and collective self-respect.

Reuniting City and Suburb
The Key to Inner-City Progress

David Rusk

Forty percent of America's central cities are programmed to fail.

This is my conclusion from studying forty years of population, economic, social, and fiscal trends for all 522 central cities in all of America's 320 metropolitan areas.

To name just a few of the cities programmed for failure: Camden and East St. Louis are already clinically dead. Gary, Bridgeport, Newark, Hartford, Cleveland, and Detroit are on life-support systems. Baltimore, Chicago, St. Louis, and Philadelphia are sinking. Although they seem fairly healthy, Boston, Minneapolis, and Atlanta are already infected.

These cities will fail despite successful efforts to reinvent urban government. They will fail despite successful programs to stimulate inner-city entrepreneurship. They will fail despite successful enterprise zones, community development banks, and nonprofit housing projects. They will fail despite new downtown office towers, festival marketplaces, and wonderful new–old ballparks.

They will fail because they are programmed to be the poorhouses for their metropolitan areas. Outside their downtown business districts, these cities are steadily and inexorably being converted into the equivalent of giant public housing projects. Very simply, they are forced to house too many poor Blacks and Hispanics.

The burden of poverty is crushing these cities. More important, the burden of poverty is crushing their residents. Most poor city dwellers cannot be rescued—most cannot rescue themselves—within these cities' neighborhoods.

How heavy is this burden? I've constructed a "fair-share poverty index" (Table 1). For example, if a city has half of the metro area's population and half of the metro area's poor, it has its fair share; its fair-share poverty index is 100. Higher than 100, and a city has more than its fair share of poor residents. At an index of 200, for example, a city has twice its fair share of poor people.

Let's look at a sample list of cities (see Table 1, column A). Their average fair-share poverty index is 263. That means they have over two and a half times their fair share of their metro area's poor.

Examining another set of sample cities (see Table 1, column B), their fair-share poverty index is 127: just 27 percent more poor people than their fair share, not 163 percent more, like the first group. And yet for that first group the percentage of poor people metrowide—10 percent—was lower than for the second group—12 percent.

How did this happen—and how was it made to happen?

Since World War II our national government has had a national

Table 1

Sample Cities' Fair-Share Poverty Index

A		B	
"Inelastic" Cities	Index	"Elastic" Cities	Index
Chicago	191	Kansas City	156
Philadelphia	201	Dallas	150
Baltimore	217	Columbus	146
Minneapolis	228	Portland	145
St. Louis	228	Houston	137
Boston	231	Indianapolis	130
Gary	241	Memphis	126
Cleveland	243	San Diego	119
Detroit	252	Nashville	119
Atlanta	273	Austin	117
Bridgeport	280	Raleigh	116
Newark	296	Phoenix	115
Camden	353	Charlotte	113
Hartford	387	Jacksonville	110
East St. Louis	406	Little Rock	108
Average	263	Average	127

urban policy. It has been a national suburban policy. Low-cost mortgages for single-family homes—$400 billion for 8 million homes. Home mortgage interest deductions—a $58 billion federal income tax break. Since 1950 over $270 billion for building suburb-serving highways and beltways—five times the amount for city-serving mass transit.

Wall Street, Detroit, Hollywood, and Madison Avenue joined in to sell the American people that the American Dream could be found only in a special place—the suburbs.

This national suburban policy has been a spectacular success. Since 1950 all population growth has been low-density, suburban-style growth. In 1950 almost 70 percent of urban-area people lived in cities. In 1990 over 60 percent of urban-area people lived in suburbs.

What happened to that first group of cities—Chicago, Detroit, St. Louis, etc.—was that they didn't grow outward. For many reasons—bad annexation laws, bad neighbors, bad city policy, above all, racial discrimination—they were trapped within their city limits. In my terminology, they were "inelastic."

The second group—Kansas City, Dallas, Columbus, etc.—did expand. From 1950 to 1990, this group of fifteen "elastic" cities expanded their city limits over 700 percent. They "captured" a lot of their suburban-style growth within their own expanding city limits. In fact, these fifteen cities captured 42 percent of all population growth for themselves. Several cities, in effect, are their own suburbs—"cities without suburbs."

It wasn't just that these "elastic" cities were located in growth areas. Yes, over these same four decades their metro areas added over 13 million new people. But the first group, of "inelastic" cities, added over 10 million new people in their metro areas. The problem was that the Chicagos, Detroits, and St. Louises didn't "capture" any growth. All growth occurred in the suburbs outside them. Not only didn't they capture new people, they "contributed" many city residents to the suburbs. These fifteen cities contributed almost 30 percent of their population to their own suburbs.

First, there was "white flight," which increased racial segregation in metro areas. More recently, there is "Black flight"—the Black middle class moving to the suburbs. This has accelerated economic segregation—yawning income gaps between city and suburbs.

How much racial and economic segregation? Both sets of metro areas have about the same percentage of Black population—17 percent for the inelastic areas, 16 percent for the elastic areas. But on a neighborhood-by-neighborhood basis, metrowide, these inelastic areas are 25 percent more racially segregated than elastic areas.

In average per capita income these inelastic metro areas appear to have higher income levels ($17,139) than the elastic metro areas ($14,835)—not taking into account cost-of-living differences. But the inelastic central cities average only 59 percent of their suburbs' income levels, while the elastic central cities essentially have income levels equal to their suburbs (96 percent).

And when rough adjustments are made for differences in cost of living, the real incomes of these inelastic and elastic metro areas are the same, while real incomes for elastic city dwellers are about 50 percent higher than real incomes for inelastic city dwellers.

No wonder that these elastic cities average AA1 municipal bond ratings, while this group of inelastic cities averages a little over BAA1—four steps below—not counting Gary, Camden, and East St. Louis, which likely cannot even sell their bonds.

These vast disparities between inelastic and elastic cities don't exist just for these two sets of fifteen areas I've illustrated. With varying

---

The Four Laws of Urban Dynamics

1. Only Elastic Cities Grow
2. Fragmentation Divides; Unification Unites
3. Economic Ties Bind Cities and Suburbs
4. Ghettos Only Become Bigger Ghettos

---

degrees of fit, they hold true for over five hundred cities in over three hundred metro areas.

Why? What are the factors? Based on regression analysis, we can answer the following questions: Does size of metro area count? No. Does percentage of minority population metrowide count? No. Does region of the country count? Some. Does the loss of manufacturing jobs in some regions and increase in others count? It's important. Does age of the central city count? Yes. Old cities have old, decaying neighborhoods that historically have become warehouses for the poor. Younger cities have less clearly defined ghettos and barrios, and have grown up in less racially intolerant times.

But nothing counts as much as how elastic or inelastic the central city is and how fragmented or unified local government is in general throughout the metro area. Why? Well, in our national mythology, smaller government may be seen as better government, but the national reality is that the more a metro area is fragmented into many small cities, towns, and school districts, the more segregated it is between Black and white, between middle class and poor. Small governments protect and promote uniformity. They act to exclude. Broad-based governments can promote diversity. They can act to include.

I suggest four laws of urban dynamics (see box). Of these, the fourth law—"ghettos only become bigger ghettos"—has the most wrenching implications for those committed to overcoming the barriers of race and poverty.

Forty cities have passed what I've identified as the point of no return—loss of population of 20 percent or more, a minority population of 30 percent or more, a city-to-suburb income ratio of 70 percent or less. Such cities continue to decline decade by decade. Not one has ever closed the income gap with its suburbs. The gap steadily continues to widen.

What's to be done? I believe that there are only two strategies that offer real hope. Either expand inelastic cities to include their suburbs through annexation and city–county consolidation to create more metropolitan governments, or make suburbs accept their fair share of responsibility for poor Blacks and Hispanics through metrowide affordable housing requirements, metrowide public housing programs, and metrowide revenue sharing.

Such strategies will not only save inner cities, they will help save inner-city people. The most effective antipoverty program is to help poor people just get out of ghettos and barrios. High levels of crime, unemployment, dependency, broken families, and illegitimacy are substantially the result of concentrated poverty. Bad neighborhoods defeat good programs. Ghettos and barrios crush too many good people.

What I've just suggested is the toughest political task in America. Inelastic cities didn't get where they are by accident. These patterns of racial and economic segregation are built on the dark fears about race and class that crouch at the heart of the American psyche.

Reorganizing urban governance isn't a task primarily for the federal government. It doesn't have the constitutional tools. I only ask the federal government: stop doing harm. Stop recycling high-rise public housing projects. Stop systematically favoring suburban growth through housing and tax policies.

Citizens of goodwill—Black, white, and Hispanic—across the country must spearhead such reforms. And their efforts must focus where the responsibility for how local governments are organized lies within our federal system—on governors and state legislators.

Such a movement to re-create our metropolitan areas as communities of shared responsibility needs all the help it can get.

It needs reinventing urban government to show that larger governments can be better, more responsive governments.

It needs inner-city economic development to broaden economic opportunity.

It needs successful inner-city community-based programs. Revitalized cities with only middle-class residents are no more desirable than decaying cities of only poor Blacks and Hispanics.

But without recognizing the dynamics of metropolitan areas—without reprogramming inelastic metro areas and inelastic cities—the record of recent decades in hundreds of communities is compelling. These other strategies cannot do the job. The social and economic forces at work are too powerful.

To many, achieving such "cities without suburbs" or forging a shared responsibility between city and suburbs that will break down barriers of both race and class may appear impossible. However, as Abraham Lincoln testified in his first inaugural address, miracles can be wrought in the American soul and spirit "when again touched, as surely they will be, by the angels of our better nature."

It is time to call forth the angels of our better nature.

Commentaries

Margaret Weir

For the past three decades urban policy has sought to improve cities as places, or to ameliorate the "pathologies" of the people who live in cities. David Rusk challenges this narrow perspective on urban problems, contending that only metropoliswide strategies will rescue ailing cities and the poor people in them. He brings a strong and cogent voice to the growing chorus now arguing that the fates of cities and suburbs are intertwined and that regional solutions are needed to remedy urban problems.

Rusk argues that traditional notions of place-based urban policy will not work in the older "inelastic" cities of the Northeast and Midwest. His arguments are persuasive. Local political arrangements, the organization of social policies, and taxing authority have overwhelmingly promoted growth in the suburbs and starved the older inner cities. Feeding this fragmentation are racial divisions that have left poor minorities paying the price for our neglect of cities. We can't expect urban policy—such as enterprise zones or nonprofit housing—to have much impact when most other policies are actively working to disadvantage cities.

Rusk's argument reflects the major changes that have occurred in our older metropolitan areas in the past few decades. In the 1980s, two-thirds of job growth occurred in suburbs. As the fiscal base of cities has eroded, the services they offer have deteriorated mark-edly. Many of the public services most important in escaping pov-erty and enjoying a reasonable quality of life are provided and—in large part—financed locally. These include such things as library and recreation services, policing and crime control, and, most cru-cially, education.

Given these circumstances, is it fair to restrict the fate of the urban poor to solutions that can be created in cities? Rusk's answer is *no*. His proposals for metrowide affordable housing requirements, revenue sharing, and public housing would begin to create more equitable re-sources across space and would offer the urban poor more choices about where to live.

However, Rusk's enthusiasm for large jurisdictions per se is less convincing. Rusk's claim that "inelastic central cities average only 59 percent of their suburbs' income levels, while the elastic central cities essentially have income levels equal to their suburbs" is tautological—and it says nothing about poverty in these elastic cities. In fact, accord-ing to a recent study by Paul Jargowsky of the University of Texas–Dallas, three of Rusk's elastic cities (Dallas, Houston, and Memphis) were among the top ten metropolitan areas with the most Black ghetto residents in 1990. Rusk notes that there is 25 percent less racial segre-gation in his elastic cities, but racial segregation there is still substan-tial.

Larger jurisdictions may make geographic mobility somewhat eas-ier, but they are no guarantee against the emergence of isolated poor neighborhoods. Likewise, they create the possibility for more equal public services, but they do not ensure that poor neighborhoods receive the services they need. In fact, equal public services rarely occur with-out mobilization of the poor—something that is often difficult in these political systems.

These drawbacks to larger political jurisdictions suggest that metro-politan strategies are only part of the solution. Even if we substantially improve the mobility of the urban poor, there still will be poor neigh-borhoods and the need for policies to help rebuild them. Increased mobility and community building are both necessary, and can be com-plementary. The notion that we must choose between them falsely polarizes the debate. The real policy question is how best to combine these strategies so that they reinforce one another.

Rusk suggests that state government is the appropriate focus for creating metropolitan policies. State governments have broad and substantially untapped powers to promote regional approaches to urban problems. Rusk's insistence on state responsibility is timely and strategic. The states' failures to exercise their power over land use has been a central component of today's urban crises. But the federal government can still play two important roles. First, it can provide incentives and penalties for states to promote regional approaches to urban issues. States have proved that on their own they will avoid acting. Second, the federal government must provide more direct aid to the poor in the form of income support, housing assistance, and employment policies.

Local political structures have encouraged an attitude of "defensive localism" that national political leaders have exploited and amplified by contending that localities are responsible for the problems that occur within their boundaries. David Rusk's metropolitan approach to urban poverty offers a critical starting point for rebuilding broader notions of collective responsibility and common citizenship.

Eric Mann

David Rusk's article offers significant empirical data on the class exploitation and racism that characterize the political economy of U.S. cities. It confirms and elaborates on what most activists and scholars working on inner-city problems already understand—that the anticipated great leap forward in the civil rights movement when Black mayors were elected in major urban centers proved to be illusory. They often took over a hollow shell, as federal policy had already abandoned the inner cities. The important, if transitory, efforts of the War on Poverty were our society's first and last effort since Reconstruction to take responsibility for the economic underpinnings of race-based poverty. Since then, from the Democratic mayors' scuttling of the Community Action Program, to the Nixonite Model Cities, to the Reagan–Bush racism as national policy, to the Clinton courtship of the suburban white "Reagan Democrats," U.S. cities have become, as Professor Cynthia Hamilton analogizes, America's Bantustans.

In this context, Rusk's work—by highlighting the economically, fiscally, and racially gerrymandered construction of cities—is a valuable contribution. This points to an important arena of political struggle: challenging America's suburban middle class and the nation's racist urban policy. His work is extremely valuable and, in some ways, I wish he had stopped there, because while his analysis of the consequences of urban policy reflects an awareness of class and race, his analysis of the political dynamics of *why* the problem exists reflects an inadequate comprehension of class and race exploitation.

Rusk's assertion that when cities become more than 30 percent people of color, they go beyond "the point of no return," has a blame-the-victim bias that confuses racist policies with "empirical" observation. For example, in Los Angeles County, where I live, there are nearly 9 million people: 3.4 million whites, 3.1 million Latinos, 1.1 million African Americans, and 1.1 million Asian Americans. With regard to the fiscal crisis of cities, it has been the corporate-initiated class and race warfare initiatives such as California's Proposition 13 (linking corporate real estate tax reduction to the middle class, addressing a real problem of too-high property taxes in some cases, but doing so in a way that gutted public services and placed greater pressure on renters and the homeless) that contribute to the decline of urban life—not the fact that L.A. is more than 60 percent people of color.

What is true in what Rusk is saying, but not addressing, is that when people of color become a near majority of the population in any city, the vast majority of whites react not just with "white flight" but also with an increasingly suburban and segregated view of "the city," even when they live within city limits. An example is Los Angeles' most recent mayoral election, in which Richard Riordan, running a Ross Perot–like "make the city safe for business and the middle class with more tax breaks and more police" campaign, was elected because the white minority voted at far higher percentages than people of color and voted overwhelmingly for Riordan.

There is a need for a long-term, antiracist movement that is not a separate movement in itself, but is a component of every aspect of progressive organizing—on the environment, labor union reform, women's rights, and every facet of urban poverty. This work has to assume a far more explicit ideological and pedagogical nature. We cannot simply seek "common interest" between people of color and whites, and between low-income and more affluent people, as if racism and class bias will go away if we just manipulate demands better. We must consciously address the racism and anti-immigrant and antipoor bias that has become institutionalized in public discourse. The middle class of all races has to be challenged for its new worship of materialism and its self-righteous, bloated, and self-aggrandizing culture.

During the 1960s, the civil rights and then Black liberation movements and the women's movement based a great deal of their moral authority on an ethical challenge to the racism and male supremacy of U.S. society and the specific ways that white people and men were often part of the problem instead of part of the solution. While we can all talk about how some of those struggles could have been handled more constructively, the overwhelming historical sum-up of that process is positive, for it proceeded not just with a liberated view of Black people, other people of color, and women, but with a strategic and optimistic view that ethical and political struggle could actually make changes in the behavior of white people and men.

Today, there is a need to dramatically reintroduce issues of ethics and personal transformation into a left politics of the city; otherwise, racism and short-term self-interest will continue to poison any bold programs for change.

Rusk highlights how the cities essentially subsidize the suburbs and recommends new urban reorganizations based on calling for "the angels of our better nature." But without a class analysis that explains the essential role that cities play as centers of low-wage labor—working people who subsidize the wealth of the middle and upper classes—and an explicit analysis of how the corporate class has effectively enlisted the middle class to support corporate priorities and abandon the low-wage working class and urban poor, and a without a conscious organizing strategy to confront white racism and middle-class reaction, his analysis will only explain why the problem is so persistent, not present any options for change.

Any strategy for urban transformation must begin with a sober assessment of how racism and poverty serve the interests of many people in U.S. society, and go beyond calls to Abraham Lincoln and angels to demand the radical redistribution of wealth and radical constraints on corporate behavior.

John O. Calmore

In 1987, more than 75 percent of America's municipalities had populations of less than five thousand people. In white suburban areas, 86 percent of whites live in areas where less than 1 percent of the population is Black. In 1986, 27.5 percent of Black students and 30 percent of Latino students were enrolled in the twenty-five largest central-city school districts, while only 3.3 percent of white students were enrolled in these districts. That is, 96.7 percent of white schoolchildren are educated outside of these problematic central-city school districts.

Over twenty years ago, urban policy makers sought to construct a coherent reorganizational framework that would establish greater parity between needs and resources. Then, as now, there were seemingly insurmountable barriers to metropolitan reform.

Racism—not race, not poverty—is the root and branch of an American society divided against itself. Racism explains more completely than any other variable the structural urban inequality, economic subjugation, spatial containment, and human expendability that afflict so many inner-city dwellers who are primarily Black. British geographer Peter Jackson is right in characterizing racism as involving "the attempt by a dominant group to exclude a subordinate group from the material and symbolic rewards of status and power." Racism's forms and expressions change over time and in response to struggle as this process of subordination continues to plague America.

Racism is a virus that affects the nation's societal organization. By "societal organization" I mean to denote William J. Wilson's reference to "the working arrangements of society, including those that have emanated from previous arrangements, that specifically involve processes of ordering relations and actions with respect to given social ends, and that represent the material outcomes of those processes." Statuses, roles, values, and norms are necessarily affected by the virus. I fear there is no cure.

America's racism is now state of the art. It reflects a picaresque genius that causes many to see it as having virtually disappeared. Does anyone sincerely believe we live in a color-blind world? This race neutrality is correctly characterized by Patricia Williams as "racism in drag." The consequences of racism are instead seen as bad luck, personal irresponsibility, acts of nature, or divine will.

Within a few years of the 1968 Kerner Commission Report, concluding that white institutions were fundamentally responsible for urban racial inequality, there developed a totally different dominant understanding, the myth that the Black community itself was responsible for its own problems, and significant governmental action was no longer necessary or proper. As Gary Orfield and Carole Askinaze note in their study of metropolitan Atlanta: "The perception of the late 1960s that America faced a fundamental racial crisis was replaced by the belief that everything reasonable had been done and that, in fact, policies had often gone so far as to be unfair to whites."

This mythology continues to contradict and distort. In 1993, Richard Riordan defeated Michael Woo in the race for mayor of Los Angeles. Los Angeles is a city with 3,485,000 people: 13 percent African American, 37 percent Anglo, 9 percent Asian/Pacific Islander, and 39 percent Latino. Within this multicultural mix, 85 percent of those who voted for Riordan were Anglo. The *New York Times* reported that Riordan voters indicated by a 2-to-1 ratio that "the problems of minorities and the inner city are problems of personal responsibility rather than problems of racism and economic imbalance, while Woo voters said exactly the opposite by the same 2-to-1 ratio."

In Los Angeles, Blacks are far from the mainstream in their electoral politics; Woo captured 86 percent of the Black vote. Among other groups, Asians voted 69 percent for Woo; Latinos, 57 percent for Woo; and Jews, 51 percent for Woo. The San Fernando Valley represents Los Angeles' suburb within the city. It accounted for 44 percent of the city's vote. The new mayor will speak primarily as the voice of the white San Fernando Valley. Although Latinos make up 33 percent of the Valley, the electorate remains white, suburban, and conservative. In the primary election for mayor, while 85 percent of the Anglos voted, only 7 percent of the Latinos voted. The predominant Valley perspective on local government since the 1920s has been that its residents pay a disproportionate amount of taxes while receiving less than their fair share of city services.

In light of prospects in Los Angeles, I cannot be enthusiastic about Rusk's prescription to expand cities through the annexation of the suburbs or through city–county consolidation. In a 1970 article, Robert Lineberry identified two beliefs that Blacks held regarding the consequences of metropolitan merger: dilution of Black voting power and redirection of urban policy away from Black issues of concern such as poverty, ghetto rehabilitation, and civil rights. As he said then, so, too, today: "Instead of stimulating concern for the poor and the Negro, the addition of a tax—and race—conscious suburbia to the metropolitan electorate probably would dilute not only their voting power, but also the dedication of urban governments to social change."

How in the world would Rusk get the suburbs to buy into being annexed by central cities? The trend is more likely to be toward suburbs in the city, like Staten Island or the San Fernando Valley, moving toward deannexation or succession. In the 1970s Michael Danielson recognized that the underlying cause of the end of annexation and the political containment of the city was "the universal desire of the periphery for political autonomy from the core." Rooted in class and ethnic conflict, the objective was tied to the desire of middle-class areas to establish local control over their relatively homogeneous communities.

In the 1980s Hadley Arkes recognized that the population movements to the suburbs were not simply a matter of convenience. Instead, they "implied a judgment about the kind of people one wished to live with, and the conditions under which one expected to live." Control over the character of the community is the epitome of home rule for suburban local governments.

In 1990 Richard Briffault observed that an important feature of suburban localism and politics is the "protection of turf through the prevention of internal racial or income differentiation." The suburban consciousness severs its historical association with the cities and regards the cities and their residents with both fear and disdain. Consider a 1985 poll of suburban Detroiters who were white, working-class defectors from the Democratic Party. As President Bill Clinton moves more toward the center, I fear that he will move closer to those who were polled: "These ... defectors express a profound distaste for Blacks, a sentiment that pervades almost everything they think about government and politics. Blacks constitute the explanation for their vulnerability and for almost everything that has gone wrong in their lives; not being Black is what constitutes being middle class; not living

with Blacks is what makes a neighborhood a decent place to live . . .
These sentiments have important implications, . . . as virtually all progressive symbols and themes have been redefined in racial and pejorative terms."

Under these circumstances, I have difficulty in seeing the key to
inner-city progress being held in the reuniting of city and suburb. What
needs to be done is (1) to obtain reparations from those suburbs whose
exclusionary policies contribute to the plight of central cities, and (2)
to obligate the federal government to compensate central cities for its
historical involvement in endorsing, maintaining, and furthering spatial
inequality and opportunity-denying circumstances associated with the
exploitation of a Black–white dual housing market.

The Economic Inequality Quiz

World Hunger Year

1. In 1995, there were 371 billionaires in the world, whose combined net worth exceeded the net worth of the bottom _____ percent of the world's population.
   A. 25
   B. 35
   C. 45
   D. 55

2. In 1974, the average American CEO made 34 times as much as the average American worker. By 1995, the difference had grown to _____ times as much.
   A. 100
   B. 134
   C. 159
   D. 179

3. In the 1940s, U.S. corporations paid about one- _____ of the nation's taxes; in 1994, they paid about one- _____. (choose two)
   A. tenth
   B. fifth
   C. third
   D. half

4. In 1995, the median weekly salary of a full-time white female was _____ percent of a full-time white male worker's salary.
   A. 35
   B. 62
   C. 73
   D. 93

5. In 1995, the median weekly salary of a full-time Black worker was _____ percent of a full-time white worker's salary; a full-time Hispanic worker made _____ percent as much. (choose two)
   A. 55
   B. 67
   C. 78
   D. 98

6. The wealthiest 10 percent of American families own about _____ percent of stocks, bonds, trusts, and business equity.
   A. 30
   B. 50
   C. 70
   D. 90

7. Between 1974 and 1994, average annual family income (adjusted for inflation) decreased by _____ percent for the poorest fifth of society, and increased by _____ percent for the wealthiest fifth. (choose two)
   A. 10
   B. 21
   C. 34
   D. 48

8. Between 1977 and 1990, _____ percent of all income gains in the United States went to the wealthiest 1 percent of Americans.
   A. 22
   B. 39
   C. 53
   D. 79

9. The Gini Index measures income inequality by analyzing the distribution of income within an economy. Based on this measure, which of the following countries has a more equal distribution of income than the United States?

A. Australia
B. Israel
C. United Kingdom
D. Germany

Answers to the Economic Inequality Quiz are on page 240.

Quiz Answers

The Immigration Quiz

The Immigration Quiz appears on page 130.

1. D
2. C. Almost 88 percent of African immigrants had a high school diploma, and 47 percent had a bachelor's degree or better. Africans, as a group, are also better educated than the general U.S. population: only 77 percent of U.S.-born adults have a high school diploma, and just over 20 percent have a bachelor's degree or higher.
3. A
4. C
5. D
6. A. True
   B. False
   C. False
   D. True
   E. True
   F. True

The Welfare Quiz

The Welfare Quiz appears on page 144.

1. The AFDC program consumes 1 percent of the federal budget and 2 percent of the average state budget.
2. C
3. In 1992, the average number of children in an AFDC family was two.
4. C
5. B
6. D
7. C
8. D
9. B

The Income and Jobs Quiz

The Income and Jobs Quiz appears on page 146.

1. D
2. D
3. B
4. A
5. A
6. C
7. A
8. C

The Affirmative Action Quiz

The Affirmative Action Quiz appears on page 187.

1. C. About 92,000 nonconstruction contractors fall into this category and must have affirmative-action plans. Another 100,000 construction contractors do not need affirmative-action plans but must abide by other OFCCP regulations.

2. D. Goals require only a good-faith effort; contractors do not have to achieve the goal. Quotas, which are often part of legal consent decrees, are more binding.

3. B. Since employers do not have to submit their plans to the OFCCP, the chances are that no federal official will ever see the affirmative-action plans of most federal contractors.

4. A. The OFCCP conducts about four thousand compliance reviews each year, and the number is decreasing. At this rate, it would take the OFCCP over forty-six years to review each of the nearly 192,000 contractors it is responsible for.

5. B. Since 1975, the average number of debarments each year has been only 1.5. It takes, on average, about three years for a company to be debarred. If a debarred company applies for reinstatement, it takes only eight months.

6. C. Using race as one of many factors was approved by the Supreme Court in 1978; gender was approved sometime later.

In March 1996, however, a federal appeals court said that this was illegal in a case involving University of Texas Law School admissions. Ultimately, the U.S. Supreme Court will have to rule on this issue.

7. C. Any school can try to recruit more qualified Black students by visiting Black high schools. The Supreme Court has ruled against special minority scholarships. In most situations, it is also illegal for a school to reserve a number of places for minorities.

8. D. In order to justify a quota, the plaintiff must first prove that an employer has intentionally discriminated and has not taken sufficient steps to stop the discrimination. There are also other legal requirements to justify quotas.

9. B. Whites are more supportive of affirmative action for women than for minorities They are more supportive of policies that don't involve quotas and that are not intended to compensate for past discrimination.

10. A. Blacks support most affirmative-action policies involving both women and minorities.

11. A. Women are more supportive than men; Black women are more supportive than white women.

12. B. White males do not have a good record in reverse discrimination lawsuits. In addition, there are many more discrimination suits filed by women and minorities. Most suits filed by white males allege gender discrimination rather than race discrimination.

13. B. The children of alumni, called "legacies," have a better chance to get admitted. Elite universities discriminated against Jews and Blacks early in the twentieth century and have been accused of discriminating against Asians in the 1990s.

14. A. Despite affirmative action, Blacks and Hispanics are still underrepresented in terms of law and medical degrees. White males still receive about half of these degrees.

The Economic Inequality Quiz

The Economic Inequality Quiz appears on page 232.

1. C. 129 of the world's 371 billionaires are American.
2. D. On average, Japanese CEOs make thirty-two times as much as their employees.
3. C, A
4. C
5. C, B. Additionally, in 1994, 12 percent of whites and 31 percent of Blacks and Hispanics lived below the poverty line.
6. D
7. A, C. In 1994, the federal poverty threshold for a family of four was $15,141.
8. D. In 1996, the wealthiest 1 percent of Americans are expected to earn an average of $438,000.
9. All four do. America has the most unequal distribution of income among the advanced industrialized nations.

Contributors

Richard America is a senior program manager in the federal government. His books include *Paying the Social Debt: What White America Owes Black America.*

The Applied Research Center, in Oakland, California, is headed by former PRRAC board member Gary Delgado.

Robert Bach is a national board member of the Changing Relations Project and principal author of the board's report to the Ford Foundation.

Julian Bond is Distinguished Professor in Residence at American University and a member of the University of Virginia's History Department faculty.

Bill Bradley has represented New Jersey in the U.S. Senate since 1989.

John C. Brittain is a professor of law at the University of Connecticut School of Law and past president of the National Lawyers Guild.

John O. Calmore is professor of law and W. Joseph Ford Fellow at Loyola Law School in Los Angeles.

Benjamin DeMott is a culture critic who writes on race and class in America. His most recent book is *The Trouble with Friendship: Why Americans Can't Think Straight about Race.*

Bernardine Dohrn directs the Children and Family Justice Center of Northwestern University.

Reynolds Farley is a research scientist at the University of Michigan Population Studies Center.

Karen Marie Ferroggiaro is a graduate student at Boston College.

Max Frankel, former executive editor of the *New York Times,* writes a weekly column on communications for the paper's magazine.

Herbert J. Gans is professor of sociology at Columbia University, past president of the American Sociological Association, and author of *People, Plans and Policies: Essays on Poverty, Racism and Other National Urban Problems.*

Nathan Glazer is co-editor of the quarterly *The Public Interest* and professor of education and sociology emeritus at Harvard University.

Henry Hampton is president and founder of Blackside, Inc., and creator and executive producer of *Eyes on the Prize I & II, The Great Depression, Malcolm X: Make it Plain,* and *America's War on Poverty.*

Chester Hartman is the president/executive director of the Poverty & Race Research Action Council (PRRAC).

David Hayes-Bautista is executive director of the Alta California Policy Research Center and professor of medicine at UCLA.

Daniel Levitas is vice-president of the Institute for Research for Education on Human Rights, Inc., based in Kansas City. He also serves as coordinator for the Georgia Rural Urban Summit.

Juanita Tamayo Lott is president of Tamayo Lott Associates in Silver Spring, Maryland.

David McReynolds is a staff member of the War Resisters League.

Eric Mann is director of the Labor/Community Strategy Center in Los Angeles. His latest book is *Mass Transportation for the Masses: The Bus Riders Union Makes a Left Turn in Los Angeles.*

Manning Marable is professor of history and director of the Institute for Research in African-American Studies at Columbia University. The most recent of his nine books are *Beyond Black and White* and *Speaking Truth to Power.*

Douglas S. Massey is the Dorothy Swaine Thomas Professor at the University of Pennsylvania and chairman of its Sociology Department.

S.M. Miller, a PRRAC board member, is a senior fellow at the Commonwealth Institute, a research professor of sociology at Boston College, and senior adviser to United for a Fair Economy.

Charles Moskos is professor of sociology at Northwestern University. His latest book (with John Sibley Butler) is *All That We Can Be: Black Leadership and Racial Integration the Army Way.*

Salim Muwakkil is a senior editor of *In These Times,* a contributing columnist with the *Chicago Sun-Times,* and a faculty member of the Associated Colleges of the Midwest's Urban Studies Program.

Samuel L. Myers, Jr., is the Roy Wilkins Chair Professor of Human Relations and Social Justice at the Humphrey Institute of Public Affairs at the University of Minnesota. His most recent book is *The Black Underclass: Critical Essays on Race and Unwantedness.*

Melvin L. Oliver is vice-president for communities, families, and livelihoods at the Ford Foundation, and former professor of sociology at UCLA and director of its Center for the Study of Urban Poverty.

Kalonji Olusegun was a first co-chair of N'COBRA, the National Coalition of Blacks for Reparations in America, a nonprofit grassroots membership organization formed in 1989.

Paul Ong, a member of PRRAC's Social Science Advisory Board, is a professor at UCLA's School of Public Policy and Social Research and chairs their Department of Urban Planning.

Leslye E. Orloff is founder of the domestic violence program and director of program development at Ayuda, a community-based legal services program in Washington, DC, serving immigrant and refugee battered women and children.

José Padilla, vice-chair of PRRAC's board, is executive director of California Rural Legal Assistance.

Sharon Parker is director of social responsibility programs for the Union Institute in Washington, DC, and former director of Stanford University's Office of Multicultural Development.

Sonia M. Pérez, the former director of the Poverty Project at the National Council of La Raza, is director of the Resident Initiatives Program at a company that manages public housing projects in Puerto Rico.

Libero Della Piana is the editor of *RaceFile,* a bimonthly publication of the Applied Research Center.

Fred Pincus is professor of sociology at the University of Maryland–Baltimore County.

john a. powell, a PRRAC board member, is on the law faculty of the University of Minnesota.

Gregory Rodriguez is a research fellow at the Alta California Policy Research Center, associate editor with Pacific News Service, and research fellow at Pepperdine University.

David Rusk is a former New Mexico state legislator and mayor of Albuquerque. He consults on urban policy in Washington, DC, and is the author of *Cities Without Suburbs.*

Werner Schink is research director for the California Department of Social Services.

Thomas M. Shapiro is professor of sociology and anthropology at Northeastern University.

Theodore M. Shaw, a PRRAC board member, is associate director-counsel for the NAACP Legal Defense and Educational Fund.

Brent Staples writes about politics and culture for the editorial page of the *New York Times* and is the author of the memoir *Parallel Time: Growing Up in Black and White.*

Ibrahim K. Sundiata is Beinfield Professor of African and Afro-American Studies at Brandeis University. His latest book is *Between Slaving and Neoslavery.* His current work is on the creation of race and ethnicity in twentieth-century America.

Cathi Tactaquin, a PRRAC board member, is director of the National Network for Immigrant and Refugee Rights in Oakland, California. She is also a member of the International Migrant Rights Watch Committee, headquartered in Geneva.

William R. Tamayo, a PRRAC board member, formerly was managing attorney at the Asian Law Caucus and now practices law in San Francisco.

John Tateishi served as the national redress director for the Japanese American Citizens League. He is a public affairs consultant with Tateishi/Shinoda and Associates in Kentfield, California.

William L. Taylor, a PRRAC board member, practices law in Washington, DC, specializing in advocacy for the rights of children. In the 1960s, he was staff director of the U.S. Commission on Civil Rights.

Ronald Trosper is director of the Native American Forestry Program at the College of Ecosystem Science and Management, Northern Arizona University. He is former director of the National Indian Policy Center at George Washington University.

Abel Valenzuela, Jr., is assistant professor at UCLA's Cesar Chavez Center for Interdisciplinary Instruction in Chicano/a Studies.

Maxine Waters, a Democratic congresswoman from California, co-chaired the Affirmative Action Task Force of the Congressional Black Caucus.

Margaret Weir, a member of PRRAC's Social Science Advisory Board, is a senior fellow at the Brookings Institution in Washington, DC, where she is studying suburban-city conflicts and emerging prospects for cooperation.

Roger Wilkins was a civil rights official in the Johnson administration and later a journalist with the *New York Times* and *Washington Post.* He is Clarence J. Robinson Professor of History and American Culture at George Mason University.

Howard Winant is professor of sociology at Temple University and the author of *Racial Conditions: Politics, Theory, Comparisons* and co-author (with Michael Omi) of *Racial Formation in the United States: From the 1960s to the 1990s.*

World Hunger Year, in New York City, is headed by Bill Ayres.

Lawrence Wright, a staff writer for the *New Yorker,* lives in Austin, Texas. He formerly worked for the *Race Relations Reporter* (Nashville) and *Southern Voices* (Atlanta).

Raúl Yzaguirre is president of the National Council of La Raza, a Hispanic research and advocacy organization.

PRRAC Board of Directors and Social Science Advisory Board

Board Member; BME: Board Member Emeritus; SS: Social Science Advisory Board; SSE: Social Science Advisory Board Emeritus. Where more than one institutional identification is given, the identification listed first was that at the time of the person's PRRAC appointment.

Richard Berk: UCLA (SS)

Angela Glover Blackwell: Urban Strategies Council; Rockefeller Foundation (BME)

John Charles Boger: NAACP Legal Defense and Educational Fund; University of North Carolina Law School

Frank Bonilla: Hunter College (SS)

Gordon Bonnyman: Legal Services of Middle Tennessee; Tennessee Justice Center (BME)

Nancy Duff Campbell: National Women's Law Center

David Cohen: The Advocacy Institute

Linda Darling-Hammond: Columbia University Teachers College (SSE)

Gary Delgado: Applied Research Center (BME)

Cynthia Duncan: University of New Hampshire (SS)

Ronald Ellis: NAACP Legal Defense and Educational Fund; U.S. District Court, Southern District of New York (BME)

Roberto Fernandez: Northwestern University; Stanford University Graduate School of Business (SS)

William Fletcher, Jr.: AFL-CIO

James Gibson: The Urban Institute

Robert Greenstein: Center on Budget and Policy Priorities (BME)

Tessie Guillermo: Asian Pacific Islander American Health Forum (BME)

247

Index